P9-DBM-917

Flash Video
for Professionals

Expert Techniques for Integrating Video on the Web

Lisa Larson

Renée Costantini

Wiley Publishing, Inc.

Acquisitions Editor: MARIANN BARSOLO
Development Editor: TONI ACKLEY
Technical Editor: OSCAR TRELLES
Production Editors: SARAH GROFF-PALERMO, RACHEL GUNN
Copy Editor: LIZ WELCH
Production Manager: TIM TATE
Vice President and Executive Group Publisher: RICHARD SWADLEY
Vice President and Executive Publisher: JOSEPH B. WIKERT
Vice President and Publisher: NEIL EDDE
Book Designer: FRANZ BAUMHACKL
Compositor: CHRIS GILLESPIE, HAPPENSTANCE TYPE-O-RAMA
Proofreader: JEN LARSEN
Indexer: TED LAUX
Anniversary Logo Design: RICHARD PACIFICO
Cover Image: © STOCKBYTE, GETTY IMAGES
Cover Designer: RYAN SNEED

Copyright © 2007 by Wiley Publishing, Inc., Indianapolis, Indiana

Published simultaneously in Canada

ISBN: 978-0-470-13113-8

No part of this publication may be reproduced, stored in a retrieval system or transmitted in any form or by any means, electronic, mechanical, photocopying, recording, scanning or otherwise, except as permitted under Sections 107 or 108 of the 1976 United States Copyright Act, without either the prior written permission of the Publisher, or authorization through payment of the appropriate per-copy fee to the Copyright Clearance Center, 222 Rosewood Drive, Danvers, MA 01923, (978) 750-8400, fax (978) 646-8600. Requests to the Publisher for permission should be addressed to the Legal Department, Wiley Publishing, Inc., 10475 Crosspoint Blvd., Indianapolis, IN 46256, (317) 572-3447, fax (317) 572-4355, or online at http://www.wiley.com/go/permissions.

Limit of Liability/Disclaimer of Warranty: The publisher and the author make no representations or warranties with respect to the accuracy or completeness of the contents of this work and specifically disclaim all warranties, including without limitation warranties of fitness for a particular purpose. No warranty may be created or extended by sales or promotional materials. The advice and strategies contained herein may not be suitable for every situation. This work is sold with the understanding that the publisher is not engaged in rendering legal, accounting, or other professional services. If professional assistance is required, the services of a competent professional person should be sought. Neither the publisher nor the author shall be liable for damages arising herefrom. The fact that an organization or Website is referred to in this work as a citation and/or a potential source of further information does not mean that the author or the publisher endorses the information the organization or Website may provide or recommendations it may make. Further, readers should be aware that Internet Websites listed in this work may have changed or disappeared between when this work was written and when it is read.

For general information on our other products and services or to obtain technical support, please contact our Customer Care Department within the U.S. at (800) 762-2974, outside the U.S. at (317) 572-3993 or fax (317) 572-4002.

Wiley also publishes its books in a variety of electronic formats. Some content that appears in print may not be available in electronic books.

Library of Congress Cataloging-in-Publication Data is available from the publisher.

TRADEMARKS: Wiley, the Wiley logo, and the Sybex logo are trademarks or registered trademarks of John Wiley & Sons, Inc. and/or its affiliates, in the United States and other countries, and may not be used without written permission. Adobe and Flash are registered trademarks of Adobe Systems Incorporated. All other trademarks are the property of their respective owners. Wiley Publishing, Inc., is not associated with any product or vendor mentioned in this book.

10 9 8 7 6 5 4 3 2 1

Dear Reader

Thank you for choosing *Flash Video for Professionals: Expert Techniques for Integrating Video on the Web.* This book is part of a family of premium quality Sybex graphics books, all written by outstanding authors who combine practical experience with a gift for teaching.

Sybex was founded in 1976. More than thirty years later, we're still committed to producing consistently exceptional books. With each of our graphics titles we're working hard to set a new standard for the industry. From the writers and artists we work with to the paper we print on, our goal is to bring you the best graphics books available.

I hope you see all that reflected in these pages. I'd be very interested to hear your comments and get your feedback on how we're doing. Feel free to let me know what you think about this or any other Sybex book by sending me an email at nedde@wiley.com, or if you think you've found an error in this book, please visit http://wiley.custhelp.com. Customer feedback is critical to our efforts at Sybex.

Best regards,

NEIL EDDE
Vice President and Publisher
Sybex, an Imprint of Wiley

To Jessica, for inspiring me to follow my bliss
—Lisa

To my Grandma, I love you always
—Renée

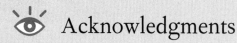 # Acknowledgments

We would like to begin by thanking our editors at Wiley. Mariann Barsolo, thank you for taking this project on, believing in us, and supporting this book. Special thanks to Toni Zuccarini Ackley, development editor, for keeping us on track and patiently spending hours sifting through our docs. And thanks to Sarah Groff-Palermo and Rachel Gunn, our production editors, for bringing it all together. And thanks to Liz Welch for copyediting.

A huge thank you to Tim Grey for introducing us to everyone at Wiley. Without Tim's encouragement, this book might never have been written (or at least never have been finished). Thanks for all the time spent reviewing our materials and guiding us through the sometimes perilous process of writing a book. We appreciate your support.

The writing of this book was certainly not just a two-person operation. We couldn't have made it through without our brilliant and ever-patient technical editor, Oscar Trelles. He graciously rewrote code for us when deadlines loomed and gently slapped us on the wrist when we violated our own best practices. Thank you, Oscar!

Special thanks also to the key contributors and consultants who helped to make this book possible:

- Jim Kremens for developing the MVC Video Player framework and writing the appendix to describe how to extend it, along with his much-needed encouragement and calm demeanor throughout the process.

- Seb Lee-Delisle (sebleedelisle.com) of Plug-in Media for his uncanny ability to debug our code, his willingness to dive headlong into AS3, and his undying patience. And for talking us down off the ledge when need be. (And did I mention he's brilliant at *maths*!)

- James O'Reilly (jamesor.com) for migrating the MVC Video Player framework, among other examples throughout the book, to AS3. No matter what we threw at him, somehow he was always able to make it work.

- Lou Klepner (klepner.com) for coming through with informative sidebars and tutorials on ridiculously short notice, and for being a great all-around go-to guy.

- Tom Kennett and Chris Sperry (http://www.flexiblefactory.co.uk) for lending their keen coding skills (on tight deadlines, to boot) to streamline some of the exercises. The bitmap examples especially were overhauled and greatly improved. These guys know their stuff, and we believe the book has benefited greatly from their help.

- André Costantini (sillydancing.com) for providing our compelling sample video clips (complete with original score), and for going along with our crazy ideas for shoots around the city.

- And let's not forget Bill Sanders (who helped to start all this by sparking our Flash video obsession with his first book on Flash Communication Server a few years ago) for offering advice on this book and helping to troubleshoot along the way, and for his ever-present support and sympathetic ear.

Our sincere appreciation also goes out to the members of the FlashCodersNY (flashcodersny.org) study group, and especially its founder and stalwart guardian, Jean-Charles Carelli. He was ever-encouraging and supportive, even when we were too busy writing to actually show up for the meetings. Thanks also to Tyler Larson, who provided feedback and valuable real-world advice all along the way. And to all the other members who shared horror stories and lessons learned, filling up our inboxes with helpful messages every time I posted to the list for feedback, thanks to you, one and all. One of these Tuesday nights we're going to hold J-C to the promise of that interpretive dance.

We owe a great debt of gratitude to the companies and individuals who graciously provided demo accounts, software, and high-level technical advice: Mike Savello of On2; Randon Morford of Sorenson; Douglas Mow and Philip Simmonds from Navisite; Richard Blakely and Paul Cunningham with Influxis; Burak Kalayci of Manitu Group, for Captionate; and Joel of Flashloaded, for hotFlashVideo. Special thanks also to Adobe's Chris Hock, who has been a great supporter in all of our endeavors in Flash Video from day one.

We also acknowledge GoogleDocs, the single tool that made the workflow of co-writing this book possible. GoogleDocs rocks.

Then there are the patient and understanding family and friends who were there through the highs and lows of the book-writing process.

Lisa's parents and sister Jennifer, who couldn't understand why she'd ever want to take on such a huge project but proudly brags about the fact that she did every chance they get. And past mentors, teachers, and friends who offered inspiration and encouragement over the years: Kevin Serbus, Ko Wicke, Stanley Rosenthal, Stuart Grigg, and Judith Moldenhauer. Then there's Tom, who was there for Lisa throughout—giving nods of understanding even when she was babbling tech-talk; consoling after missed deadlines; holding space patiently, knowing that someday this book was going to be finished... then choosing to propose to her right in the middle of it (of course, she said yes)!

Renée's brothers, André and Michael, who have always supported their little sister. My mom, who has always encouraged me to pursue all of my interests (and there have been many). My dad, thanks for continuing to be such a great influence and inspiration. You both always take the time to coach me on life. I thank all of my friends and family, who repeatedly had to hear the excuse "I can't because I'm working on the book" over the past few months. My teachers, who helped me explore all my interests in design, photography, film, and architecture and find ways to combine them. This was made possible with some help from many of my teachers, namely Abby Goldstein, Stephen Apicella-Hitchcock, and Jack Lach.

About the Authors

Lisa Larson, a developer/designer living in New York City, is co-founder of go:toGroup, a digital media studio specializing in Flash video applications. She began working in print design back in 1988, when graphic design still meant shooting "stats" in the darkroom, keylining with wax and a t-square, and composing type on a Compugraphic 7200. Always drawn to emerging technologies, though, she latched onto the Mac as quickly as she could, then taught herself HTML and Flash along the way. She now has more than eight years of experience in web and other electronic media.

A graduate of Wayne State University in Michigan with a BFA in Graphic Design, Lisa also received a New Media Certification from the Rhode Island School of Design/Fraunhofer CRCG in 2003. After spending two years as a freelance designer/developer, Lisa co-founded go:toGroup. She is currently the firm's Technical Director, specializing in Flash Video and Flash Media Server applications.

Whether it's interactive design, print design, or application development, Lisa has an award-winning approach to all her work. She has written technical articles for the Adobe.com Developer's Center and StreamingMedia.com and is an active member of the FlashCodersNY user group. She was recently selected as one of ten Flash developers spotlighted by Adobe for their 10th Anniversary of Flash commemorative website.

She is also actively developing iFoxCam, a consumer video surveillance product using Flash Media Server.

When she's not glued to the computer screen, Lisa enjoys yoga, belly dancing, and geeking out with her FlashCodersNY buds. She tries to blog just about every day on FlashConnections.com, where she posts news, tips, and ramblings about Flash video, workflow issues, and life in the big city.

Renée Costantini has more than seven years of experience in print and interactive design, specializing in marketing and strategic planning. She started as a freelance graphic designer in 1999 in New York and is currently the driving force behind go:toGroup, Inc.'s business development.

She holds a B.A. in Visual Arts from Fordham University at Lincoln Center and received her New Media Certification from the Rhode Island School of Design/Fraunhofer CRCG in 2003. She also earned a Web Design Certification from Parsons School of Design.

Renée is cofounder of go:toGroup, Inc. She specializes in integrating marketing concepts with print and web design, with an emphasis on usability.

If not tethered to technology, Renée can be found traveling, running, reading, or making notes on paper cups, and is busy trying to discover the next big idea.

Lisa and Renée met in Providence, Rhode Island, when they arrived at RISD. Initially, the Cliff Walk, Red Bull, and "The Sopranos" brought them together. Intrigued by the possibilities of digital media, with an understanding of traditional design, and the desire to bring the two together, they found common ground. After working together briefly interning with Hasbro, it seemed only natural to go into business together a couple of years later. Luckily for Renée, Lisa still humors her by going along with ideas such as this book.

Founded by Renée and Lisa, go:toGroup Inc. offers consulting and application development for clients ranging from start-up companies to large media corporations. Their recent projects range from custom Flash video players, to fully interactive video applications, to integration of ad display functionality into existing applications. They also have experience in user interface and usability design and bring that sensibility to all of their projects.

Renée and Lisa can often be seen speaking at, or attending, industry events and conferences such as Flash in the Can, Flash on the Beach, FlashBelt, FlashForward, and StreamingMedia. They can always be reached through their company website, http://gotogroupinc.com, or through their blog, http://flashconnections.com.

Foreword

Eric Schumacher-Rasmussen, Editor, *Streaming Media* magazine

When I started covering the world of streaming media in 2003, the jury was still out on whether or not this "web video" thing would ever really take off. Sure, large enterprises and educational institutions had been able to exploit the cost-saving advantages of delivering communications and e-learning via online video, but only because they didn't have to send those relatively huge files out over the public Internet to users whose bandwidth access ranged from paltry 28.8kbps modems to the occasional 128kbps ISDN line.

The widespread access to media and entertainment video—promised by so many in the heady, pre-bubble years of 1999–2000—still looked like a pipe dream. It wasn't until broadband access reached something close to critical mass that the promise of Internet video delivery began to resemble reality. And even as recently as late 2005, when U.S. broadband penetration crept up toward 50 percent of Internet users, video was still low on most consumers' list of web priorities.

We all know what happened then. User-generated video sites, YouTube chief among them, became *the* entertainment and technology story of 2006, the vanguard of the Web 2.0 revolution that led *Time* magazine to name "You"—as in the users who contributed all of that content, video and otherwise—as its Person of the Year. For the first time, Internet surfers were watching video in droves, even if the video on most of those sites was either juvenile or, shall we say, "repurposed" television content.

What was missing from most of the discussion about YouTube was any mention of the technology that made YouTube and other user-generated video sites possible. But even if that omission seemed glaring to those of us who'd been following streaming video for years, it was really the best thing we could have hoped for. It meant that users don't have to think about what's going on behind the curtain when they watch video online. It just *works*.

And what is the video technology behind YouTube? Adobe Flash Video. Users upload their videos, in whatever digital format they wish, and that video is transcoded into Flash Video. Why Flash Video? Because, unlike so many other video formats, Flash Video plays on virtually every computer on the planet, whether or not you build it into a Flash Player, without the viewer having to install additional software. And though other online video formats have their strongholds—Windows Media Video in locked-down corporate IT environments, QuickTime for Hollywood movie trailers—Flash Video has emerged over the last few years as the leading video format on the Web.

I know what you're thinking: "But so many of those videos on YouTube look horrible!" Maybe it really *is* a good thing that most people don't know that YouTube uses Flash Video; the grainy picture and often choppy playback just might give Flash Video a bad name. That's got everything to do with the fact that YouTube can't control the quality of the source videos and places a premium on quick-and-dirty transcoding rather than having a professional video editor or Flash developer work with each and every clip submitted to its site.

That's fine for YouTube, but it's not representative of even one-tenth of what Flash Video is capable of, not only in terms of video quality but—and most importantly—the entire viewing experience. You can see *that* on hundreds of high-impact, interactive advertising and marketing campaigns, with custom-branded players running crystal-clear video that features clickable spots that will lead viewers deeper into their content. Or in dynamic training courses that combine video seamlessly with Flash animations and other Adobe tools like Contribute. Or myriad other applications where what's going on behind the curtain *is* exceedingly complex, and subtle nuances in encoding and embedding can make all the difference between the dull and the dazzling.

That's where this book comes in. What Lisa Larson and Renee Costantini have done here is put together an exhaustive resource for developers who want to take advantage of everything Flash and Flash Video have to offer. And when I say "exhaustive," I mean it. From the client proposal to the encoding to the correct use of ActionScript and BitmapData objects, this book offers both high-level and quite granular information. It's a technical book, to be sure, but it doesn't ignore the fact that all of this technical information doesn't mean a thing if you lose sight of the big picture. So whether you're an experienced Flash developer looking to add Flash Video to your toolkit or a novice who's just beginning to explore Flash, let this book be your guide.

Contents

Introduction   *xvii*

Chapter 1   Project Archaeology   **1**

Scout the Site: Define Client Needs 2
Getting the Lay of the Land: The Site Survey   3
Excavation: The Interview   4

Piece Together the Artifacts: Determine the Appropriate Solution 5
Anticipate the Pitfalls   6

Construct the Project Map: The Proposal 8
Price It Right   11
Offer Alternate Routes   12

Summary 13

Chapter 2   Raw Materials: Encoding Basics   **15**

Footage Fundamentals 16
Receiving Source Video from Your Client   16
Producing Your Own Video   17
Getting Fancy: Transparent Video   19

How Do I Create FLVs? 21
Helpful Tips, No Matter What Encoder You Use   24

Obtaining and Encoding Video 26
Your Handy-Dandy Encoding Reference   26
Where the Rubber Hits the Road: Let's Encode   29

Summary 35

Chapter 3   Creating a Video Delivery Roadmap   **37**

Functionality and Flow 38
Flow Chart   39
Start Building   40
Testing 1, 2, 3   40
Back Button Considerations   40
Flash Player Detection   41
Flash Video Navigation   42
Keep It Simple   42

Progressive or Streaming? That Is the Question 42
Embed Video in SWF   43
Progressive Download   44
Streaming   44

On to the ActionScript!..................................46
Progressive Delivery: AS2   46
Progressive Delivery: AS3   48
Streaming Delivery: AS2   50
Streaming Delivery: AS3   51

Publishing and Hosting Choices 52
What Is a CDN, and Why Do I Need One?   53
What Is an FVSS?   53
What If I Need More Services?   54
What About Offline Video? FLV to DVD   54

Don't Copy That Floppy: Digital Rights Management 55

Summary..56

Chapter 4   OOP and the Video Application   57

Why All This Hoopla About OOP? 58
What Is OOP?   58
What Are the Key Elements of OOP?   58
Why Is OOP So Useful in Flash Development?   59
And What Does OOP Have to Do with Flash Video?   59

Design Patterns and Flash Video...........................59
Model-View-Controller (MVC)   60
State Design Pattern (SDP)   62

The Fork in the Road: AS2 vs. AS3 64
Which Language Do You Speak Fluently?   64
What Does Your Application Have to Do?   65
What's Your Target Player?   65

Setting Up Your Work Environment 66
Doing It Our Way: Setting Up Eclipse, FDT, and MTASC for AS2 Development   67

Viva la Open Source! 73

Summary..74

Chapter 5   The Video Player   75

So You Need to Play a Video—Where to Begin 76

Creating a Player Using Components 76
What the FLVPlayback Component Can Do   77
What It Can't Do   77
Using the FLVPlayback Component in Flash CS3   78

Roll Your Own: Creating a Custom Player....................86
Our Player Structure   89
Dissecting the Code   92
Skin It!   98

Summary..99

Chapter 6   Getting It Out There: Test, Optimize, and Deploy   101

Test It, Then Test It Again. Repeat. 102
Test-Driven Development vs. Testing While Coding   102
Tests, Tests, and More Tests   104

Nobody Likes to Wait: Bandwidth Considerations 109
Video Buffering: Not If, but How Much   109
Bandwidth Detection: How Much Can We Push Through That Pipe?   110

3, 2, 1... Ready to Launch! 118
Progressive Deployment   119
Streaming Deployment   121

But Wait, There's More: Project Wrap-up 124
Revisiting the Spec Sheet   125
Final Walkthrough   126
Launching   126
Deliverables: Documentation and Asset Files   126
Schedule a Meeting   127
Archiving   127

Summary. 128

Chapter 7   Dynamic Playlists   129

When Clients Attack: Handling Content Updates. 130

Playlists in the Wild: Your Options 131
PlaylistListBox.fla: Simple Array into a ListBox   137
PlaylistListBox_XML.fla: XML Data into a ListBox   139

Mixing It Up: Sequential and Shuffle Playback 144
PlayListAutoPlay.fla: Sequential Playback   145
PlaylistShuffle.fla: Playing Random Videos from Your Playlist   146

Integrating an XML Playlist into the MVC Player 148
test_playlist.xml   148
AS2: MediaPlayer.as   149
AS3: Main.as   152

Summary. 154

Chapter 8   Demystifying Metadata and Cue Points   155

Metadata Magic 156
Reading Metadata   159
How Long Is This Video?   161

Cue Point Power 165
Why Would You Want to Use Cue Points?   165
What Data Does a Cue Point Contain?   165
Now That You Want to Use Cue Points, How Do You Add Them?   166
What Are the Three Types of Cue Points Used For?   167
How to Read Cue Points on a NetStream   168

Adding Dynamic ActionScript Cue Points   170
Adding Captions   173
Adding Chapter Links   177

Progressive Sleight-of-Hand: Scripted Psuedo-Streaming 184
Traditional Progressive Download   184
Scripted Pseudo-Streaming   185
Now That You're Enlightened...   189

Summary 189

Chapter 9   **Bending Pixels with Filters and Masks**   **191**

What Can I Do to My Video? 192

One Video, Many Masks 192
ActionScript 2: FunWithMasks.as   193
ActionScript 3: FunWithMasks.as   199

Alpha Channels, Revisited. 207

Fun with Filters and Tints. 208
ActionScript 2: FunWithFilters.as   210
ActionScript 3: FunWithFilters.as   215

Lost in Transitions 220
ActionScript 2: FunWithTransitions.as   221
ActionScript 3: FunWithTransitions.as   225

Summary 230

Chapter 10   **Video and the BitmapData Object**   **231**

What Is This BitmapData Object, and Why Should I Care? 232

Dynamic Thumbnails: Video Snapshots 235
ActionScript 2: FLVBitmapThumb   235
ActionScript 3: FLVBitmapThumb   239

Transitions and Dissolves 246
ActionScript 2: FLVBitmapTransition   247
ActionScript 3: FLVBitmapTransition   258

The FotoBooth Application. 265
ActionScript 2: FotoBooth Application   266
ActionScript 3: FotoBooth Application   270

Summary 280

Chapter 11   **Live Video and Webcams: FMS**   **281**

The Video Revolution Will Be...Webcast 282
What FMS Is and How It Works   282
Why It's So Cool   283
Where/How You Can Use It   283

FMS2 Live! What You Need to Know 283

Hosting: Choices, Choices, Choices   284
Setting Up a Development Environment   287
File Structure   288
The Basics   289
The Media Classes   291

From Your Webcam to the World 293

videoConf.fla   293

What Else Can This FMS2 Thing Do? 306

File Class   306
Server-Side Data Manipulation   306
Server-to-Server Communication   307
Bandwidth Management   307
Server-Side Streaming   308
Load Balancing   308
Control Access to Streams and Recording   308
Secure Applications   309

Smart Bandwidth Streaming 310

FMS Hit List: Lisa's Tips and Tricks 311

Summary 313

Appendix: Real-World Deployment of an MVC Media Player   315

Our Client's Requirements 316

Refactoring Higher-Level Framework Code 317

Implementing EventBroadcaster   317
Using a Code-Based Animation Library   318

Refactoring MVC Media Player Code 318

Changing How MVC Connections Are Made   318
Adding Necessary Methods to the Interfaces 320
Implementing New Methods in the Classes   324

Adding Multiple Components to the View 331

Core Component Class   332
Elapsed/Total Time Display   335
Mute/Unmute Buttons   336
Fast-Forward and Rewind Buttons   337
Play/Pause Button   339
Volume Slider   342
Seek Bar   343
Download Progress Bar   343

Media Player Wrapup – MVC pays off! 344

Taking It to the Next Level 345

Index   349

Introduction

You may notice as you read this book that we have developed quite a passion for Flash video. With all the technologies out there to build a business around, why did we specifically choose this one? The way we see it, Flash Video chose us.

Back in 2003, Lisa had an opportunity to learn Flash Communication Server while working with (and cofounding) a start-up company called iFoxCam, in Providence, Rhode Island. She already had experience with Flash and ActionScript development, but this immersion into interactive video got her to thinking. Video can be played right in the browser using Flash, Flash offers an almost unlimited amount of interactivity, and Action-Script is accessible to even novice programmers—she knew this was gonna be big.

Meanwhile, Renée was in New York City, working as the marketing director for a major magazine. Although her past experience was in print and interaction design, she, as always, was keeping her eye on the latest trends—trying to discover what the next one was going to be. As she watched old media struggling and new media thriving, she said to Lisa one day, "One word. Broadcast!"

All the pieces began to fall together. Flash video started to gain momentum as developers and marketers began to realize the power of video in the browser. Yahoo! Video, Google Video, YouTube, ABC, MTV...video was on the rise. Then, in 2004, Lisa joined Renée in New York City and go:toGroup was born. Through Lisa's published articles on video and her experience with iFoxCam, along with Renée's networking and business strategies, clients began to come to go:toGroup almost exclusively for Flash video projects.

So, you ask, why did we write this book? This is the book we wished we had next to us when we began working with Flash video. The one we could have referred to when trying to figure out what the best keyframe rate was, and why. When we wanted to know how to create a playlist, or mask a video. The book that would have told us the pitfalls we might run into when accepting video content from a client, or transitioning from development server into deployment. The book that laid out the hosting choices available and the pros and cons of each. This is that book.

Every day, we developers wake up and work in the real world. We get projects, we spec them out, we code and build applications, we manage to avoid some pitfalls and fall headfirst into others. We don't just need to know how to stream a video—we need to know how to handle the situations when the video won't stream, or the XML won't load, or the client changes the specifications on the player we just spent two weeks developing. Code is important, sure, and there's plenty of it in this book. But we're also here to teach you what to do with that code, and most importantly, what's possible with Flash video.

We hope this book is inspirational, informative, and useful to you. We hope you read it through from start to finish, and keep it by your side for reference and guidance.

Who Can Benefit from This Book

We've targeted this book toward intermediate-level developers who need to integrate Flash video into their skill set. If you're comfortable in ActionScript 2, the side-by-side comparisons of AS2 and AS3 code can help ease the transition to ActionScript 3. If you're already familiar with AS3, this book should help to clarify the differences in how AS3 treats video, and specifically the syntax changes introduced in the video-related classes.

With the release of ActionScript 3, a solid grasp of object-oriented programming (OOP) will become more crucial to developing professional applications in Flash. Many developers who consider themselves to be at the intermediate level haven't taken the leap into object-oriented programming. We understand. We've been there. In this book, we aim to ease you into the concept, with a clear overview of OOP principles and lots of class-based examples to help you understand the approach. When you finish reading this book, you will have a better understanding of class-based structures and design patterns that you can put into place in your video applications.

Like it or not, no matter if you're working in an in-house department or as an independent developer, you'll need to deal with some level of project management. For this reason, we've also spent a good deal of time discussing the up-front considerations involved in planning and managing real-world Flash video applications. Hopefully you'll be involved in, if not heading up, the planning process. You'll need to deal with clients directly and manage expectations and deliverables. And it is ultimately your responsibility to avoid technical stumbling blocks that can trip up deployment of your project. This book will help give you the big-picture perspective, and also alert you to common gotchas that can occur in Flash video projects, saving you time, money, and face.

If you are a developer, designer, or even a project manager working on Flash video applications with solid deadlines and high client expectations, this book is for you. We do our best to avoid esoteric exercises and clearly give you the knowledge, reference, and practical code examples you need to get the job done.

About This Book

This book takes a holistic approach to covering Flash video projects. It's not just a process guide, and it's not just an ActionScript reference. By covering all aspects of the development process, we give you the perspective you need to create rock-solid, professional—and profitable—Flash video applications.

We've culled not just from our own experience, but also from the tried-and-true experience of colleagues specializing in Flash video (or those who have struggled themselves to integrate video into their Flash projects). From determining the scope of a project to creating a reusable player structure, we share our common pitfalls, tips and tricks, and lessons learned along the way. Both ActionScript 2 and ActionScript 3 code will be covered, with special attention given to helping you transition from one version to the next.

You'll start by learning the basics of project planning and dealing with clients. In Chapter 1, we give you the tools you need to get the most relevant information out of your clients before starting the job. With a sample preliminary project survey, suggestions for determining the appropriate solutions, and pricing guidelines, you'll be armed with everything you need to put together a proposal and project spec.

Next, in Chapter 2 we'll dive into the intricacies of encoding video into the FLV format. We'll give you a detailed primer on video in general, tips on shooting your own video, and recommended FLV encoding guidelines. We'll guide you through the encoding process and discuss your software options. Alpha-channel video considerations, DVD source conversion methods, and helpful tips will round out your knowledge.

In Chapter 3, we step back again to the planning stage, where you actually begin to sketch out the underlying structure of your application and determine the best method of video delivery. This step is crucial to the success of your project, so we cover details such as basic functionality, flow charting, planning for testing, digital rights management, and player version detection. A variety of hosting and delivery options are available for Flash video as well, so we cover these in depth and offer some suggestions.

Chapter 4 offers you a primer in OOP, with special attention to how it can be useful in Flash video applications. We define OOP for those who are not familiar with the concept, and explain why we extol its virtues as a basis for robust applications. Common ways to structure applications, known as design patterns, that can be particularly useful in video applications are discussed. Here we also compare the differences in AS2 and AS3, and help you to decide which version to use for the project at hand. Then, as an added bonus, we discuss options for setting up your work environment to program using class-based methods. There are lots of open source programs and utilities that can help streamline your workflow, so we introduce you to a few of those as well.

Next, we dive into the ActionScript. In Chapter 5, we introduce the basic code used to play a video in Flash, and explain the basics of the NetConnection and NetStream objects. Then, we discuss the FLVPlayback component, its benefits and shortcomings, along with our recommendations for when and where to use it. This leads us into the basics of creating your own custom player, where we present a basic framework for a player that is based on the Model-View-Controller design pattern. This player structure will be referred to, and extended, in later chapters.

Chapter 6 will bring you back to project planning a bit, but gets more into technical considerations and solutions for final deployment. Here we point out things you'll need to plan for in advance (but this chapter can also be a reference for you when you're rolling out the project as well). Formal testing, bandwidth considerations, video buffering, and progressive versus streaming deployment are all explored in detail. Important procedures such as final client testing and rollout, final deliverables, client wrap-up meetings, project follow-up, and archiving are covered, and we provide some tips to help you keep your clients happy and satisfied.

Then, in Chapter 7, we dig right into the meat and potatoes: creating dynamic playlists. Implementing a dynamic playlist gives you a reusable player, allowing your clients to update their content themselves. We discuss your playlist options, from simple arrays, to XML data, to playing an FLV dynamically from a specific directory, and we offer code examples to get you started. Methods for playing videos in sequence and playing random videos are also covered.

Then, diving even deeper into the inner world of the FLV, we explore metadata and cuepoints in Chapter 8. Here we unravel the mystery of metadata and demonstrate some of its useful applications. Then we explain the intricacies of the various types of cuepoints and how you can use them to create some pretty cool dynamic video applications. Video navigation, chapter markers, event triggers, and captions are just some of the options we discuss. Code examples and encoding methods are presented, so you can understand the entire process of working with cuepoints and metadata.

In Chapter 9, we have some fun with the new pixel-level control that Flash offers, applying filters and transformations to video. Drop shadows, color matrix, color transform, and blur filters are demonstrated in a little "switcher" application that you can play around with. Then we give you examples of dynamic masking of video and show you ways it can be used creatively in your applications.

Then, in Chapter 10, we'll explore the uses of the BitmapData object for creating thumbnails, still-frame placeholders, and video transitions. We included lots of code examples in this chapter, including a full application we created that simulates a retro photo booth, snapping pictures of a video every few seconds and displaying them in a filmstrip. We even introduce the code used to grab snapshots from a webcam.

Finally, in the last chapter, we give you a crash course in Flash Media Server (FMS) and live video. Along with a basic overview of client-side and server-side communication classes, we give you ideas about how FMS can be used in interactive applications that utilize real-time video, audio, and data sharing. Your hosting options are discussed, and we outline what's needed to develop and test FMS applications. We briefly discuss alternatives to FMS as well. As a demonstration, we show you how to create a two-person videoconference with audio and utilizing remote shared objects.

The appendix is a nice little bonus case study written by Jim Kremens, the architect of our MVC player framework from Chapter 5. He explains the framework in great detail, and shows you how to extend it into a robust player application that you can re-skin easily, and reuse again and again for your real-world projects.

Overall, this book will provide a basic framework and building blocks to make custom Flash video more accessible. It will give you insight into the entire process—customer engagement, planning, development, review—all the way through project launch.

The Companion Website

All exercises and examples discussed in this book are available for download at both the official Wiley website, http://www.sybex.com/go/flashvideo/, and our blog, http://www .flashconnections.com. The downloadable resources will include all source files, published SWFs, sample FLVs, and related scripts. Our blog is updated often with new resources, links, tips, answers to frequently asked questions, and Flash video-related news.

Project Archaeology

Starting a new Flash video project, especially with a new client, is much like arriving on an archaeological site. There's important information under the surface that you need to uncover. What is the overall focus of the application? What are the audience bandwidth targets and file size restraints? What type of video navigation and interaction is needed? As the developer, it's your job to drill down to the main objectives and functionality of a project, and create a realistic map to get there. This chapter will walk you through the steps of mapping out a successful Flash video project.

1

Chapter Contents

Scout the Site: Define Client Needs
Piece Together the Artifacts: Determine the
    Appropriate Solution
Construct the Project Map: The Proposal

Scout the Site: Define Client Needs

As any good archaeologist would tell you, you don't start digging without first scouting the site. Before you get started on any project, especially one involving video, you have to clearly define its scope. All too often we developers jump eagerly into the technical aspects of a project, delivering exactly what the client asked for, only to end up with a disappointed client. It can be frustrating to deliver exactly what they said they wanted, only to have them tell you it doesn't achieve their goals. "I want DVD quality!" is a common request, but when a video of that quality is not properly deployed on the Web, disaster ensues. The video stutters and stops as it squeezes through on its limited bandwidth. The client isn't happy, the viewer isn't happy, and neither are you.

As an expert (if you aren't one now, this book will help you get there), you play a critical role in helping to define these realistic project specifications with your client. You need to truly see this as a partnership. Doing so always works to your advantage and will set you apart from the less-involved developer. This approach will lead to a better overall relationship with your client, and you will gain their trust as the expert.

They may not be able to articulate it, but you need to trust that your clients *know* what they need. It is important that you spend time listening and asking the right questions to develop a full understanding of their goals. Excavating the real job scope from this exchange is your challenge.

Note: Listen more than you talk. You can't hear what your client is communicating to you if you're too busy telling them what you know!

Read Between the Lines (or, Is the Customer Really Always Right?)

"I want the video to play automatically when someone comes to the site—and it needs to play FULL-SCREEN."

Wow, this guy really wants attention. He wants every visitor to see that video, in their face, in high quality. But as anyone involved in the execution of Flash video on the Web knows, many of those visitors won't see that video in high quality at full-screen size—it'll be a jerky, jittery slideshow—if they don't get so annoyed at the full-screen pop-up that they leave the site altogether, that is.

So, reading between the lines here, what does this client really want?

He wants to entice the visitor to watch the video, and he wants them to see the best quality possible. There are many ways to prompt the visitor to view video content. Playing an animation or a very short clip of the video to draw attention on the page is one option. Except in special applications, it's almost always best to let visitors *choose* to play a video and not make that choice for them.

The Flash Player does now have a full-screen video option built in, but keeping in mind bandwidth issues, as well as user preference, it's best to let users specifically choose that option too. Either let them choose low- or high-bandwidth options or, if you are streaming, dynamically serve the optimized video for their connection automatically.

Explain your proposed solution to your client in a way that is positive and makes them feel that you respect them and their ideas, and your slap of reality will sting a bit less. Even though these are mostly usability considerations, they almost always have a technical counterpart, as in extra work. Clients are usually hesitant to spend extra money in usability, but presenting it as an investment in their corporate image is known to yield results.

Getting the Lay of the Land: The Site Survey

So, how do you partner with your client in this "dig?" You begin by asking lots of questions. Their answers will help you define the overall goal and offer solutions.

What are the key components and features? Will there be user-generated content? Who is the audience? What are their limitations? Browser? Platform? Connection speed? What version of Flash will be required?

One of the best ways to extract that information from your client is to prepare a survey document with pertinent questions for the client to fill out prior to the initial meeting. It is meant to provide an overview, covering questions in such categories as general information, project information, content, marketing goals, and technical considerations. We have found this to be a great way to get started because it allows the client to complete it at their convenience and get input from others who may not be available for a phone call or meeting. Also, the sheer act of putting thoughts in writing will offer clarity. In short, it efficiently gets your project under way.

Flash Video Survey Sample Questions

Here are some of the questions we've found helpful to include in the survey for a new Flash video project:

- What are your primary objectives? Secondary?
- Who will be the primary contact person for this project? Who makes the final decisions?
- When is the expected launch date of the project?

Continues

Flash Video Survey Sample Questions *(Continued)*

- Do you have a specific budget range? Can the project be divided into phases to accommodate budget and timing constraints?

- Describe the user interface look and feel of the application/website. Are designs/screen layouts being provided?

- Will this site use existing content from the current site? If not, who will be providing the content, and when?

- How do most people find out about your website or application?

- How many people (as far as you can tell) access your site on a daily, weekly, or monthly basis? How do you measure usage?

- Will the content need to be dynamic (changing often or automatically)? Will a content management system be required to allow you to update the content?

- Will you be providing source video? If so, what are the specs (dimensions, frame rate, file format)? Can you provide a sample file now?

- If utilizing long-form video, will "seek" functionality be required? In other words, do you want a "scrubber" bar that viewers can use to scan through the video?

- If predetermined, in what format(s) will the project be executed (i.e., Flash, a Flash-HTML hybrid, or other technology)?

- What deliverables will be required?

- Do you have a target file size for the final application?

- Will the project be deployed on a new server or on an existing server? What level of access will be provided (i.e., FTP, SFTP, Root access)? Who will be the IT point of contact?

We've provided a complete sample survey for you to download at http://www.flashconnections .com/flash-pro/.

Excavation: The Interview

In archaeology, the excavation process involves the exposure, processing, and recording of data. In our scenario, you "excavate" the information you need by conducting an interview with your client. The interview is an opportunity for you to understand what the client's real needs are. You are an active participant here, and need to take charge of the process. You'll be taking the valuable survey information and digging deeper for more meaningful answers.

You'll want to walk through the completed survey with your client, in person if at all possible. This will allow you to ask questions and clarify details. This is your chance to ask things like:

- Will your visitors want to view the site on mobile devices?
- What are the most important features?
- What are your plans for the future? Does this application need to be scalable?
- How solid is the deadline date? Is there a tradeshow or other event that you need to accommodate?
- What happens when a deadline isn't met? How will delays on the client's side affect the expected delivery date and final price?
- Any other questions that your client may not have considered.

Note: Break down "geek speak" into plain English. Keep the tone informative, never condescending.

Having a strong understanding of your client's goals will also help you maximize the project's value. Giving them verbatim what they say they need may lead to a proposal so cumbersome that you'll never get the job, or never get the job done. Understanding their needs and defining your own solution will likely result in a much leaner project. We'll talk about the importance of providing multiple pricing options later in this chapter.

Piece Together the Artifacts: Determine the Appropriate Solution

Now you have nailed down what this application needs to do. The next step is to figure out how to get it done. Video projects are complex and demanding in nature, and mistakes are expensive. We have listed some common example projects that can help point you in the right direction. They reference chapters in this book that would be useful in these common scenarios.

Video Playlist with Variable Bandwidth Options

Design a smooth user experience (Chapter 3: "Creating a Video Delivery Roadmap")

Detect user bandwidth and display appropriate clip (Chapter 6: "Getting It Out There: Test, Optimize and Deploy")

Determine the source of clip names (Chapter 7: "Dynamic Playlists")

Player with Chapter Links

Add bookmarks using Cue Points (Chapter 8: "Demystifying Metadata and Cue Points")

Live Webcam Conference with Text and Sound

Use Flash Media Server (Chapter 11: "Live Video and Webcams")

Choose deployment solution (Chapter 3: "Creating a Video Delivery Roadmap")

Note: The costs for hosting video content can vary significantly and often are not considered by the client ahead of time. Many delivery options are available, ranging from hosting your own streaming Flash Media Server 2 to using a content delivery network; we'll cover those topics in detail in Chapter 3. You will want to make your client aware of the options and pricing structures from the beginning of the project.

Anticipate the Pitfalls

Managing Flash video projects is often like navigating an obstacle course. This section will give you an overview of the major obstacles so you can avoid them, or at least plan ahead.

When dealing with video in Flash specifically, you'll consistently run into certain problems. We've outlined some (including some of our own hard lessons) in the "What You Don't Know *Can* Hurt You" sidebar, and also included a few general project-related problems that we found cropping up often. You'll find the survey document very helpful in ferreting out these potential issues early on.

Overall, the best approach is to keep the project as simple as possible. It is difficult to make something cutting edge that is 100 percent fail-proof. When you start adding various connection options, compatibility requirements, and all the bells and whistles, the potential problems will grow exponentially. Even the simplest of applications can have some serious complexity behind the scenes. This is why this first "project archeology" step is so crucial.

Many of the pitfall examples may seem like common sense, but it's easy to gloss over them when planning and pricing a project. You want to be as thorough as possible in these preliminary stages so that you encounter fewer surprises along the way. Having an experienced associate play "devil's advocate" and point out potential flaws in your project plan is always a good idea. "What happens if the video file specified in the XML does not exist?" "What happens if the visitor loses their Internet connection while broadcasting?" "What if the video goes viral and traffic spikes?" We've seen this happen, and it's not fun. Developers should plan for "unplanned" traffic increments; this means making sure the hardware will not break down with the overhead, and that there's enough bandwidth allowance in the case of shared hosting. It's difficult to anticipate every possible scenario, but with experience and the information in this book you will be able to spot potential pitfalls early and avoid them.

What You Don't Know *Can* Hurt You

We've learned the hard way, so you don't have to! Here are our top eight gaffes (that we're willing to admit to); some were more expensive than others:

1. Trying to make do with existing subpar hardware; we lost sleep and missed deadlines in the process.

2. Implementing ActionScript 3 (AS3) in the middle of a project; learning a new language as you go is never a good idea.

3. Caving in to client demands to deliver their website before testing was complete. The site still didn't launch on time.

4. Not having a written contract. Enough said.

5. Realizing we needed a DV camera without including it in the budget. Doh!

6. Traveling offsite with no remote access to files. Figures—our biggest client called us for changes on an old project shortly after our plane landed.

7. Expecting that the client knew how to encode good-quality Flash video files (FLVs) because they said they did.

8. Not having a plan B. A colleague of ours had a photoshoot where the client washed and prepped a fleet of limousines — and his camera broke on-site. Thankfully, there was an electronic store nearby that had his exact camera in-stock (whew). Without a replacement camera, his specialty 360-degree lens would have been useless. Rescheduling the shoot would have been a nightmare as the limos get booked for events.

Some other common pitfalls to avoid:

- Getting incompatible assets from the client after the application is already built.

- Not planning for NTSC/PAL conversion issues (e.g., audio and video out of sync, video flicker, etc.).

- Video encoded using square versus nonsquare pixels (there are reasons for both; we'll cover that in Chapter 2).

- Failure to use a high-quality microphone to record audio.

- No limit or goal set for final file size.

- Not getting crucial content from client prior to starting the project (most clients don't understand that DVDs do not make the best source video). The earlier you get involved, the better. If you can monitor the shoot, please do. Often producers are not knowledgeable about the video formats required for Flash video. We will arm you with the information you need to know in Chapter 2.

Continues

What You Don't Know *Can* Hurt You *(Continued)*

- Not accommodating low-bandwidth situations.

- Not planning for interrupted connections in streaming applications.

- Not anticipating traffic spikes (load balancing).

- Not getting input from the real decision makers early in the process.

- Not leaving enough time for torture testing.

- Poor communication with IT staff responsible for final project deployment.

- Attempting to incorporate new technology on a tight deadline.

- Not planning for future uses (scalability of application).

- Trying to get by using inefficient software or hardware (not using the right tools for the job). This last one's pretty important. *Never try to dig with a teaspoon when the job calls for a shovel!*

Construct the Project Map: The Proposal

Using the data you've unearthed from the survey and interview (while steering clear of the pitfalls), you are now ready to construct a map of the project—in other words, a formal proposal. This document will define the actual project scope. Its purpose is to have the project specifications clearly defined in writing for both client and developer. It also provides a benchmark to ensure that the project is on time and on budget, and is built to specification. If the client decides in the middle of the project that they want to add on-the-fly alpha channel video, you can whip out the proposal document and remind them that, though you'd be thrilled to add it, it's not in the spec so you'll issue a change order. (Yes, those need to be in writing, too!) When it appears you're off course, you can always use the map as a reference to get back on track.

The most useful maps are detailed. Be as specific as possible, and include:

- Overall objective, stated in one sentence

- Deliverables

- File formats

- Milestones

- Who will be providing assets, when, and in what format

- Functionality of application/navigation

- Browser and bandwidth targets

- Additional programming languages required

See Figure 1.1 for a real world example of a typical Proposal. This file is also available for download at http://www.flashconnections.com/flash-pro/.

Project Specification :: Multimedia Playlist Widget
PREPARED FOR Sample Client, Jan 1, 2007

User interface and programming of custom Flash multimedia "player" to be integrated with existing [url address here] website. Deliverables: FLA, SWF and associated JS files.

PLAYER VERSION 1 : Basic Multimedia Player with Playlist and Other Stories Block

- Working with project team, finalize look and feel of simple multimedia player interface to coordinate with company branding. Have this look finalized by Monday, 1/23 EOD.
- All content including copy, FLVs, JPGs, SWFs and HTML/CSS page template provided by client.
- Layout and copy for initial splash to be provided by client.

Create basic XML-based Flash Multimedia Player with the following functionality:

- Read widget headline, media captions, thumbnail filenames and media filenames from XML file. This file can be edited by client. (This is a text file, no editing interface.)
- Ability to display JPG, SWF, or FLV files. *Initial design will accommodate 355x244 max size.*
- Support for display of extended characters in copy.
- Show thumbnails and short captions for each, in a single scrolling playlist. These captions will be limited to a certain number of characters (to be determined).
- Video player will have basic functionality (play/pause toggle, jump to start, progress bar, volume control, sound mute toggle).
- On initial page load, visitor will choose Low Bandwidth or High Bandwidth experience.
- Optimized for Flash 8/ON2 codec, served as progressive video through [service provider]
- Target audience: Internet Explorer 6, Javascript enabled.
- Integrate with [service provider] tracking, providing basic statistics: video filename and number of times played. Need access to a test account for development.
- Dynamic article title (or other headline copy) displayed at top of widget.
- Dynamic caption displayed with media file.

continued

Web » Print » Interactive » Design + Development

www.gotoGroupInc.com

9
■
CONSTRUCT THE PROJECT MAP: THE PROPOSAL

Figure 1.1 Sample proposal

go:to Group

- If there is only one video for the article, no scrolling playlist will show. The video will center in the space.
- HTML/javascript links from html article text to load media files (SWF, JPG or FLV)
- Second SWF that displays a scrolling playlist of the Other Articles, which are pulled from another XML document. This document will be common to all articles in the series, so it will detect what the current article is, and omit it from the list. Height of widget will accommodate two articles at a time.

ESTIMATED: 10 days @ $[dayrate]: [Total Cost]

Since timing is imperative and deadlines are tight, we will set aside these 10 days between 1/20 – 2/6, finishing Phase 1 by EOD Friday, 2/6. If there are delays in approval or receipt of materials, this will affect the delivery date accordingly. If the deadline or receipt of materials is delayed by client, we'll need 3 working days' notice to rearrange reserved schedule or a fee of 50% of day rate will be incurred for the days not utilized.

PLAYER VERSION 2 : Added Functionality to Player v1

- Additional [service provider] tracking: session tracking, video viewing duration
- Larger size media overlay (scale existing FLV) This size TBD by client before coding begins.

ESTIMATED: 5 days @ $[dayrate]: [Total Cost]

We will set aside these 6 days between 2/7 – 2/17. If there are delays in approval or receipt of materials, this will affect the delivery date accordingly.

*TERMS: **50%** UPON ACCEPTANCE OF PROJECT PHASE, BALANCE UPON COMPLETION*

Thank you for the opportunity to quote on this project.
Please contact us with any questions regarding this estimate.

Figure 1.1 Sample proposal *(contiued)*

The proposal ultimately serves the important function of "managing your client." Managing your client really means managing their expectations. A good proposal is the clearest way to set these expectations. It plays a critical role in your client interaction, partnership, and therefore project success. We can't stress enough how important this step is. If you don't have a map of where you are going, chances are you will never get there!

Note: The devil is in the details. Play out all the nightmare scenarios you can think of from the beginning so you aren't living them later.

Price It Right

Developers and creative professionals use several time-based ways to determine their rates, including hourly fees, day rates, and project fees. Often it's not up to you. It is common for clients to have a system in place that you will have to follow, such as "project not to exceed" clauses, a predetermined purchase order amount, or an approved hourly rate. It's just important that you set a project scope that is reasonable within any time or budget limits.

The more experience you have in pricing, the more accurate you will be in estimating realistic labor hours. The most common problems with calculating pricing involve misjudged rates or projected hours, and not the formulas themselves. To help estimate project fees, or if you are new to pricing, it's a good idea to keep a project time log. This is something you can refer to for future projects to achieve more accurate estimates.

Note: Notice if a potential client is in need of "hand-holding." Expect them to be more hands-on, thus requiring more in-person meetings and phone calls. This is not necessarily a reason to run away—just build extra hours into your estimate for management time.

Here are some common formulas for determining fees:

Hourly Fee (Monthly Overhead Costs / 160) + Hourly Labor Costs + Profit Margin

Take your total monthly overhead costs and divide by the number of working hours in a month (based on five 8-hour days per week). Then add your real hourly labor cost and a profit margin (usually 15–30% of the total).

Day Rate (Standard Hourly Rate × 8) × 90%

This approach applies a 10% volume discount to the standard hourly rate.

Project Fee (Standard Hourly Rate × Number of Hours Estimated) × 2
This multiplier covers the estimated costs of management time, overhead, etc.

Although most clients have a budget in mind in advance, these guesstimates are often made to the best of their ability without having a benchmark for such a project. It's common to state how much a project should cost without having any experience in the industry to know a realistic amount. In our experience, the budget they have in mind is not definitive and they usually have some flexibility depending on the priority the project has in their overall budget for the year.

Once the fee is determined, you will want to update your client about hours spent, either weekly or when you reach a milestone. Even if it is not required of you, it's a good practice to have a procedure to keep them informed along the way in order to avoid a shocking invoice at the end.

Working for Equity: A Word on Startups

With all your fresh, in-demand Flash video skills, you may find yourself being approached by entrepreneurs who would like you to help them bring their startup ventures to life—in exchange for a share in the company's profits.

There are a few things you should consider carefully. First, working for equity is risky, paying off only when (and if) the company is actually profitable. Then there's the expense of having a lawyer draft or review the formal equity agreement. Add to that the significant time investment (and as we know, time is money). Remember that often your services are among the venture's most critical needs. Consider this fact when negotiating an agreement. Evaluate the opportunity carefully; the chances of buying in to the next YouTube or Revver are quite slim (though we have to admit, it's tempting!).

Offer Alternate Routes

When estimating complex projects, we almost always break the proposal down into "a la carte" options. Beginning with the core functionality of the application, we then add either project phases or feature add-ons that the client has requested. These are listed as separate menu items with their own price estimates. Often, we add features here that we think would improve the application (or would just be "cool"). This allows us to get creative and introduce ideas to the client that they can assign value to.

Breaking down the project this way also gives the client perspective of the work involved in each phase, and gives them the freedom to choose options rather than a "take it or leave it" bottom-line number. However, be careful not to create so many options or phases that clients are overwhelmed, or worse, confused. Keep in mind that you are the expert here, and the client is looking to you to best group these options together to streamline the project.

Even if your numbers are perfectly reasonable, allowing the client to see these options itemized will tell them what they are paying for and give them confidence in their investment.

Note: Note that a proposal is different from a contract because it does not contain all the legal verbiage of an agreement. Although we do not cover contracts in this book, we strongly recommend having one drafted by a lawyer, based on the proposal, for both parties to sign. The contract, unlike the proposal, addresses legal issues such as copyright, payment, and liability. This is especially important when creating Flash video applications, as they tend to be complex and large in scale.

Summary

In this chapter you've learned how to:

- Develop a partnership with your client.
- Grasp an understanding of the project at large and clearly define your role.
- Conduct the survey and interview.
- Create a detailed written proposal.

So you've surveyed, excavated, and created a detailed map. You've got everything you need to prepare for a successful Flash video project. It's time to gather your assets and start digging!

Raw Materials: Encoding Basics

OK, here's the ugly truth: there is no camera available that is going to record video directly to Flash video format. If this magical camera existed, we would certainly buy one for each of our clients. With all the various video formats out there, it's truly unrealistic to expect your clients to know how to make web-ready FLVs and hand them over to you ready to publish. To those not familiar with the intricacies of video, creating a good final product may seem like video voodoo.

In this chapter, we'll demystify the production and encoding process, and offer a basic overview of terminology, along with tips and best practices. You can use these guidelines to produce your own video or to provide guidance to your clients so they can give you what you need.

2

Chapter Contents

Footage Fundamentals
How Do I Create FLVs?
Obtaining and Encoding Video

Footage Fundamentals

The longest journey begins with the first step (and a good map, which you should have from Chapter 1). So let's get going and begin with the basics. FLV (Flash Live Video) is the format Flash uses for video. It is designed for delivery via the Web, offering high rates of compression. Depending on your targeted Flash version, you'll encode using either the Sorenson Spark codec (Flash 6 and higher) or the On2 VP6 codec (Flash 8 and higher). OK, now, don't get freaked out about this "codec" business—we'll cover that in detail later in this chapter. Regardless of the file format you start with, you will need to end up with an FLV to play back in Flash. We'll talk about all the different encoding software you can use to create FLVs later in this chapter, but first we'll look at what's involved in evaluating and producing source video.

When you are beginning a Flash video project, you'll either be: (1) receiving source video from your client or (2) producing it yourself. Both approaches can have their benefits and pitfalls. Receiving video from your client is great when the footage is delivered to you early on in the process and it's high quality. However, producing it yourself gives you more control over the overall product, which can be a good thing— if you know what you're doing. If you are new to shooting video, it can be a huge undertaking, and you may end up asking yourself why you agreed to do it in the first place. We'll give you a rundown of the production guidelines to be mindful of, but experience goes a long way. You can use this section to just familiarize yourself with the process, or take it further and play around with producing your own video. Remember, although it's possible to create professional video on your own, it's also a profession in itself. There are well-paid professionals out there who specialize in post-production and editing. But if you decide to produce your own video, you can use this chapter as a guide to create the best source video you can.

Receiving Source Video from Your Client

Bottom line: the key is to start with the highest-quality video possible and then compress it once. You'll want to work with high-definition or uncompressed video source files. It's best to stress this to your client up front because original source sometimes takes time to acquire. Often, high-quality source needs to be sent to you from a third party, and usually the files are too large to transfer electronically. There can also be confusion about what "high-quality" video really means. Many clients don't understand that they have to send an uncompressed video, not the pretty-good-quality MPG video file they just exported for you. Ultimately, you can only deploy what is provided to you, so be clear about expectations up front.

Note: Garbage in/garbage out: Flash can't do anything to make bad video footage better. Always start with the best quality possible.

What If My Client Gives Me a DVD?

Give them a good scolding. Seriously, regardless of how many times you ask, the reality is that often the final assets are provided to you at the last possible moment and in an undesirable format, such as the dreaded DVD. (Note that we're referring to playable DVDs here, not data DVDs.) Being handed a DVD is not ideal because the video is already in a compressed format. A standard playable DVD stores its data in MPEG-2 format and is always security protected. Because of this security measure, you'll have an additional step of converting it to an encodable file. Assuming you have the rights to use the content, of course, and it's not available to you any other way, you can use legal DVD ripping software (DVD Ripper on a Mac or DVD Shrink on Windows), both of which are free. Convert the files to MPEG-4, MPEG (at the highest settings), or MOV before converting them into an FLV with Flash or another FLV encoder.

Note: When getting footage from your client, ask for a sample clip up front, encode it, and get approval of the sample.

Producing Your Own Video

Continuing with our obsession about planning, you'll want to start with a storyboard. Storyboards are composed of a series of sketches (usually in comic strip format) that show the planned shots, convey the mood, and correspond to the scripts. They can be very simple. They typically indicate the shot framing and lighting style. If your video is long (say, 5 minutes or more), you may want to break it up into smaller clips for Flash, depending on your final application.

Note: Always get a release from your subjects to ensure that you can freely use the footage. In addition, check the legal considerations when shooting for commercial use (not as a tourist) in public spaces. Requirements vary by location, and in many cases you will have to obtain a permit or a location release.

Determine the format in which you will be shooting (miniDV, DVCAM, Beta, VHS, MPEG, etc.; see the sidebar "Video Standards and Formats: What You Need to Know" later in this chapter). When shooting your own video content, use a 3-CCD camera if possible. 3-CCD cameras have three RGB optical sensors, thus recording three times as much data as the typical consumer-level camera, which generally has only one CCD. If your camera gives you the option, choose progressive mode instead of interlaced. Interlaced format is configured for TV broadcast, and progressive is best for display on computer screens. (We'll discuss the differences between interlaced versus progressive formats later in this chapter.)

Audio is crucial. Your audience will tolerate poor picture quality far more than bad sound. Poor sound can include inconsistent volume level, noisy audio, use of on-camera microphone (which can yield dull, echoing audio), or music drowning out the dialogue. Invest in a boom mike or wireless clip-on microphone to record your audio. Plan microphone placement for the cleanest sound, avoiding background noise and echo. Sometimes it's impossible to avoid environmental noise, such as when shooting street scenes or crowds. Consider adding an audio track in postproduction, or if narration is appropriate, consider voiceovers.

Never shoot without a tripod. Each tiny movement of your camera changes a majority of your pixels, drastically increasing your final FLV file size, increasing encoding time, and making your viewers a bit dizzy. (You'll learn why this is so important when we talk about encoding later in this chapter.)

Avoid fast pans and zooms. Encoding will be slow, and your final video can be blocky. This also applies to transitions; avoid the temptation to use fades, wipes, and dissolves. You'll thank us later, when you've saved hours of encoding time. If you are going to use transitions, make them quick or simple jump cuts. If you want to include a fast pan or zoom because you have a reason for using the effect, be sure to do two takes of the shot, one with the effect and one without. If the fast zoom doesn't encode well, you can swap it out. Another option is to add fades and effects in Flash. For example, a fade to black can be achieved by covering the video with a black square, then applying an alpha transition—this transition could then be triggered by cue points in the video. (We'll discuss how to add cue points in Chapter 8.)

Another important point: Avoid using your camera's autofocus and autoexposure. Always manually light and focus your subject to avoid the random fluctuations that occur when using autosettings. These subtle fluctuations tax the encoder, forcing it to process extraneous data.

Properly light your scene. You don't need to invest in expensive lighting; you can use standard clip-on lights from your local hardware store. Just be sure your lighting is sufficient to avoid "artifacts," the blocky static that creeps into dark areas of your video. In general, harsher lighting will compress better in digital video. Just be sure to keep your lighting and exposure consistent whenever possible.

Finally, when editing, plan ahead for interactivity. If you plan to have event triggers or other interactive functions at certain points in your video, write down the time-codes for easy reference later.

These are obviously very general guidelines, but all relevant to squeezing the best FLVs out of your video shoots. Follow the basic tenets we've outlined, and your product will be closer to being a Cecil B. DeMille production, instead of one of *America's Funniest Home Videos*.

Getting Fancy: Transparent Video

One of the coolest new features in Flash 8 is its ability to utilize alpha-channel transparency for video. This allows you to do clever things like have a person, complete with drop shadow, walk right across your dynamic website content. Being the creative genius you are, we're sure you can come up with tons of even more imaginative things to do with video transparency and compositing, so let's review just how its done.

First, you'll need to shoot your subject against a background of solid color to create an alpha channel or a transparency layer in your video file. You have a choice when filming to use either a green screen or a blue screen as a background. How do you choose? The green screen is preferable for digital video whereas the blue screen is preferable for film. Also keep in mind the colors of the subjects you're filming. For example, if you're filming a person dressed as a frog, you may want to use a blue screen; if you're filming a man painted blue, you may want to use a green screen. Generally, either color will work, but since the green channel in digital video has the highest sampling rate, you'll want to stick with green in most cases to get a better-quality alpha channel.

When shooting on a green or blue screen background, painted or fabric, be sure to smooth out any creases, wrinkles, or bumps. Spandex is a good choice for a smooth surface. Again, pay attention to your subject's clothing color—you wouldn't want them to be wearing a green shirt in front of a green screen because all you'll see is a floating head (unless that's the effect you're going for!). Also avoid white clothing because it may reflect the background. Avoid anything shiny such as metal watches or jewelry. Creating an even contrast between your subject and the green or blue screen will make keying using your video-editing program easier. *Keying* is the process of removing the green or blue screen by creating a transparency layer. You may use another program such as the Keylight plug-in in Adobe After Effects to remove the green or blue screen with greater precision.

It is very important that you light the background evenly. To produce flat light over the complete background, you'll want to use at least three lights. The lights must be placed behind the subject to avoid shadows on the background. Place one light on each side and one shining down. Use soft light such as fluorescent lights or try achieving soft light by bouncing the lights off a white surface.

Next, light your subject. These lights should not point on the background. Be careful not to create a backlight of your subject, either. Also, be sure that the final composite elements all have consistent lighting to create a realistic scene.

Once you have captured footage that you are satisfied with, you can transfer it from your camera to your computer and start the keying process in video-editing software such as Adobe Premiere Pro, Final Cut Pro, or Adobe After Effects.

When you've got a video with a clean alpha channel, you'll want to export it in QuickTime format with the Animation Codec set to Millions+ colors. It will then be ready to import into your favorite encoding software. We'll discuss encoder options a bit later in this chapter.

Video Standards and Formats: What You Need to Know

Here's a rundown of the most common video standards and formats that you may run into out there:

Display Standards

Five major video display standards exist. These formats are used to encode the signal that is fed to a television or video monitor. You'll likely have to deal only with NTSC and PAL formats when receiving source video from clients, but all five are listed here. Note that each format is incompatible with the others.

- NTSC (National Television System Committee): 30 frames per second (fps); used in North and Central America, the Philippines, South Korea, and Taiwan
- NTSC-J (National Television System Committee—Japan): 30fps; used in Japan
- PAL (Phase Alternating Line): TV standard introduced in the early 1960s in Europe; 25fps; used in Europe, parts of Asia, and South Africa
- PAL-M: 30fps; used in Brazil
- SECAM (Sequential Color and Memory): 25fps; used in France, Russia, the Middle East, and North Africa

Video Formats

The following are the basic digital and analog video formats that you will likely be using to record your own source video. They are listed from lowest to highest quality. Digital video, although considered "low end," is high enough quality for web deployment. Remember, you can always decrease quality but you cannot increase quality.

- DV (Digital Video): miniDV, DVCPro-25, DVCAM
- SD (Standard Definition Video): DVCPro-50, Betacam SX, Betacam SP, DigiBetaCam
- HD (High-Definition Video): HDV, DVCPro-HD, HD

How Do I Create FLVs?

There are several options for encoding videos into the FLV format. The best solution for you depends on your budget, system configuration, and project requirements.

Before we get to those, let's clarify what "encoding" actually is. *Encoding* is the compression of a video file using a codec. *Codec* stands for compressor/decompressor. It is an algorithm that encodes video (when writing the file) and decodes video (when viewing the file). The goal of a codec is to create the smallest file possible with the best quality.

> **Note:** If for some reason you just want to distribute your video without having to construct a player, you can encode directly to an SWF format or create a projector, using an encoding program such as Flix or Squeeze. There will be no player controls, but it's a quick and easy way to get your Flash video to anyone with a Flash Player installed.

The following formats can be encoded into FLV format (of course, we can't say it enough: you want to use uncompressed whenever possible):

- Active Streaming Format (.asf)
- AVI (.avi)
- DV (.dv)
- QuickTime (.mov)
- MPEG-4 (.mp4)
- MPEG (.mpg, .mpeg)
- Windows Media Video (.wmv)

The most straightforward way to create an FLV is to use the Flash Video Import Wizard directly in Flash. To do this, in Flash Professional 8 choose File > Import > Import Video. You can then choose a source video from your hard drive, choose how you'll be deploying it (progressive, streaming, or embedded), configure compression settings, and encode (see Figure 2.1).

Another option, if you own Flash Professional 8 (FP8), is the Flash 8 Video Encoder. This program, which ships with FP8, allows you to batch-process and perform basic video editing in addition to basic editing. Flash CS3 will also ship with a Video Encoder with similar functionality.

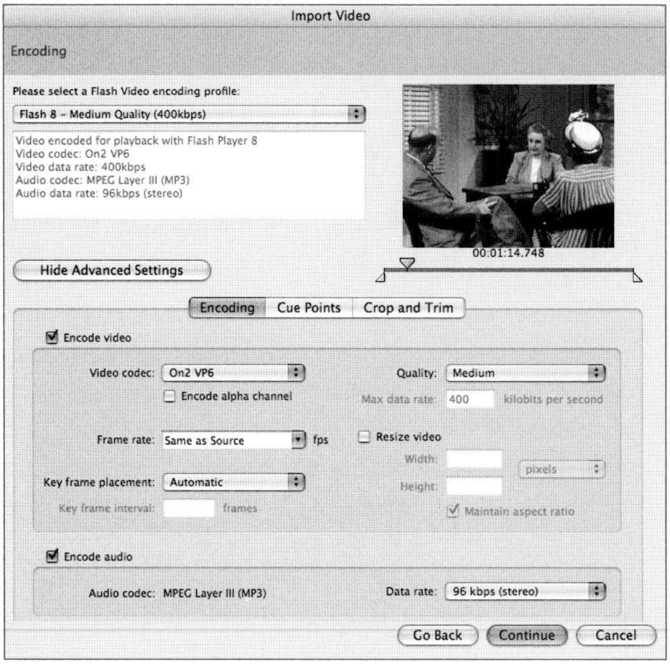

Figure 2.1 Importing video into the Flash Video Import Wizard

A third option, if you have FP8 or newer and QuickTime 6.1.1 installed, is the FLV QuickTime Export plug-in. This plug-in allows you to export FLV files from within supported video-editing applications. The following applications are currently supported, utilizing the VP6 codec:

- Adobe Premiere 6.5
- Anystream Agility
- Apple Final Cut Pro (Mac)
- Apple Final Cut Express
- Avid Media Composer
- Avid Xpress
- Canopus ProCoder
- Discreet Cleaner

If you have a bit more of a budget and more complex encoding functions are needed, you'll want to invest in one of the professional-grade third-party encoders such as On2 Flix Pro or Sorenson Squeeze. Using Sorenson Squeeze you can create your own audio/video compression settings as seen in Figure 2.2. Figure 2.3 shows the settings applied in the Sorensen Squeeze interface.

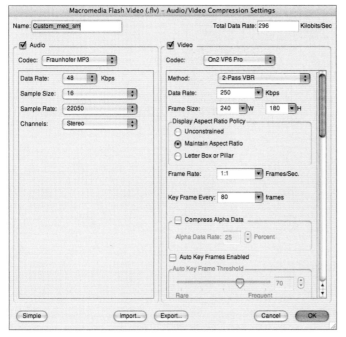

Figure 2.2 Creating custom settings in Sorenson Squeeze

Figure 2.3 Sorenson Squeeze showing how to create an FLV

There are also some down-and-dirty shareware encoders out there:

- Riva Encoder
- ffmpeg (command-line encoder for PC)
- ffmpeX (command-line encoder for Mac)

Though you likely wouldn't be using these yourself, they can offer an affordable solution to those who don't own Flash Professional 8 or Flash CS3, or need a server-based encoding solution.

 Note: Links to these encoders can be found at www.flashconnections.com or www.sybex.com/.

Helpful Tips, No Matter What Encoder You Use

If you are editing your source in a video editor such as Adobe Premiere, Final Cut Pro, or Adobe After Effects, you'll want to encode directly from that program if possible to avoid an intermediate compression step. To do this, you'll need either the Flix Exporter plug-in, the Sorenson Squeeze plug-in, or the FLV QuickTime Export plug-in, if available for your editor. Remember, if your source video is interlaced (see Figure 2.7 later in the chapter), you'll need to deinterlace it at this point (check the option in the export settings). If you don't want to spring for an FLV encoder plug-in for your editing software, you'll want to choose a lossless export format such as QuickTime using the Video codec on Mac or uncompressed AVI on Windows.

If you want to use Flash 8 as your encoding application, you should note that two-pass VBR encoding is not available. We explain exactly what that means later in this chapter, but for now, just know that two-pass VBR encoding is highly recommended for the best-quality video. Flash 8 also does not perform deinterlacing or offer filters (such as lighten, darken, and color shift), which the more robust third-party encoders do (as shown in Figures 2.4 and 2.5).There are subtle, but potentially crucial, differences between the third-party encoders Squeeze and Flix that you should take into account if you are deciding between the two. If you want the ability to perform basic green or blue screen keying, along with vector video options, you may want to choose the more inexpensive On2 Flix Pro. If you want more control over batch encoding (including watch folders), automatic keyframe placement, and FTP uploading within the software, you may want to go with Sorenson Squeeze. Weigh price versus features before deciding which third-party software is the best investment.

Note: Set up an encoding preset in Sorenson Squeeze or On2 Flix Pro and you can send the settings to your client (so they can do all the video encoding for you). Just be sure that your deadlines don't hinge on getting this video content back on time. This is a great option, however, for clients who will be updating their content on their own later.

Figure 2.4 Applying a filter in Sorenson Squeeze

Figure 2.5 Exporting in Vector Video format in On2 Flix Pro

Obtaining and Encoding Video

So, now you've got a nice, clean, uncompressed digital video file, and you've fired up your encoder of choice. What are all these options and settings, and how do they affect your encoded video? Let's start by walking through them and getting familiar with what they mean.

Your Handy-Dandy Encoding Reference

Regardless of where your video comes from, or what encoding software you're using, you'll need to be familiar with the basic settings discussed in this section and how they affect your final FLV.

The following parameters will affect the image quality, audio quality, and playback smoothness of your final video. Your goal is to get the right balance of all the settings to get the best out of these three attributes, within your target bandwidth limit. The main settings you'll be tweaking will be frame size, frame rate, data rate, keyframe interval, and audio compression. You'll also need to take into account the type and method of compression, encoding methods, and video format settings.

Frame Size and Aspect Ratio

Frame size is the width and height of the video, measured in pixels. The *aspect ratio* is the relationship between the width and the height. Two common frame sizes used in Flash video and their aspect ratios are shown in Figure 2.6. The most common aspect ratio is 4:3, used for television and most computer monitors. Widescreen video aspect ratio is 16:9. When reducing or enlarging your source video frame size, you'll want to maintain the aspect ratio.

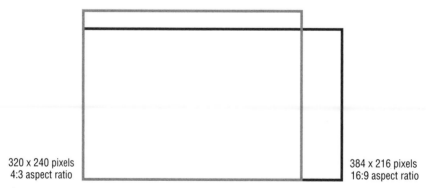

320 x 240 pixels
4:3 aspect ratio

384 x 216 pixels
16:9 aspect ratio

Figure 2.6 Common Flash video frame sizes and corresponding aspect ratios

Data Rate or Bit Rate

Data rate is a measure of bandwidth; it measures how many kilobits per second (kbps) need to be transferred to view the video. Higher data rates mean better image quality and, inevitably, larger file sizes. No two videos are exactly the same, however, so you'll have to experiment to determine the best data rate for each video you encode.

> **Note:** *Don't get bit by bytes!* It's easy to confuse the two commonly used units of measure, bits and bytes.
> 8 bits = 1 byte
> 1,000 bits = 1 kilobit
> 1,000,000 bits = 1 Megabit

Audio Compression

Two parameters control audio compression: sample rate and bit rate. The *sample rate* refers to the number of times per second the source file's bits are referenced. (The more you reference, the higher quality the compressed sound will be.) It is measured in kilohertz (kHz). Like the video data rate, the *audio bit rate* refers to how much audio data is being transferred each second.

Keyframes

Flash video is composed of keyframes and delta frames. *Keyframes* are complete video frames saved at consistent intervals, along with information about the differences between that frame and the next (the delta frames). This is similar to tweening on the timeline in Flash. Flash will calculate the frames in between each keyframe for you; these are the *delta frames*.

Frame Rate

The frame rate is the number of frames that appear each second (fps). Common standards include:

- NTSC: 29.97fps
- PAL: 25fps
- Film: 24fps

Types of Compression

There are two types of video compression: spatial and temporal. *Spatial* (intraframe) compression is applied to a single frame of data, independent of any other frames. *Temporal* (interframe) compression is a more complex and efficient approach. This method detects differences between frames and stores only those differences. Frames are then rendered based on their difference from the previous frame (only encoding what has changed, or what is moving). This is the method used in Flash video.

Methods of Compression

When encoding FLVs, you have a choice of constant bit rate (CBR) or variable bit rate (VBR) compression methods. CBR is best for streaming video or local playback, and has a much faster encoding time than VBR. Variable bit rate is the optimal method for compressing progressive videos. In VBR compression, the bit rate per frame fluctuates based on the complexity of the frame data.

Encoding Methods

Working hand in hand with the compression method is the encoding method. In most professional encoding software, you can choose either one-pass or two-pass encoding. The one-pass method just begins encoding, looking at past frames to determine the surplus or deficit in data rate and readjusting as it goes.

That is good to know, but you should always use two-pass encoding, when available. Two-pass encoding analyzes the entire video once, remembering the complexity of each frame, and then begins to encode, distributing the bit rate appropriately. Frames with lots of color or motion get more bits and the simple or low-motion frames get less, keeping the "bit budget" balanced. This results in much more efficient bit rate distribution and thus better overall quality, with the same final file size as one-pass encoding. However, keep in mind that two-pass encoding does take, well, twice as long to encode, so you'll definitely want to consider encoding time in your workflow plan.

As mentioned earlier, the encoder built into Flash 8 and Flash CS3 does not offer two-pass encoding; you'll have to spring for one of the more robust third-party encoders to have this option.

Deinterlacing

Broadcast TV and camcorder video is interlaced (see Figure 2.7). Interlaced video is composed of horizontal scan lines that are numbered consecutively and grouped into the odd field (consisting of the odd-numbered lines) and the even field (consisting of the even-numbered lines). Computer monitors show only progressive video (full frames, not interlaced). If your source is interlaced, you'll want to apply deinterlacing during the encoding process, set to "upper field." Most professional encoding software offers this option. If your camera gives you a choice of shooting modes, you'll want to choose progressive mode when shooting your own content. This is especially important for alpha channel video.

Figure 2.7 Interlaced video

Where the Rubber Hits the Road: Let's Encode

We've already mentioned this, but we can't stress it enough: start with uncompressed or lossless source video! Avoid double-compressing; quality will be noticeably lost with every new generation. It's like recopying a photocopy—pretty soon you have a blurry mess.

Of course, in reality you can't always control what you get from your client, so you just have to do the best with what you've been given. Be sure to communicate the importance of good source material to your client early on, so they have clear expectations of quality in the final FLV.

Step 1: Watch the Video

Yes, from beginning to end. Then watch it again. Analyze the content: Is it mostly talking-head footage with minimal movement? Are there cuts and transitions you can't edit out? Is there a lot of fast motion? Make a determination of whether the video overall is fast, medium, or low motion. The more motion you have to accommodate, the higher the data rate will need to be. You'll also want to note the dimensions and the frame rate of the source video. You can get this information from most video players, encoding software, or video-editing packages. It's important to get this information, because you'll never want to encode a video at a size or frame rate greater than the source.

Step 2: Determine Bandwidth Target

Next, determine the bandwidth capabilities of your target audience. Will many of them be on cable or DSL connections, or still on dial-up? Or will they be viewing the video locally on a CD-ROM?

Be Realistic about Bandwidth

Think your connection's fast? Believe your cable provider when they tell you you've got a 1.2Mbps connection? Check your own bandwidth, and you may be surprised. Here are a few free online test sites; keep the results in mind when you're choosing a bandwidth target:

- http://reviews.cnet.com/7004-7254_7-0.html
- http://www.bandwidthplace.com/speedtest/
- http://specials.zdnet.co.uk/misc/band-test/speedtest50.html

Try the tests at different times of day, and from different locations. You will likely see differences between tests run minutes apart, showing you just how radically actual bandwidth can fluctuate.

Another handy tool for testing what user experiences will be like at different bandwidths is the Charles Web Debugging Proxy (http://www.xk72.com/charles/index.php). This handy tool can actually throttle your Internet connection to give you an accurate picture of what your application looks like to visitors with various connection speeds.

Step 3: Choose Data Rate

Video playback is much like a flowing river: the water is composed of the bits of video and audio data, and the banks of the river represent the available bandwidth on the user's connection. Your goal is to keep this river of bits flowing as your video plays. If the river flows too fast for the banks to hold, it will back up, or buffer, and your video will stall until there's enough data to start playing again. And no one likes an, um, buffering river.

So, based on the information you gathered in steps 1 and 2, choose the appropriate data rate from Table 2.1.

▶ **Table 2.1** Recommended Data Rates for Various Connection Speeds

Connection Speed	Description
1024kbps	850kbps
768kbps	620kbps
512kbps (DSL target)	**410kbps**
310kbps	**248kbps**
256kbps	205kbps
128kbps	**80kbps**
56kbps (Dial-up target)	**47kbps**

bold = a common rate

Don't attempt to use all of your viewers' available bandwidth. They could be trying to have a chat with a friend, download a file, or listen to an audio stream in the background. Use bit rates that are 70–80% of the theoretical connection speed.

You should rarely go over a 512kbps target bandwidth. You can send really good 320 × 240 video using this data rate. Unless you're serving full-screen video, the quality improvements of higher data rates are negligible. The VP6 codec also tends to perform poorly over 512kbps, as the decoding becomes complex, bogging down your viewers' processors. It's just too much math! Remember, data rate alone does not equal video quality. If your data rate is too high, the experience will be poor no matter how much data is contained in each frame.

Note: If you're stuck with a low-quality video or one with areas of low light, you'll want to increase your data rate to accommodate the extra noise. Another option, if you're using Sorenson Squeeze, is to use the Black and White restore settings, which will smooth out the shadow and highlight areas, removing all of the slight variations in color. This will make your video smoother, thus decreasing the amount of data being processed in each frame.

Step 4: Choose Frame Size

Determine the appropriate frame size for your video. The frame size should be based on your target audience's bandwidth (refer to Table 2.2 for suggestions) and your desired final application dimensions.

Pixel Aspect Ratio

Here's a tricky one for you. DVD and DV video use nonsquare pixels. Computer screens use square pixels. If your source video is composed of nonsquare pixels, you'll need to use the scale function in your encoder to scale the image nonproportionately down to a 4:3 aspect ratio. For example, if your source file is 720 × 480 (standard DV NTSC), then scaling to 640 × 480 (correct 4:3 ratio) with square pixels will require a nonproportional scale (a greater change in the X-axis than in the Y-axis). This will prevent your video from appearing stretched.

▶ **Table 2.2** Suggested Applications for Common Video Sizes at Both 4:3 and 16:9 Aspect Ratios

Dimensions	Local or CD	High speed connection (~)	Dial-Up (~56k)
Common 4:3 Frame Sizes:			
640 × 480	X		
512 × 384	X		
320 × 240		X	
240 × 180		X	
160 × 120			X
120 × 90			X
Common 16:9 Frame Sizes:			
704 × 396		X	
448 × 252		X	
384 × 216			X
192 × 108			X

Note: When bandwidth is limited, and frame rate and image quality are most important, you'll want to reduce your frame size.

Step 5: Choose Optimal Frame Rate

If you wish to reduce your frame rate in the encoding process, you'll want to use an even divisor of the source frame rate. For example, if your source rate is 29.97fps:

- ½ = 14.98fps
- ⅓ = 9.99fps
- ¼ = 7.49fps

Any of these frame rates would be acceptable. The one you choose would depend on your source video content and desired playback quality. If your clip has medium to high motion, you may want to use 14.98fps. If it's just a talking head, or if your target bandwidth is limited, you may want to go with 7.49fps.

> **Note:** If your video is longer than 10 minutes and you don't adhere to the even divisor rule, your audio will tend to drift out of sync.

Step 6: Set Keyframe Interval

This part can get a bit tricky; it's easy to get confused and lower your keyframe interval when you mean to increase it. A keyframe interval of 4 is actually a higher rate than an interval of 8. You are telling the encoder how often to place a keyframe in the video: one every 4 frames, or one every 8 frames.

If "automatic" is an option, let the encoder choose where to place the keyframes. If your resulting file size is too large, however, you may need to set a specific keyframe rate. For average motion, try one keyframe every 4 seconds (fps × 4) as a starting point. If you need to reduce your target data rate, reduce the keyframe rate. A lower keyframe rate will reduce your bandwidth demand, but also will lower your video quality. If you have a lot of fast motion in your clip (more differences from frame to frame), you'll need to use more keyframes to smooth out the transitions. Remember, keyframes are much larger than the frames between them, so the fewer you can get away with, the smaller your file will be.

> **Note:** If you want to have a scrubber so the viewer can navigate the video in your final application, it's important to note that Flash can only jump forward and backward to keyframes. So for a smoother scrubber, you'll want more keyframes. (Flash Media Server 2 makes keyframes on the fly while scrubbing, so this isn't as relevant for videos that will be streamed through FMS2.)

So, to review:

- More frequent keyframe interval = better quality and larger file size
- Less frequent keyframe interval = lower quality and smaller file size

 Note: For high-motion clips, you'll want to increase the keyframe rate, the frame rate, *and* the bit rate.

Step 7: Set Audio Compression

Hopefully, while you were viewing your video in step 1, you also listened to the soundtrack. Your audio bit rate choice, as with video, will depend on the audio content. For example, music should generally be encoded in stereo at 64kbps or higher, but voices can be encoded as low as 24kbps in mono and still be clear (Table 2.3).

▶ **Table 2.3** Bit Rate Quality Guidelines

Bit Rate	Comparative Quality
24kbps	AM quality
64kbps	FM quality
96–160kbps	Typical "acceptable" quality
192 kbps	Typical "good" quality
224–320kbps	Near audio CD quality

Generally, you'll want to encode at 48 kbps or better for most audio content. Just remember to add this number to your video data rate to get the real data rate total for the FLV. Unless you have a very good reason for doing otherwise, always use MP3 audio encoding.

 Note: Make sure your source clip has audio. Flash uses the audio track to keep the frame rate in sync. (If the audio controls in your encoder are grayed out, it generally means there's no audio track in your clip.)

Step 8: Determine Alpha Channel Video Settings

If you've gone to all the trouble of green or blue screening and chroma keying, you'll need to go through a couple of extra steps to import your fabulous masked video. First, you'll want to crop the video down to the active area. Even though there won't be any pixel data in the empty areas, it will still increase your file size. Then, sit back and wait. Expect that the encoding process will take a bit longer than usual, because alpha channel video is much more complex to encode.

Summary

In this chapter you've learned:

- Basic video terminology and standards, as they relate to Flash video
- Guidelines for accepting video files from clients
- Best practices for shooting your own video
- Options for creating FLVs
- Optimal settings for encoding

Now that you've dispelled the "voodoo" of FLV creation, it's time to figure out the best way to deliver it to your audience. The next chapter will walk you through the process of setting up your workspace and choosing between ActionScript 2 and Action-Script 3, and will introduce some programming techniques for killer video applications.

Creating a Video Delivery Roadmap

The best way to get your awesomely designed video application on the Web is to understand your options early on. As we've said before, you need to know where you're going before you set out on this exciting and sometimes perilous journey that is Flash video.

In our early days of coding, we would often get so anxious to get into a project that we'd sit down and start coding immediately after leaving the first client meeting. Sure, we can do that! Let's try it...OK, that works; now how about that other feature? Great! And before you know it, we'd end up with a bunch of unrelated code, but not anything close to an efficient application.

3

Chapter Contents

Functionality and Flow
Progressive or Streaming: That Is the Question
On to the ActionScript!
Publishing and Hosting Choices
Don't Copy That Floppy: Digital Rights Management

We'd grudgingly go back and map everything out and start over. We're smarter now. We plan, test, adjust the plan, then code. But we always have a clear vision of which direction we're headed in, and why.

This chapter presents you with the final considerations you need to make before getting your head down and starting to code. You've got all of your ducks in a row with the client, such as the project budget, type of content, and quality of video, and now they want to see some video—*pronto*. This chapter outlines the steps to get you there. You'll start by learning best practices for Flash video application design and the differences between progressive and streaming video. Then we will introduce you to some content delivery networks to serve up your content. When you finish this chapter, you'll have a solid deployment plan, and you'll have gotten your feet wet with some basic code to get video into Flash.

Functionality and Flow

As we're sure you know by now, Flash is a flexible platform for developing applications and websites. Sometimes it can be too flexible, however! If you neglect basic usability principles, you can easily get yourself into trouble. How do you feel when presented with a video that has no controls, for example, or when you click a link and nothing happens for about 15 seconds while the video loads? Frustrated, confused, maybe even angry, we suspect. The planning stage is the time to think about these issues.

In Flash, everything is wrapped in a single page, so you don't necessarily have linear functionality, as visitors might expect from a typical web page. There are entire books written on ways to compensate for this (and we advise you to read one or two of them if you haven't already), so we'll just review the most basic best practices we've found relating to Flash video application development.

Ultimately, you want your user experience to be a positive one. For example, nothing is worse than having to spend time figuring out how to use a site's navigation. "Don't make me think!" as usability guru Steve Krug would say. Except in extreme cases (such as some games or conceptual art projects), navigation should always be intuitive. There should be as few steps as possible between your users and the information they want. Visitors to YouTube, for example, most likely want to see the most popular viral videos, so they're right on the front page. If users aren't looking for those, they're likely looking for something specific, so the search bar is right there, too.

A good user experience is good customer service. There are a few basic steps to laying out an intuitive and positive user experience, starting with a functionality flow chart, a document we mentioned as part of the project archeology back in Chapter 1. As you may have guessed, good flow involves some planning.

Flow Chart

You may already have created a flow chart (if you haven't—naughty, naughty!) during the project planning stage outlined in Chapter 1. You'll want to at least start by writing a concise "mission statement," spelling out the overall purpose for your website or application. For example:

> *Deliver video, audio, and other multimedia elements relating to an accompanying HTML article, all within a single player.*

Next, attempt to define the overall user experience in a sentence or two. Something like this:

> *The player should operate seamlessly with the HTML article. Viewers should be able to interact with the FLV playlist, or choose items from the FLV playlist via links in the HTML. Oversize items will overlay the text, furthering integration.*

Using this mission statement as a guide, create rough schematics, like the one in Figure 3.1, illustrating the flow of the application—how users get from point A to point B and how different elements interact with each other. This will clarify in your mind what the key parts of your application need to accomplish. The schematic shown in Figure 3.1 illustrates the scenario from the previous paragraph. Creating this sketch is a great exercise, and can illuminate potential logic and design problems quickly.

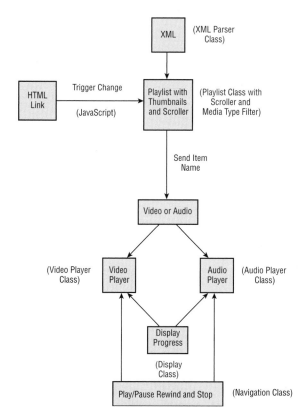

Figure 3.1 Flow chart sketch

You can start thinking in terms of objects and methods here, and the application will begin to take shape. (We will talk more about programming styles in Chapter 4.) You'll of course want to refine this sketch as you get closer to building your application, especially if other developers will be involved. Defining tasks and breaking down the functionality into small parts is critical here as well. You've created the model that will serve as your code blueprint. We'll also discuss video application–specific design patterns in Chapter 4 that you can apply to this "code sketch" as you refine it.

Start Building

Build the simplest thing you can, and then build the next simplest thing. Develop a stripped-down prototype that achieves the core functionality of your application and build on top of that. This will ensure that you understand what each part of the application is doing and make it easier to troubleshoot. We also catch usability mistakes or oversights at this stage before we have too much time invested.

Testing 1, 2, 3

Never build ahead of user feedback. If you follow this golden rule, you will avoid a lot of unnecessary development once you get deeper into the project. There are entire books on this subject as well, but there are some down-and-dirty testing techniques you can use when budget and time are tight.

Whenever you can, conduct usability tests, preferably with small groups of about five people; these can even be friends, family, or coworkers. Let them think out loud as they try to navigate and accomplish a task, allowing you to observe their actual process. If you find yourself having to give them instruction, it's probably an indication that you need to simplify your navigation. We avoid giving guidance here as much as possible in order to simulate the average user figuring it out. Design and develop around the way the testers actually use the application. We'll talk more about the specifics of testing the functionality of Flash video applications in Chapter 6. For now, just take into consideration testing as part of your preliminary design process and less of an afterthought.

 Note: Don't get offended, and don't argue with your testers! It's tempting to interject and say, "No, no— just click there!" Watch, listen, and learn, and then adjust your user interface accordingly.

Back Button Considerations

Flash should act as the user expects, and users expect to be able to use the back button in web browsers. Unfortunately, since Flash applications are encapsulated in a single

SWF, the back button takes users to the last page they visited and away from your application. This is contrary to the users' expectations, and many users find this frustrating. At a recent project meeting, our client had difficulty navigating to a page because he kept clicking the back button in his browser, despite knowing that it would take him out of the website application. He was a creature of habit, as many of us are.

There are workarounds for this issue, many of them open source, that allow you to "fake" page changes, so the back button acts as it is expected to in the browser window. These generally involve JavaScript and ActionScript integration. If the design of your application prompts test users to go for the back button, you may want to implement one of these workarounds.

Basically, these solutions work by keeping track of the current "page," or state, of the SWF through a variable in Flash. This variable is then passed from the SWF to the HTML page and is added to the browser history. Then, when the visitor hits the back button, the JavaScript sends the variable back to the SWF, which changes content accordingly. Of course, if this is a player that exists within an HTML site there is probably no need, but if it takes over the browser completely, then you should consider implementation. You can find several related solutions, including the open source project SWFaddress (http://www.asual.com/swfaddress/) at http://www.flashconnections.com /flash-pro/.

You'll want to decide if this navigation issue is important to the usability of your project early on, so it can be implemented in the initial code structure.

Flash Player Detection

In the project planning stage, you should have specified the target Flash version for your project. Be sure to let your audience know which version of Flash Player is required to view the site. Version detection should be automatic, and you should prompt your visitor to upgrade if needed, providing a link to the latest player. This can be done very smoothly by taking advantage of Express Install available for Flash 6.0.65.0 and later. Express Install is a handy little option included in Adobe's Flash Detection Kit (available for free on http://www.adobe.com) that allows developers to trigger the installation of upgrades to the Flash Player from within Flash.

If you don't deal with detection issues, you risk displaying only a blank page—the worst example of usability, which is no usability at all. We know it's difficult to hold back from building the latest and greatest, but if only a handful of people are viewing your video because they don't want to upgrade, then it's better to build to the oldest player version that has the functionality required by your application. For example, if your video quality is most important, you'll want to use at least Flash 8 to take advantage of the higher-quality VP6 video codec.

Flash Video Navigation

Flash comes with a set of user interface (UI) components such as text input fields, buttons, scroll bars, and video player components. You can skin these components and add all sorts of customized options such as closed captioning. You can also purchase third-party components from companies such as Flashloaded, Proxus, and Metaliq. In some cases, these tools are all you need to deploy simple video applications. Most have all the controls needed to navigate video—play, pause, rewind, scrubber bars, audio controls—built in.

However, since you've bought this book, you likely will be developing your own video players because some of these components (especially the v1 and v2 components that ship with Flash) tend not to be customizable, and are often "heavy," implementing extra features and added code that you may not be using in your application. Ultimately, you want to be sure that all video controls are intuitive and operate as expected by the viewer and that the application is responsive, not bogged down by unneeded code.

In Chapter 5, we'll discuss the new ActionScript 3 FLVPlayback component—a completely rebuilt and optimized component architecture.

Keep It Simple

Certain interactions may make perfect sense to us as developers but may not make sense to the average visitor. Make the important content large and obvious, paying close attention to critical copy and navigation so that they appear concise and clear. If you miss the mark, your usability testers will be the first to let you know. Sometimes this is challenging because you can be too close to the content to distinguish between what's obvious to you and what's obvious to the average Joe. For example, it may be intuitive to you that the slider bar on the right, below the video, is a volume slider. But if you don't label it, some of your viewers may interpret it to be a scrubber bar.

At critical points in development, stop and refer back to the "mission statement" and user experience goals. Is your application still fulfilling those requirements, or has it strayed? Be sure to ask yourself at each stage if what you're developing enhances the user experience. Then test it to be sure your users agree.

Progressive or Streaming? That Is the Question

Now that you've got the interface and functionality under control, it's time to answer the eternal question: What method will you use to deliver the video? You have three options:

- Embed the video in an SWF.
- Provide a progressive download FLV, loaded into an SWF.
- Stream from Flash Media Server (FMS), viewed through an SWF.

Note that in each method, you will need an SWF shell to play the FLV through. This shell will contain all the ActionScript needed to load the FLV. (Yea! Finally, some ActionScript!) First, let's look at each delivery option in detail.

Embed Video in SWF

This is the most basic option, available for Flash 4 and up (see Figure 3.2). In most professional applications, though, you'd never use this method. It's good for very short clips (5 seconds or less) whose quality is not so important. The only reason you'd ever want to use this method would be if you needed to deploy one single encapsulated SWF or if you needed to deliver short clips to older versions of Flash. Also, some older versions of the Linux Flash Player have reportedly had issues with FLV playback, so it's common to use SWF videos when delivering short videos to Linux clients.

This embed method can actually be helpful because it gives you visual feedback if you need to develop animation overlays and interactivity. It lets you actually see each frame on the timeline in Flash as you animate.

Note: Embedded video is limited to 16,000 frames, and audio can quickly fall out of sync with the video. Also, the SWF's frame rate must match the video frame rate, which can sometimes create headaches.

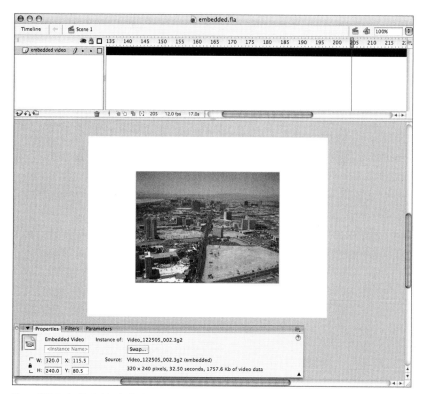

Figure 3.2 Embedded video in Flash

Progressive Download

This is most likely the method you'll end up using in your application. It is the most commonly used, being compatible with Flash Player 6 and up. "Progressive" means that as the FLV file is downloaded to your computer, or "cached," it starts to play. This method is most efficient for clips that are 5–90 seconds in length, but longer clips can be accommodated with well-planned caching. There is no limit to file size or duration, and there are no audio synchronization issues. Because the FLV file is external to the SWF shell, it is relatively easy to swap video content without republishing your SWF. This gives you great flexibility in developing dynamic video applications. The frame rate of the video can be different from the SWF, which is also invaluable when swapping videos, allowing you to accommodate files with differing frame rates into the same shell.

Progressive download isn't the perfect solution, however. There are three issues that you'll want to be aware of. First, viewers can't seek ahead in the video beyond the portion that's been downloaded, which can be a problem with large video files. Often your viewer wants to skip ahead to a part of the video or see if the content is something they want to watch. Second, when viewers do jump ahead in a fully downloaded video, they're constrained to jumping between keyframes. This results in a "choppy" feel to the video, which can be undesirable.

Finally, there's the issue of digital rights management (DRM). The FLV file is actually downloaded to the viewer's machine after it's cached, and is stored on their hard drive. This can be a big problem if you're delivering copyright-protected video. If this is an issue for you, you'll be glad to know that we'll talk about DRM in more detail later in this chapter.

Streaming

If progressive download is the workhorse of Flash video delivery, streaming is the luxury model. Delivered through a streaming server such as Flash Media Server (FMS) and compatible with Flash Player 6 and up, this method features built-in bandwidth detection, high-quality playback, faster video start time, advanced logging and monitoring, and real-time data synchronization. With its persistent connection between the client and server, streaming allows on-the-fly changes to FLV content. For example, you could change to a lower-quality video if the viewer's connection slows down during playback. Or with live video, you could switch camera angles based on user interaction. You can even use the persistent connection to send data along with the video, such as a chat room or synchronized slides controlled by a live presenter. Scrubbing is streamlined as well; you can smoothly jump ahead in a video without having to download the file to that point, and without the jerkiness of jumping to the nearest existing keyframe (as in progressive download); keyframes are created on the fly by FMS.

As with progressive download, the SWF acts as a shell containing the video content, so updating does not require republishing the SWF. Streaming also saves on bandwidth and hardware resources; viewers only download the portion of the video they watch, and nothing is stored on their hard drive. This brings us to another pretty significant benefit—the video is never cached, providing more security for copyrighted content. Currently this is the extent of DRM offered by Flash video. So, if you don't want your viewers to have a copy of your video somewhere on their hard drive after viewing, streaming is your answer (though we will show you some tricks to add extra barriers to downloading later in this chapter). If you have large quantities of stored video, very long video clips, or live video (such as live event broadcasts or webcam chat rooms), you'll want to choose streaming.

The downside to streaming, of course, is its significantly higher deployment cost. Programming for FMS is also complex, as is setting up your own FMS server. Luckily, there are options such as Flash Video Streaming Services (FVSS) that can help streamline the deployment process in many cases. We'll cover your various deployment options later in this chapter as well, and will cover live video in depth in Chapter 11.

Table 3.1 shows the features of all three video delivery methods.

▶ **Table 3.1** Video Delivery Methods at a Glance

	Embed Video in SWF	Progressive Download	Streaming
Short clips (5 seconds or less)	X		
Long clips		X	X
Timeline authoring	X		
Audio sync problems	X		
Caches content locally	X	X	
Ability to seek ahead without downloading entire video		X	
No special hosting required	X	X	
Expensive to develop and host			X
Least buffer time			X
Built-in bandwidth detection			X
Most secure (DRM)			X

On to the ActionScript!

We'll be diving deeper into this book's scripting conventions in Chapter 4, but let's get our feet wet now by looking at the most basic scripts for loading and viewing a video in Flash. To help those who haven't transitioned yet or who need to script for older versions of Flash, we are going to include both ActionScript 2 (AS2) and ActionScript 3 (AS3) examples throughout the book. In both cases, the code will be class-based, but you can extract it from the class file and place it on the timeline in Flash if you prefer. (If object-oriented programming [OOP] and classes make you break out in hives, relax—we'll get you set up in the next chapter!) All code examples are available on our companion website, http://www.flashconnections.com/flash-pro/.

Progressive Delivery: AS2

Here is the most basic code you need for video playback, wrapped in an AS2 class:

```
class net.flashconnections.FLVPlayerBasic {

    var ns:NetStream;
    var myVid:Video;

    public function FLVPlayerBasic(target:Video, filename:String,
⟹  nc:NetConnection){

        myVid = target;

        // Connect to the NetConnection
        nc.connect(null);

        // Construct NetStream and connect to flow through NetConnection
        var ns:NetStream = new NetStream(nc);

        // Attach NetStream to video object on the stage
        myVid.attachVideo(ns);

        // Tell the NetStream which FLV to play
        ns.play(filename);
    }
}
```

This code is then added to the first frame of your Flash file, assuming you have a Video object with the instance name myVid on the Stage.

```
import net.flashconnections.FLVPlayerBasic;
var nc:NetConnection = new NetConnection();
// Instantiate an instance of the FLVPlayerBasic class,
// passing in your parameters
var FLVPlayer:FLVPlayerBasic = new FLVPlayerBasic(myVid,
⇒"video/myvideo.flv",nc);
```

That's it! Pretty simple, isn't it? If you are new to classes, it may seem somewhat complex at first, but don't worry—working with classes will become second nature in no time (and you'll need to master OOP when you move on to AS3).

Figure 3.3 shows the code in Eclipse, while Figure 3.4 shows you the import code needed in the Flash IDE.

Figure 3.3 ActionScript 2 code in Eclipse

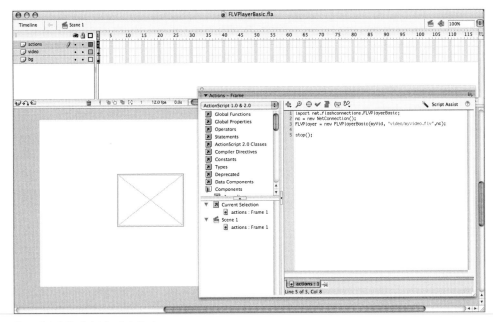

Figure 3.4 ActionScript 2 code in Flash

Progressive Delivery: AS3

Now let's look at an example in AS3, using Flex Builder2.

1. Open Flex Builder 2 and create a new ActionScript Project.

2. Name the project **FLVPlayerBasic** and enter the following code:

```
package {
        import flash.display.Sprite;
        import flash.net.NetConnection;
        import flash.net.NetStream;
        import flash.media.Video;
        import flash.display.MovieClip;

        public class FLVPlayerBasic extends Sprite {

           public function FLVPlayerBasic() {
               // Construct NetConnection
               var nc:NetConnection = new NetConnection();
               nc.connect(null);
```

```
        // Flash is looking for an onMetaData method,
        // route all calls to an object
                var metaObject:Object = new Object();
                metaObject.onMetaData = onMetaData;

                // Construct NetStream and connect to
                // flow through NetConnection
                var ns:NetStream;
                ns = new NetStream(nc);
                ns.play("video/myvideo.flv");

                // Route all onMetaData calls on NetStream to the metaObject
                ns.client = metaObject;

                // Construct video object with dimensions
                 var video:Video = new Video(160, 120);

                // Attach video to the NetStream, and add to the display list
                video.attachNetStream(ns);
                addChild(video);
        }

        private function onMetaData(data:Object):void {
        // Satisfies Flash's need to send metadata with Flash Video
        // This is considered to be a bug and may be fixed
        // in the final AS3 release
        }
    }
}
```

3. Compile directly in Flex Builder.

There's no need to create a Flash file or put anything on the Stage. It's all handled in code (see Figure 3.5).

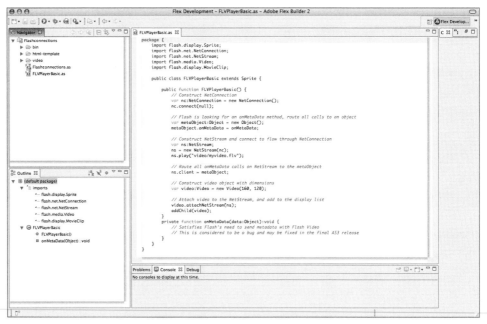

Figure 3.5 ActionScript 3 code in Flex Builder 2

Streaming Delivery: AS2

The only thing that changes between progressive and streaming is the NetConnection string, highlighted here:

```
class net.flashconnections.FLVPlayerBasic {

    var ns:NetStream;
    var myVid:Video;

    public function FLVPlayerBasic(target:Video, filename:String,
    nc:NetConnection){

        myVid = target;

        // Connect to the NetConnection
        nc.connect("rtmp://www.domain.com/FLVPlayerBasic/_definst_");

        // Construct NetStream and connect to flow through NetConnection
        var ns:NetStream = new NetStream(nc);
```

```
            // Attach NetStream to video object on the stage
            myVid.attachVideo(ns);

            // Tell the NetStream which FLV to play
            ns.play(filename);
        }
    }
```

In the connect method shown here, you're telling Flash to connect to a Flash Media Server to stream the video file. The code in Flash will remain the same, and the FLV will be retrieved from the _definst_/streams folder in the Applications folder on your Flash Media Server, rather than in the video folder on your web server, as in the progressive option. Most examples in this book will be progressive, but we'll cover more specifics about configuring your application for FMS in Chapter 11.

> **Note:** To test these streaming examples, you'll need either your own Flash Media Server 2 setup (the developer version is free) or an account with an FMS2 hosting service. Check our companion website, http://www .flashconnections.com/flash-pro/, for an updated list of providers and potential deals.

Streaming Delivery: AS3

Again, the only difference between this and the progressive example is the location of the FLV and the NetConnection path, highlighted here:

```
package {
    import flash.display.Sprite;
    import flash.net.NetConnection;
    import flash.net.NetStream;
    import flash.media.Video;
    import flash.display.MovieClip;

    public class FLVPlayerBasic extends Sprite {

        public function FLVPlayerBasic() {
            // Construct NetConnection
            var nc:NetConnection = new NetConnection();
            nc.connect("rtmp://www.domain.com/FLVPlayerBasic/_definst_");
```

```
// Flash is looking for an onMetaData method, route all calls to an object
var metaObject:Object = new Object();
metaObject.onMetaData = onMetaData;

// Construct NetStream and connect to flow through NetConnection
var ns:NetStream;
ns = new NetStream(nc);
ns.play("myvideo.flv");

// Route all onMetaData calls on NetStream to the metaObject
ns.client = metaObject;

// Construct video object with dimensions
var video:Video = new Video(160, 120);

// Attach video to the NetStream, and add to the display list
video.attachNetStream(ns);
addChild(video);
}

    private function onMetaData(data:Object):void {
// Satisfies Flash's need to send metadata with Flash Video
// This is considered to be a bug and may be fixed in the final AS3 release
    }
  }
}
```

Now that you've got an idea of how to get video into Flash, let's look at your options for getting your video on the Web.

Publishing and Hosting Choices

So, you've ruled out embedding your video into an SWF and are going with a progressive or streaming deployment. Now you need to decide how to handle account hosting. For simple progressive video applications with minimal traffic, you can, of course, just use a standard website hosting account. But as you develop more enterprise-level applications or deploy streaming video, you'll want to look into content-delivery networks (CDNs), Flash Video Streaming Services (FVSSs), Flash Media Server 2 hosts, or even converting to DVD. Let's look at each option in more detail.

What Is a CDN, and Why Do I Need One?

A content-delivery network (CDN) is a hosting company that specializes in serving rich media files, quickly and efficiently. These networks are engineered to be load balanced and fast, delivering large video, audio, and file downloads on demand. (Load balancing is when work is spread over multiple computers so that one server does not get overwhelmed.) The larger CDNs work by caching content on servers located around the world, then serving it from the server closest to the client.

In addition, CDNs offer detailed traffic reports and tracking, which can be very valuable for commercial applications. If you have a small-scale progressive video application and you expect slow, steady traffic, you likely wouldn't need a CDN, and can store and serve your FLVs from your website's standard server. If you have a large quantity of progressive video, long videos, or have a possibility (or hope) of traffic spikes, you would definitely want to use a CDN.

The largest players in the CDN market for Flash video currently are Akamai, VitalStream, Limelight Networks, NaviSite, and Brightcove.

What Is an FVSS?

A Flash Video Streaming Service (FVSS) is a CDN that specializes in Flash Media Server (FMS) hosting for streaming video or simple FMS applications. Hosting costs for streaming video are definitely more expensive than for progressive video. Luckily, several pricing tiers and hosting packages are available, allowing you to scale your application and traffic.

Because FVSSs offer load balancing, the video or audio streams will be delivered faster than if they were hosted on a single FMS server, with less buffering and timeouts. FVSSs are generally more popular than setting up your own FMS. Licensing and operating your own Flash Media Server can be quite costly, and you need to have expertise in server administration and troubleshooting, along with 24/7 monitoring to use it in commercial applications. FVSSs offer these services for you. You may want to set up your own FMS locally for testing purposes, but deploying it in a real-world application yourself, without server administration knowledge, can be daunting and downright dangerous.

That said, where can you find a good streaming service? The current Adobe-certified FVSSs are Akamai, Limelight Networks, Mirror Image Internet, and Vital-Stream. These are the more robust enterprise-targeted providers, generally focused on straightforward streaming video.

What If I Need More Services?

If your streaming application uses more custom FMS features, such as server-side scripts, server-side streams, or data integration, you may want to turn to the more FMS-centric FVSSs. These companies specialize in FMS application hosting, and even have some plug-and-play applications you may be able to utilize in your projects. You can choose between shared and dedicated hosting plans. A shared plan will be cheaper, but sometimes you'll want your own dedicated server because it's more secure and scalable—and you have the control to get in there and play around with it.

Some of these FMS hosts offer their own prebuilt video players and other FMS applications. As with any plug-and-play option, specific features such as size and configuration of the player may mean you need to create a custom solution. These applications may have standard functionality, but likely won't have custom features, such as adding cue points, multiple playlists, multiple channels, special configurations, or custom advertising solutions. Again, keep in mind the final goal of your application, and use components and plug-and-play widgets only if they meet those requirements. Don't try to "shoehorn" a ready-made video player into your application if it doesn't fit.

The most popular FMS hosts currently are Influxis, Uvault, and MoreMX. The authors host all of their FMS projects with Influxis and have found their support and reliability to be great. If you're looking for a CDN that handles the gamut of small to large-scale applications, you might find Brightcove to be an interesting solution. It also features simple plug-and-play video playback widgets, and even offers advertising solutions that include shared-revenue models.

What About Offline Video? FLV to DVD

You spend all that time and energy creating those beautiful FLVs, and inevitably your client will ask, "Cool...can we put that on DVD? And PSP too?"

Well, if you have the right equipment for the job, anything is possible. There are several third-party utilities for converting FLVs and/or SWFs to various video formats. Unfortunately for Mac devotees (like us), utilities on this list are only available for Windows. PC users currently have several choices:

- Total Video Converter
- ConvertXtoDVD
- GeoVid Flash to Video Encoder PRO (not VP6)
- Moyea's FLV to Video Converter (3GP, VP6, and more)
- AoA DVD Creator
- SWF Toolbox

The overall goal of these utilities is to convert FLV format videos (either Spark or VP6 codec, depending on the program) to another format compatible with another device. If you'd like to play back your video on a DVD player, unlike with a data DVD you'll need to use software that authors the MPEG-2 file directly onto the DVD itself. For a Playstation Portable (PSP), you need to save it in Third-Generation Platform (3GP) format.

Some of the utilities are more full-featured, such as Moyea's FLV to Video Converter. You can add custom watermarks and even batch-process multiple files with this handy little program. Don't forget to test your final DVD on many different machines to ensure compatibility. DVD is a fussy medium.

Don't Copy That Floppy: Digital Rights Management

It's a battle that's been raging since the beginning of time—well, since the beginning of video anyway. Copyright issues, piracy, digital rights management (DRM)—the recording industry and Hollywood are the highest-profile warriors (and the biggest spenders) in this fight, and they are losing. Just as fast as the next clever DRM scheme is implemented, it's cracked by an equally clever hacker. The best we can do to prevent piracy is, well, the best we can do. Flash does have some inherent security such as obscured URLs and media file locations, but these are not generally considered enterprise-level protection. Regardless, there are some measures you can take to protect your FLVs.

Streaming through Flash Media Server is the most secure DRM option available for Flash. The video is downloaded as it is viewed and expires immediately; nothing is saved on the viewer's computer. In addition, FMS uses a unique transfer protocol, Real-Time Message Protocol (RTMP), which can limit stream ripping. FMS also offers support for Secure Sockets Layer (SSL) and encrypted streams and stream authentication using server-side scripting. Keep in mind, however, that anything viewed on a computer screen can theoretically be recorded using a screen-capture utility. So streaming is not the perfect solution but is adequate for most DRM needs.

Progressive video is inherently insecure, because the FLV file is cached on the viewer's computer after playback and can be retrieved from the cache. The DRM options for progressive video therefore involve "security through obscurity." Let's take a look at some of the approaches:

Watermark You can add a visible watermark to your video (either when editing or in some encoding software such as On2 Flix or Sorenson Squeeze) to at least get credit, if not a little traffic, if someone steals your video. You can also add an invisible watermark by adding metadata to the FLV. This can be stripped out by crafty pirates, but it's an extra step, and they may not know it's there. We'll cover metadata in Chapter 8.

Expire from Cache After Viewing In the meta "Expires" header in HTML documents, you can tell the browser when a cached document should expire from the cache. Insert the following tag between the <HEAD></HEAD> tags of the HTML document containing your SWF file:

```
<META HTTP-EQUIV="Expires" CONTENT="-1">
```

The content of the page will expire from the cache immediately after being viewed.

Don't Cache at All Using the following code, you can instruct the browser not to cache the content at all. Note that this method does not work in Internet Explorer versions 5 or older, and it does break standard HTML rules. If you still want to give it a try, you'll need to insert this tag at the very end of your HTML document, after the closing </BODY> tag:

```
<HEAD>
<META HTTP-EQUIV="PRAGMA" CONTENT="NO-CACHE">
</HEAD>
```

As a catchall, you may want to use both the "Expires" and "No-Cache" methods in the same HTML document.

Of course, none of these methods is totally hack-proof, but they do serve as roadblocks to the casual pirate and can give you (and your client) some sense of security.

Summary

Now that you know what's involved in the architecture of a video application, you should have everything you need to plot a course. You learned about

- Best practices for user experience
- Streaming versus progressive download, and which is best for you
- Basic code for each delivery option
- Deployment and hosting choices
- Digital rights management issues and possible solutions

In Chapter 4, we'll review object-oriented design principles, introduce some relevant design patterns for Flash video, help you decide between ActionScript 2 or 3, and get you set up with the best development tools. Let's go get your workspace and workflow in order so you can get busy coding!

OOP and the Video Application

As a Flash developer, you're likely already familiar with object-oriented programming (OOP) concepts. You may have adopted OOP practices in your daily work, or maybe you've just started centralizing your code into external files. If you're still not quite embracing objects and classes in your workflow, now is the time! Whether you're currently using ActionScript 2 or 3, fully utilizing OOP practices will allow you to create more professional applications. This chapter is here to give you a refresher and tie in the principles directly to Flash video projects. We'll also review options for configuring your work environment, and walk you through setting up our recommended Eclipse-FDT- MTASC workflow. When you've finished this chapter, you'll be fully armed and ready to start developing some serious video apps.

Chapter Contents

Why All This Hoopla About OOP?
Design Patterns and Flash Video
The Fork in the Road: AS2 vs. AS3
Setting Up Your Work Environment
Viva la Open Source!

Why All This Hoopla About OOP?

Object-oriented programming has been a standard in programming languages for over a decade, currently with support in languages such as Java, JavaScript, C++, PHP, and Ruby, just to name a few. OOP support is native to ActionScript 3 and, a bit more loosely, to ActionScript 2. You may already be familiar with the basic principles of OOP, but we feel it's important to offer you a refresher and show how you can use its benefits to your advantage in Flash video applications.

What Is OOP?

Object-oriented programming (OOP) is a language model composed of self-contained, modular objects. Some languages, such as ActionScript 1, just use a collection of functions (though it could be "hacked" into an object-oriented framework by very determined programmers). OOP-structured languages can be much more powerful because of their modular nature, making application structure more flexible and easier to understand. The modules, or objects, can send messages and data to one another while remaining compartmentalized. By adopting an OOP structure, ActionScript has joined the ranks of enterprise-level programming languages.

What Are the Key Elements of OOP?

Glad you asked. Let's start with *classes*. A class defines an abstract object and all of its properties and features. In a classic example, the class Vehicle would define all the characteristics that make up a vehicle. These characteristics, or properties, could be things like year, make, model, and color. In ActionScript, these properties could be accessed by referencing vehicle.year or vehicle.color, for example. Instances of a class are *objects*. An object has specific methods, data, and properties as defined by its class.

Another key object-oriented principle is *inheritance*. If you need more specialized versions of an object, you would create a subclass that *inherits* all the properties of its parent and adds additional properties. Back to our vehicle example—you could subclass the class Vehicle to create the new class called Garbagetruck. The new class Garbagetruck would have all the characteristics of a vehicle but could also have the added method compactGarbage().

The object's abilities, or functions, are referred to as its *methods*. In the vehicle example, the functions of a car might be forward, reverse, steer left, or steer right. In ActionScript, you'd say vehicle.steerRight(). You can think of each object as its own self-contained machine with its own defined functions and abilities.

This brings us to the next key concept, the crux of OOP, *encapsulation*. Encapsulation dictates that what goes on inside of a class is its own business. You should be able to make a change to a class, provided its name, method names, parameters, and return values stay the same, without having to change any other classes in your application. This also promotes code re-use, and allows you to test individual units of an application on their own when troubleshooting (referred to as unit testing, which we'll get into in Chapter 6).

Why Is OOP So Useful in Flash Development?

OOP techniques with Flash are a winning combination. You can encapsulate your code and reuse it, eliminating the need to write the same code over and over. This saves you tons of time, speeds up your application, and reduces time spent debugging. It also promotes something Flash was crying out for—centralization—by forcing you to organize your code all in one place, not scattered on various nested frames of the Flash file. The encapsulation of modules, or objects, keeps the logic clear and is invaluable when working in teams and on complex projects such as Flash video applications. Bottom line: OOP makes development more efficient.

And What Does OOP Have to Do with Flash Video?

As you'll soon see, Flash video projects, especially enterprise-level applications, can quickly become quite complex. Dealing with buffering, bandwidth detection, dynamic playlists, cue points, and the like, you can easily end up with an application full of seemingly haphazard "spaghetti code." By following object-oriented design principles, you are forced to encapsulate specific functions into classes and adhere to a more organized overall structure. For example, you could have one class that loads the video filenames, another that displays that data in a playlist, and another that actually plays the selected video. Without an OOP approach, you may have been tempted to group all of those functions into one ActionScript file. They are related functions, after all, aren't they? This is true, but grouping them together limits flexibility and doesn't allow you to reuse the code. For example, you might want to reuse the class that plays the video to also play MP3 audio files.

There are also established object-oriented design patterns that you can rely on to help you. A design pattern is a repeatable approach to a common problem in application architecture. The model-view-controller pattern and the state design pattern are particularly useful for Flash video applications. Let's take a closer look at how they are structured, and how you can use them in your projects.

Design Patterns and Flash Video

When developing an application, it's helpful to have a birds-eye view of its overall composition. Utilizing established OOP design patterns can help guide you to create a solid underlying structure and can speed up your development process because you're relying on tested, proven design principles. Design patterns also can offer solutions that save you from having to reinvent the wheel—dealing with those recurring problems you run into, like functionality or behaviors that always need to be created or dealt with, ranging from simple button toggling to more complex view changes.

Admittedly, in ActionScript development it's often difficult to adhere rigidly to a single design pattern. We do find them very helpful in envisioning the underlying structure and planning of complex applications, so we use them as a guide. Remember, if a pattern is not practical, don't try to force your code to fit the pattern. That being said, let's review two common patterns that can be very useful in Flash video applications.

Model-View-Controller (MVC)

In the MVC pattern, all of your code is encapsulated in one of three areas: models, views, or controllers. In short, models store the data (such as video filenames); views create the method of display (a video display object, for example); and controllers trigger changes in either the model or the view (such as stopping the video or changing the video being played). Figure 4.1 shows what a basic MVC structure looks like.

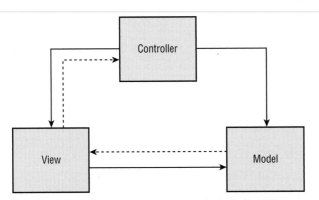

Figure 4.1 A basic MVC structure. Solid lines are method calls; dotted lines represent dispatched events.

This structure ensures that items can only communicate in certain ways, which keeps your application from becoming a tangled mess. Encapsulation is the key. The model class imports the data and stores it; it doesn't care how the data is presented or how input is received. The view class creates the application's display interface; it doesn't care about how the data is parsed or how input is processed. The controller listens for changes and initiates calls to update the interface and the model; it doesn't care how the data is parsed or how it is displayed. This separation of duties is the basis of the MVC pattern.

MVC can be a bit confusing if you're new to using design patterns (and even for seasoned programmers from time to time), so let's examine the functions in more detail:

Model functionality

- Stores data in properties
- Contains data management methods
- Maintains list of registered views
- Updates all registered views when notified of state changes
- Implements all logic of the application

View functionality

- Watches for changes in the model
- Updates the display in response to changes in the model
- Sends input events to the controller
- Can retrieve information directly from the model

Controller functionality

- Listens for events from the view
- Notifies the model of changes (sometimes translating changes into meaningful commands before sending to the model)
- Calls methods on the view directly in special cases (simple implementations or visual changes with no effect on the model)

Note: It's important to note that the *model* implements all the logic of the application. Too often, the logic that should be in the model ends up in the controller or (worse) in the view. The common error is to treat the model like a dumb holder of data and nothing more. In reality, you have one data model and many controllers and views that need to interact with that model. This is why most of the logic needs to live in the model. If the logic is in the controller: The minute you have more than one controller, you will have duplicate code.

Now let's walk through an example so you can understand the MVC structure more clearly (also take a look at Figure 4.2). An event occurs, such as a button press, in the view. The view notifies the controller of the event. The controller then sends the change to the model, which then sends the update to the view to change its display. Changing the display could consist of updating data, pausing the video, or playing a new video, for example.

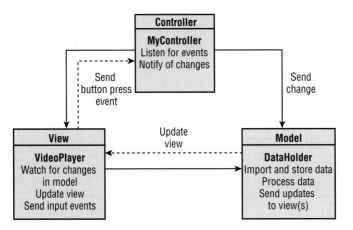

Figure 4.2 Sample MVC framework in a simple video application

This may seem like a roundabout way to update the view, but it allows for greater scalability. Say later you want to add an additional view, such as captions with each video chosen from a playlist. You wouldn't have to change the structure of your application; you'd just add a new view that displayed the caption in addition to the original view that played the video.

State Design Pattern (SDP)

The state design pattern (SDP) is based on the idea that an application has various states and behaves differently depending on its current state. You might easily see how this could be adapted to video applications. For example, a very simple video application could have two states: (1) video playing and (2) video stopped. If the play button is pressed while in the play state, this would have no effect, but if it is pressed when in the stop state, it would trigger the video to play.

The state design pattern allows you to set up methods that create different results depending on the current state of the application. This streamlines your code by preventing you from having to write multiple conditional statements to address every possible scenario.

There are three areas of an application built using the state design pattern (referred to as a state machine): context, state, and concrete state. Let's take a look at each element to gain a better understanding of how it works:

Context functionality
- Defines the interface
- Maintains instances of each concrete state
- Gets and sets the current state

State functionality

- Defines an interface template for concrete state instances

Concrete state functionality

- Extends state, implementing specific methods (behaviors) for each state change

So, the context is the main user interface that controls what the visitor sees. The state is a basic template that establishes the methods, or behaviors, for all concrete states. The concrete states then customize these methods to react appropriately to changes.

States are changed through transitions. In more complex applications, you may need to go through several transitions to get from one state to another. For example, theoretically you can't get to a fast-forward state from a stop state; you first need to go to the play state, then the fast-forward state.

State transitions are initiated through triggers. Triggers can be anything from a button click to an expiring timer. They are basically functions being called on a specific concrete state. For example, if the current state is stop and the play button is clicked, the videoPlay() function in the stopState class would be called. Figure 4.3 diagrams this logic, applied to a very basic video application.

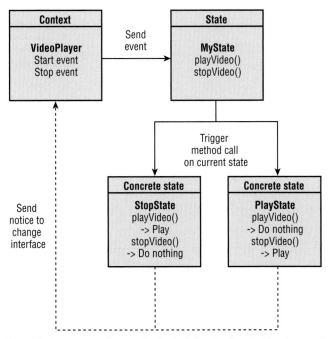

Figure 4.3 A state pattern diagram, showing basic functionality of a video player application

If you're interested in using this pattern and want to learn more, Bill Sanders has written an excellent article for Adobe demonstrating the state design pattern applied to video; it's called "Creating a Video Player Using the State Design Pattern and ActionScript 3.0" (http://www.adobe.com/devnet/flashmediaserver/articles/video_state_machine_as3.html).

Note: This section was meant to introduce you to the concept of design patterns and provide you with useful examples of how to use them in your Flash video applications. When you get into large-scale Flash applications, if you're working with a development team, or if you just want to improve the quality of your code, you'll likely want to learn more about design patterns. We have links to some helpful articles on the subject on our companion website, http://www.flashconnections.com.

The Fork in the Road: AS2 vs. AS3

One of the first choices you'll have to make before you dive into programming is "ActionScript 2 or 3?" Your answer lies in three factors: (1) which language you are most familiar with, (2) what functionality and processing speed your application requires, and (3) what Flash Player version you're targeting.

Which Language Do You Speak Fluently?

For those of us who come to the table with a design background, the jump from AS2 to AS3 may feel like traversing a canyon, but to those with a computer science background it will seem much more intuitive and less limited than AS2. Flash Player 9 is a remarkable step forward from previous versions in its speed and efficiency. Although AS3 requires more coding time up front, your AS3 applications will require less troubleshooting later. If you're relatively new to ActionScript we recommend that you start with AS3 and don't try to learn AS2 and expect to build upon it. AS3 truly is a different beast.

Note: As we recommended earlier in Chapter 1, you want to avoid learning a completely new language during a new project. Take it from us; we've learned the hard way. So if you haven't studied AS3 yet, and haven't worked through some tutorials and made a few small sample projects, stick with AS2 for now if you can.

What Does Your Application Have to Do?

As far as video applications go, the quality of the video will be the same in either Flash Player 8 or Flash Player 9; both use the VP6 codec. You won't need to worry about backward compatibility either; Flash Player 9 will still play older SWFs. Really, the major differences are under the hood, not in remarkable added features. (The biggest functionality benefit that may sway you to choose AS3 is the new components in Flash 9—but you didn't buy this book to go and just use the components, now did you?) The major advantage of AS3 is going to be its performance. For example, if you have any complex animation or data parsing in your application, AS3 is the winner here, hands down.

What's Your Target Player?

Another factor in your version decision will be your target audience. If your client wishes to target Flash Player 8 and under, then you will require AS2. If you are targeting Flash Player 9, your applications will run faster using AS3. You may be able to persuade your client to go with Flash Player 9 by pointing out its rapid adoption rate. Here are some other convincing reasons:

ActionScript 3.0 is a powerful, ECMA-standard-based object-oriented programming language. OK, that may not mean much to your client, but it's important. It puts Flash on the same playing field as other enterprise-level languages such as Java.

AS3 is faster because of the brand-new highly optimized ActionScript Virtual Machine (AVM2). This is the internal engine that runs Flash; completely rewritten from AS2, it supports full runtime error reporting and industry-standard debugging. And it's remarkably faster than AS2.

AS3 has stricter code rules and better error checking, leading to less troubleshooting. You'll spend less time debugging, so maybe you can add that extra feature they were asking for, after all.

AS3 has commonly used classes and objects repackaged as APIs. Again, too much geek-speak for your clients, but you know that efficiency = less development time. You do the math.

AS3 is much faster and more intuitive when working with XML. Support is included for regular expressions and E4X (an XML extension that adds native XML support and streamlines parsing).

Of course, AS2 is still a viable option, and will likely be needed for some time to come as many large companies are slow to upgrade their computers to the latest plug-in versions.

Once you decide on your ActionScript version, you'll need to set up your work environment, if you haven't already. Even if you have a workflow setup now, you may want to skim the next section to be sure you know your options.

Setting Up Your Work Environment

A number of development environment choices are available for ActionScript. The configuration you choose depends a great deal on your working style, your programming background, and personal preference. You likely have already established a good workflow for your Flash projects, but if you want to consider alternatives or streamline your process, or if you are transitioning from AS2 to AS3, read on. Though this section doesn't pertain exclusively to Flash video projects, the complexity of a good video application is going to require that you have a solid working environment from the start.

Some of the common configurations for ActionScript 2 authoring include:

- Flash IDE, Actions panel
- Flash with Dreamweaver AS editor
- Flash with any text editor
- Flash with XCode editor (Mac)
- Flash with Emacs editor (PC)
- FlashDevelop editor with Flash
- FlashDevelop editor with MTASC compiler
- SEPY with MTASC compiler
- Eclipse editor with Flash
- Eclipse with the FDT (Flash Development Tool) plug-in and MTASC compiler

For ActionScript 3 authoring, your options are currently:

- Flash CS3 IDE, Actions panel
- Eclipse with the FDT plug-in (upcoming release) and Flash CS3
- FlashDevelop 3 with MTASC
- FlexBuilder2

Of course, for both AS2 and AS3, the most straightforward way to build SWFs is to edit ActionScript on the timeline directly in the Flash application, also referred to as the Flash IDE (Integrated Development Environment). This approach is good for those who may be new to programming, are comfortable working in the Flash authoring environment, or for simple projects. But as your projects get more complex and you work more with OOP design frameworks, you'll want to move out of the Flash IDE and into the realm of more powerful development tools. If you're programming in more than one language (PHP, Ruby, etc.), it's best to pick one editor and master it. For example, if you choose Eclipse, as we suggest, you'll find it easier to switch to FlexBuilder or the FDT Eclipse plug-in for AS3 development.

Though both XCode and Emacs are professional-level code editors, neither currently has robust support for ActionScript. FlashDevelop is a free, open source ActionScript editor with a solid toolset, but it is not as full-featured as Eclipse. Eclipse is a versatile development tool used by many professional Flash developers, and it's the one we used to develop the examples shown in this book. A Java-based, cross-platform code editor, Eclipse is used by professional coders for working with many different programming languages. Plug-ins for each language can be downloaded, often for free, offering code hinting, error-checking, and other language-specific functions. Two popular Eclipse plug-ins are available for ActionScript: ASDT and FDT. ASDT is open source and free; FDT costs 199 Euros, or about $275. (FDT is currently available for AS2, but an AS3 version is scheduled to be released by the time this book is published.) Although, admittedly, we are usually tempted to go for the free or cheap option, ASDT can be a bit more complex to configure, so we use FDT.

For those of you working in AS3, Adobe's FlexBuilder2 will be your best all-in-one choice for development. It is built on top of the open source Eclipse framework, with plugins for Flex/AS3. The cost will likely be higher than the FDT AS3 plug-in, but you'll also get Adobe's Flex components, which can potentially offset the cost with efficiency and productivity gains. We generally will use FlexBuilder2 or the Flash IDE throughout the book in our AS3 examples, since the FDT AS3 plug-in is not yet available.

Note: The setup that follows is for AS2 development; our recommended setup for developing AS3 code is FlexBuilder2. If you don't have a copy, you can download a 30-day trial from http://www.adobe.com. (Unlike the AS2 setup shown here, no special configuration is required for FlexBuilder2.) Alternatively, you can download a 30-day trial of the FDT AS3 plug-in for Eclipse at http://fdt.powerflasher.com.

Doing It Our Way: Setting Up Eclipse, FDT, and MTASC for AS2 Development

Let's go through the process of installing and configuring your work environment, the way we have it set up. You may already be comfortable with your own workflow, but even so, it would be helpful to you to read through this section so you understand how the examples in this book are set up.

Install Eclipse

To install Eclipse, follow these steps:

1. First go to http://www.eclipse.org and download the latest software development kit (SDK).

2. After downloading and unzipping the SDK, place the entire Eclipse folder in your Program Files folder (or Applications folder on a Mac).

3. Launch Eclipse by double-clicking the application file.

 Note: To run Eclipse, since it is a Java-based program, you need a version of the Java Runtime Environment (JRE) installed. You likely already have this, but if you get a runtime error when first launching Eclipse, or if it won't launch at all, you may need to install a JRE. Consult the Eclipse website for more information or go to http://www.java.com to download and install it. (The Eclipse documentation lists a number of possible JREs; we recommend starting with Sun Java 5.)

4. The program will ask you where you would like to store your files (your "workspace"); choose a folder or create a new one. Check the box to make this your default workspace.

5. You'll now see a welcome screen presenting you with some options to learn more about Eclipse (see Figure 4.4). Choose Go to Workspace. Easy as pie so far, right?

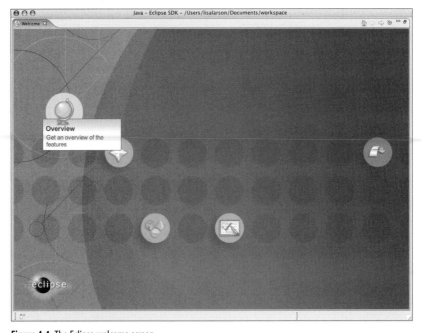

Figure 4.4 The Eclipse welcome screen

Note: We recommend setting your workspace to be inside the web root of your local dev machine. This way you can test your pages via your localhost server. This is especially important when you're building apps that depend on server-side data (PHP, Ruby, FMS).

Note: We recommend that you take some time to get familiar with the basics of the program before you proceed to installing plug-ins.

Install FDT

The ActionScript plug-in we recommend is FDT. It does cost a few bucks, but the productivity you'll gain definitely offsets the cost. We know several developers who'd rather lose a limb than be forced to work without FDT. It offers live error highlighting, code completion, wizards, and "quickfixes" (which create missing methods for you with a single click). A fully functional 30-day trial is available, so you can give it a try for yourself and see if it fits into your workflow before committing to a purchase.

To install the FDT plug-in, follow these steps:

1. Open Eclipse.

2. From the Help menu, choose Software Updates > Find and Install (see Figure 4.5).

3. On the dialog box that appears, select Search for New Features to Install, then click Next.

4. Choose New Remote Site. Insert FDT as the name and the URL http://fdt.power-flasher.com/update and click OK.

5. Check the FDT selection box and click Finish. Another dialog box will appear; check the FDT selection box again and click Next.

6. Accept the License Agreement. Finally, in the next dialog box, confirm the latest version of FDT to be installed by checking the FDT selection box. Click Finish.

7. You may be asked to confirm you want to install an extension that is not digitally signed. Click Install.

8. You'll be asked to restart Eclipse; say OK.

That's it—you've installed FDT!

Note: FDT should be automatically configured to find Flash's Core Libraries, ASO directory, Flash IDE, and Flash Player upon installation. If you are having trouble getting FDT to work, consult the help files and follow the instructions to configure your FDT preferences.

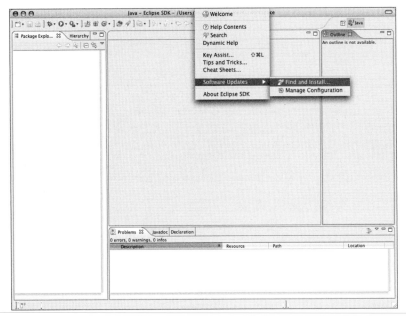

Figure 4.5: Eclipse plug-in installation menu

Configure MTASC and Test

MTASC (pronounced *EM-task*) is an open source command-line compiler that can be used by Eclipse/FDT to build SWFs. It is much faster than the built-in Flash compiler, provides more robust error checking, and is completely free. It takes a bit of configuration but can cut out hours of valuable idle development time. We know one game developer who was saving as much as 3 minutes from each compile using MTASC, adding up to several additional productive hours a week. (He did have difficulty finding the time to keep up with his e-mail and IM conversations after making the switch, however!)

Installing MTASC at this point is optional. You could choose to write your code in Eclipse/FDT, then just compile using the Flash IDE. However, if you have a large project with lots of classes, or just need to compile often, you may want to choose MTASC.

To set it up, follow these steps:

1. First, download the latest build for your operating system from http://www. mtasc.org and unzip it.

2. Place that folder inside your Eclipse application folder.

3. Choose Window > Preferences.

4. Within the FDT dropdown menu, open the Tools menu and choose MTASC.

5. Click Browse and navigate to the MTASC.exe file and click OK.

OK, you've almost finished configuring MTASC. First, you'll want to create a new Flash Project to work with.

6.　In Eclipse, choose File > New > Project.

7.　In that dialog box, if FDT was installed correctly, you'll see a Flash dropdown menu. Open that menu and choose New Flash Project (Figure 4.6). Click Next.

8.　Call the project **MyFlashProject** and choose Finish.

9.　You'll be asked if you want to open the Project in the Flash perspective; click Yes (Figure 4.7). In Eclipse, a perspective refers to the custom workspace menu configuration for a specific plug-in.

Figure 4.6 Creating a new Flash project in Eclipse

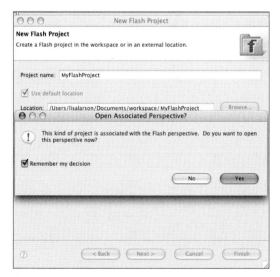

Figure 4.7 Opening the new Flash project in the Flash perspective

Next, you'll need to create a new Source folder to hold your class files for this project.

1. Right-click (or Ctrl-click on Mac) on the myFlashProject folder in the Flash Explorer pane and choose New > Source Folder. Call it **Classes** and click Finish.

2. Right-click on the Classes folder you just created and choose New > Other. Then choose Class from the Flash dropdown menu and click Next.

3. Make the class name **MyFlashProject** and click Finish.

4. You should see the new class file in the Source folder, and it will be open in the main Editor pane. FDT has created "stub" (basic framework) code for you; replace what's there with the following code (also available for download on our site):

```
class MyFlashProject {
    function MyFlashProject () {
        _level0.createTextField("test_txt",1,0,0,300,200);
        _level0.test_txt.text = "Hello World, I'm compiled by MTASC.";
    }

    //MTASC trace function
    public static function main() : Void {
        var h = new MyFlashProject();
    }
}
```

5. Save the file with your changes. This step seems a bit fiddly, but it's essential to test your installation.

To finish the MTASC configuration:

1. Select Run > Run. Then, in the FDT dropdown menu, choose FDT-MTASC Support. Right-click, select New, and give the configuration the name **MyFlashProject**.

2. Select the Main tab, click Browse, and select MyFlashProject as your Project.

3. Next, choose your main class; click Browse, and choose MyFlashProject from the list.

4. Choose the Miscellaneous tab, check the Start SWF After Compilation box, and choose Open with External Flash Player.

5. Click Apply, and then Run.

6. You should get an "SWF not found" message in the Eclipse console.

7. Again, select Run > Run. Then, in the FDT dropdown menu, choose your MyFlashProject configuration in the FDT-MTASC Support dropdown menu.

8. Select the Miscellaneous tab. Now browse to your project folder for MyFlash-Project on your hard drive and choose the SWF that is there. (It should be called mtasc_default.swf.)

9. Click Apply, then Run.

The Flash Player should launch, and your screen should look something like Figure 4.8. Congratulations—you're configured and ready to rock and roll.

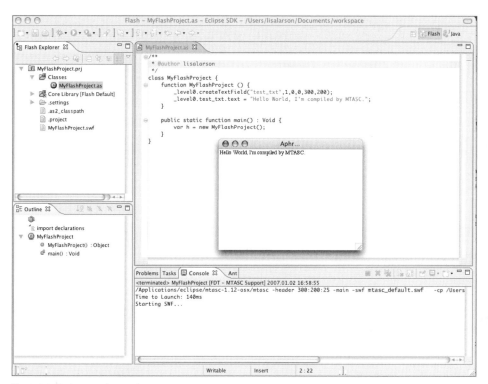

Figure 4.8 Flash test project results

Viva la Open Source!

The open source Flash community offers a wealth of helpful tools and utilities to make your life as a Flash developer easier. From tweening libraries to debugging tools to compilers, projects are being worked on every day that can take Flash further and streamline your workflow.

Notably for Flash video, many helpful utilities are available. Utilities such as FFmpeg and flv2mpeg4 can come in handy for transcoding video on the server side. These can be useful for sites that feature user-generated content, allowing server-side conversion of video to and from FLV format. FLVTool2 can be used to update FLV metadata and add cue points. All of these utilities are available for download—free of cost—at http://osflash.org/. Then there's always the illustrious FLVMDI (Burak's FLV Metadata Injector), for updating and injecting custom metadata into FLV files. This tool is indispensable for adding captions and watermarks, which we'll cover in more detail in Chapter 8. (Whew...so many acronyms!) Despite their sometimes cryptic names, know that many groundbreaking Flash video applications have been developed using these free tools and others. Use the tools, participate in the forums—maybe even contribute to a project—and the entire Flash community will benefit.

OK, that's enough of our pontificating; let's get back down to the business of building a sturdy Flash video player—on to Chapter 5!

Summary

In this chapter we gave you a quick overview of object-oriented programming, and got you set up to start some efficient coding. You learned about:

- What object-oriented programming is, and why you should care
- How OOP principles are applied in Flash
- Design patterns, and why they are useful
- Specific design patterns—MVC and SDP—that are useful for video applications
- Common workflow configurations for AS2 and AS3, and the pros and cons of each
- Setting up the recommended AS2 work environment and recommendations for AS3 development

You're now fully set up and ready to start coding! Let's dive in and build us a basic video player, shall we? In the next chapter we'll do just that.

The Video Player

So you've developed the "deployment roadmap" for your application. You know whether it needs to be progressive or streaming, where it'll be hosted, and what the overall functionality is. You and your client have agreed on all the details of the project. You've even set up your workspace and decided on a target Flash Player version. Now it's time to actually code this beast. Where do you begin? Don't fret, this chapter's here to get you started, and headed in the right direction.

Your approach will depend on a few factors: How much custom functionality does your application need? Is it critical that the file size be as small and optimized as possible? Does the player itself need to fit seamlessly into a larger Flash application? Here we present the options, as well as their pros and cons, and walk you through the steps to a finished app.

Chapter Contents

So You Need to Play a Video—Where to Begin
Creating a Player Using Components
Roll Your Own: Creating a Custom Player

Prepare yourself, though—this chapter runs the gamut from just dropping a video playback component onto the Stage to creating a Model-View-Controller–based customizable video player in both ActionScript 2 (AS2) and ActionScript 3 (AS3). So strap in and hold on—let's build a video player, shall we?

So You Need to Play a Video—Where to Begin

All video applications have a few things in common, one always being the playback of an FLV, of course. Beyond that, what else does your application need to do? How much customization does the interface need? Do you need playback controls? Are you projecting the video onto a shape or using alpha-channel transparency? Will there be a playlist, and if so, what will the data source be? Will you need to integrate with a larger application structure? Your answers to these questions will determine the best approach to building your player.

For example, if you're simply playing a video with alpha transparency, or projecting a single video onto a shape (say, for a "video billboard" inside an animated scene), you'd just instantiate a video object in the right place and configuration, hook up a NetConnection and NetStream, and play your specified video file. If you're targeting Flash Player 9 (or even 8, if you don't need a custom skin) and have a video you'd like viewers to be able to control easily, you may want to use the FLVPlayback component. However, if you have an application that requires more complex functionality, you'll want to build a more robust player structure that will give you the ability to access and control playlists, metadata, dynamic buffering, and the like.

In this chapter we walk you through your options when using the CS3 video playback components (we recommend the CS3 versions over v2 components available in AS2), and then dive into the structure of our sample video player framework based on the Model-View-Controller design pattern. It was originally designed for us by a rock-star programmer and all-around great guy, Jim Kremens, and ported to AS3 by equally amazing developer James O'Reilly. It's a solid object-oriented design, which gives us a robust API for extending functionality in later chapters.

Let's start out by taking a look at the components and examining the pros and cons of using them in your video applications.

Creating a Player Using Components

OK, we hear what you're saying: you bought a book on Flash video for *professionals*, right? If you had wanted to work in the Flash IDE and use the prebuilt playback components you would have just dropped one on the Stage and gone on your merry way? Well, hold your horses. Let's not go dissing the components just yet. Adobe has employed some very talented developers from the Flash community to rebuild them from the ground up in AS3 for Adobe Flash CS3. Though you likely are reading this book because you have a custom application in mind, it's worthwhile to take a look at the latest prebuilt components to see if they can serve your needs.

What the FLVPlayback Component *Can* Do

There are a number of benefits to using the FLVPlayback component:

- It can be useful for quick implementations of video. You can drag it onto the Stage, set some parameters, and off you go.
- It plays both progressive and streaming video files.
- It can be skinned much more easily than the previous v2 components in Flash 8.
- It provides the ability to add cue points. (We'll go over this in Chapter 8.)
- It can implement standard captioning through the FLVPlayback Captioning component (using Timed Text Files, a subset of Synchronized Multimedia Integration Language [SMIL]).

What It *Can't* Do

The FLVPlayback component does have some shortcomings, however:

- It can't apply bitmap effects or filters to the video. (Any transformations would need to be applied to the whole component.)
- It's not useful for live chat applications.
- We wouldn't use it for alpha-channel video.
- It can be difficult to add custom functionality without having to pull apart the underlying code. It's almost always better to write your own code rather than try to decipher someone else's.
- And the real deal breaker—it's overkill for live video or simple video players that don't require the full function set built into the component. Even if you're not using it, all that extra code is still included in your SWF.

So why would we recommend using the component at all for developing professional-grade video applications? Because it's so darn quick. If you need to mock up a working prototype, you want to show your client proofs of an encoded video, or you're just feeling lazy that day (OK, not the best reason!), then the FLVPlayback component can get the job done.

By now you know how we feel about the v1 and v2 components, which shipped with previous versions of Flash. Because their code is too bloated and they're too difficult to skin in our opinion, we won't be covering them here. Of course, you can always use them if you don't need a custom skin or don't mind a bit of overhead in file size. (We do use them in some of our AS2 examples later in the book.) In this section, though, when it comes to components, we'll only be going over the new version of the FLV-Playback component that comes with Adobe Flash CS3. Let's take a look at how it's used, and learn about ways you can customize it.

Note: The FLVPlayback component is compatible with Flash Player 9.0.28.0 and later.

Using the FLVPlayback Component in Flash CS3

There are two ways to implement this component:

- By dragging one out of the components library onto the Stage
- By instantiating one dynamically through ActionScript

To get you familiar with what the component looks like and what the parameters are, we'll start with the first approach.

Note: You must create a new ActionScript 3 Flash File to have access to the AS3 components. If you are working in any other type of Flash file, they won't be available.

Old-School: Dragging It onto the Stage

FLVPlayback components are easy to implement. Creating a Flash video player, complete with player controls, can be achieved in six simple steps:

1. Create a new ActionScript 3 Flash file in Flash CS3.
2. Select Window > Components if the Components panel is not already open.
3. Click Video > FLV Playback and drag the component onto the Stage.
4. In the Properties panel, give the component an instance name.
5. Still in the Properties panel, click the Parameters tab. This is where you specify your parameters for this instance. The parameters outlined in Table 5.1 are available in the Component inspector for an FLVPlayback instance. Each of these parameters has a corresponding ActionScript property of the same name. When you assign a value to these parameters, you are setting the initial state of the property in the application. Setting the property in ActionScript will override any value you have set in the Parameters panel.

    There are really just two important parameters to set for most simple uses: source and skin.

The source can be:

- A local path to an FLV file
- A URL to an FLV file
- A URL to an XML file with information about how to play an FLV file

To choose a skin (with playback controls) for your video player, select the skin parameter in the Properties panel, and then click on the magnifying glass icon. From here, you can choose a skin in three ways:

- Choose one of the skins included with Flash CS3 from the dropdown menu.
- If you've created a custom skin, select Custom Skin URL from the dropdown menu. In the URL text box, type the URL for the SWF file you created.
- Select None, and add playback controls by adding individual FLVPlayback Custom UI components to the Stage.

(We'll cover what's involved in customizing the skin in more depth later in this section.)

6. After choosing a skin, click OK and then publish the SWF to watch your video, complete with playback controls. See, wasn't that just too easy?

Note: In most cases, if you walk through the video wizard to add your FLVPlayback component, you won't need to touch the Parameters panel.

▶ **Table 5.1** CS3 FLVPlayback Component Parameters

Property	Description
Align	Specifies the video layout when the scaleMode property is set to VideoScale-Mode.MAINTAIN_ASPECT_RATIO or VideoScaleMode.NO_SCALE. The video dimensions are based on the registrationX, registrationY, registrationWidth, and registrationHeight properties. The default is VideoAlign.CENTER.
autoPlay	Set to either True or False, this determines if the video will begin playing automatically. The default value is True, which means that the FLV will play immediately when loaded. If you're using player controls, you'll likely set this to False, so the viewer has control of the video playback right from the start.
source	A string that specifies the URL of the FLV file and how to deliver it (either streaming via Real-Time Message Protocol [RTMP] or progressive delivery).
preview	Only used for live preview. Reads in a PNG file for a preview of the FLV.
cuePoints	An array that contains the cue point // data for the FLV, as added manually in the Properties panel. Cue points allow you to synchronize specific points in the FLV with Flash animation, graphics, or text by triggering events at specified points in the video. The default value is an empty array.

Continues

Property	Description
scaleMode	scaleMode specifies how the FLV will resize after it is loaded. Options are maintainAspectRatio, noScale, and exactFit.
	maintainAspectRatio resizes the video to the size of the FLVPlayback component on the Stage, maintaining the proportions of its original dimensions.
	noScale forces the component to respect the original video dimensions. (There is no autoSize parameter in the latest version of the FLVPlayback component.)
	exactFit stretches the video to fit the dimensions of the FLVPlayback component on the Stage.
skin	A string that specifies the URL to a skin SWF file. This string could contain a filename, a relative path such as Skins/MySkin.swf, or an absolute URL such as http://www.yourdomain.com/MySkin.swf.
skinAutoHide	A Boolean value that, if true, hides the component skin when the mouse is not over the video. This property affects only skins that are loaded by setting the skin property and not a skin that you create from the FLV Playback Custom UI components. Defaults to False.
skinBackgroundAlpha	The alpha for the background of the skin. The skinBackgroundAlpha property works only with SWF files that have skins loaded by using the skin property and with skins that support setting the color and alpha. You can set the skinBackgroundAlpha property to a number between 0.0 and 1.0. The default is the last value chosen by the user as the default.
skinBackgroundColor	The color of the background of the skin (e.g., 0xRRGGBB). The skinBackgroundColor property works only with SWF files that have skins loaded by using the skin property and with skins that support setting the color and alpha. The default is the last value chosen by the user as the default.
volume	A number from 0 to 1 that represents the fraction of maximum volume at which to set the video's audio. The default is 1, full volume.

Instantiating and Configuring the FLVPlayback Component in ActionScript

Let's kick it up a notch and create the player entirely in ActionScript:

1. Create a new ActionScript 3 Flash file in Flash CS3.

2. Drag the FLVPlayback component from the Components panel to your new document's Library.

3. Choose frame 1 of the timeline, then add the following code to the Actions panel. Save the file.

```
import fl.video.*;
var myFLVPlaybk = new FLVPlayback();
```

```
myFLVPlaybk.x = 115;
myFLVPlaybk.y = 60;
addChild(myFLVPlaybk);
myFLVPlaybk.skin = "SkinOverAll.swf";
```

Modify the skin path to reflect the location of the Skins folder on your hard drive, or copy the skin into the same folder as your published SWF, as shown in the example above. (The default path of the AS3 Skins folder on Windows is file:///*my_harddrive*/Program Files/Adobe/Adobe Flash CS3/en/Configuration/ Skins AS3/. Just replace *my_harddrive* with the name of the drive where you installed Flash CS3.)

4. Publish the SWF and watch your video play, complete with playback controls (Figure 5.1).

Now that was pretty easy as well, eh? You'll notice that the previous code isn't in a class, though, so you'd have to wrap it in one for a good OOP application. But it works great in a pinch.

Figure 5.1 FLVPlayback component on the Stage

Note: To stream FLV files from Flash Media Server (FMS) through the FLVPlayback component, you have two choices. The first option is to add a specific main.asc file to your FMS application, which makes some required bandwidth checks before accepting the connection. This main.asc file can be found in your Flash CS3 application folder in Flash CS3/Samples and Tutorials/Samples/Components/FLVPlayback/main.asc. Or, if you don't need the bandwidth detection (or your Flash Video Streaming Service doesn't allow custom main.asc files), you can add the following lines to your ActionScript instead:

```
import fl.video.*;
VideoPlayer.iNCManagerClass = fl.video.NCManagerNative;
```

In both cases, your source URL would be formatted like this:

```
rtmp://your_fms_server/your_app/your_instance/stream_name
```

Or, if you don't specify an instance name in your source URL, FMS will use _definst_ as the default:

```
rtmp://your_fms_server/your_app/stream_name
```

We've noted that there are a lot of things you can't control when using components, often making them difficult to integrate into specialized applications. There are certain things you can control more easily in AS3 components, however, such as changing their look and feel—affectionately known as "skinning." Let's take a look at how it's done.

Customizing the FLVPlayback Component in Flash CS3

There may be many ways to skin a cat, but there are only three ways to skin an FLVPlayer component. Your options are:

- Choose one of the default predesigned skins provided with the application or created by third-party designers.
- Customize each UI control individually (you'll have control over both their look and their behavior).
- Create your own custom skin.

Let's go through the process for each option.

Choosing a Predesigned Skin

This is the option used in the examples earlier. In both the Parameters panel and in ActionScript, we just chose one of the slick skins provided by Adobe. The next option gives you much more control, but is a bit more involved. Let's take a look.

Note: The skin and the video are two separate SWF files. You must upload the selected skin SWF file to the web server along with your application SWF file for the skin to work with your FLVPlayback component.

Customizing UI Controls

If you'd like to use this skinning method, you need to start by specifying the skin property of None. This assures that you have full access to all of the individual UI controls without any conflicts.

> **Note:** Possible showstopper: The UI components are not meant to be scaled. So be sure you create artwork for the skin that is sized to 100 percent of your final usage size. You'll also need to set the FLVPlayback component scaleMode property to noScale.

The first step to skin the individual UI controls is to drag each one you'd like to use onto the Stage. The video control components available to you in CS3 are:

- BackButton
- BufferingBar
- CaptionButton
- ForwardButton
- FullScreenButton
- MuteButton
- PauseButton
- PlayButton
- PlayPauseButton
- SeekBar
- StopButton
- VolumeBar

Once you have the UI controls you want to use on your Stage, you can just edit them like you would any other symbol. Each control has its own unique internal structure. These details are documented in the Help files; we didn't feel an in-depth discussion is worthwhile here.

You'll notice that the controls all have ActionScript inside that you can edit, if you wish to change the symbol's behavior. Having code here is usually a *huge* no-no, but it's the most straightforward way for Adobe developers to give us easy access to the functionality. Fully encapsulated code, as in the previous component versions, just wasn't customizable in reality.

The controls can be placed anywhere on the Stage that you like. You can create a custom UI using each of the individual elements that make up the full FLVPlayback component. Here's how you do it:

1. Create a new Flash CS3 document. Begin playing a video in the FLVPlayback component with no skin selected.

2. Create a second layer on the timeline for your ActionScript, and name it **Actions**.

3. Give the component an instance name of **video** and place it on a new layer called **ui**.

4. In the Components panel, open the Video folder. Below the FLVPlayback and FLVPlaybackCaptioning components you will find the list of controls to choose from. Choose the PlayPauseButton and drag it onto the Stage.

5. Next, connect the PlayPauseButton to the video. To do this, you just need to give your PlayPauseButton the instance name of **playPause**.

6. Highlight the first keyframe in the Actions layer and insert the following ActionScript:

```
video.playPauseButton = playPause;
```

Now the control is connected to the video component and will control playing and pausing of the video. See Figure 5.2 for an example.

Figure 5.2 Skinned FLVPlayback UI buttons

Creating Your Own FLVPlayback Skin

It's very easy to create and customize your own skin in the new Flash CS3. When you decide you want to skin this component, the best approach is to sort through the existing skins and find the one closest to the one that you'd like to create. You can find them in your Flash installation folder, in a folder called FLVPlayback Skins within the Configuration folder. Here you'll find the FLA folder containing the ActionScript 3.0 source FLAs and the ActionScript 3.0 folder containing the SWF files. Your final skin will need to be in this ActionScript 3.0 folder with the other SWFs in order for it to be recognized in the dropdown menu in Flash.

Let's dive in and edit a skin, just to see how it's done:

1. Start by opening one of the existing FLA files in the FLA\ActionScript 3.0 folder. Before doing anything else, save it as a new file so that you don't overwrite the default. You may also want to edit your publish settings to save your SWF directly into the ActionScript 3.0 folder within FLVPlayback Skins to save a step later when you want to test the skin in Flash.

2. The various controls are laid out for you on the Stage. We recommend working directly from the Library when editing them. Edit the larger pieces first, such as the background or the background color. Choose the background in the Library and right-click to edit it. Make your changes just as you would to any symbol, adding layers to create highlights or gradients.

3. Test the movie to see your changes. To change the button states, don't select the states from the individual buttons. Instead, edit the items in the folder in the Library that all the buttons use as their base (in most cases, the first folder in the Skins folder). This folder will have the down state, normal state, and over state. Again, make your desired modifications to the design. Save your file.

4. Open a new AS3 Flash file and drag a new FLVPlayback component onto your Stage. Find the skin parameter in the Parameters panel. Clicking on the magnifying glass will allow you to browse the different SWF skins, including the custom one you just made. (Since you've already published your SWF into the AS3 skins folder, you will see your new skin in the list.)

5. After you've selected your skin and an FLV to play, you can test the button states before you publish by clicking on the magnifying glass next to the preview parameter in the Parameters panel. A dialog box will pop up showing you your FLV, with your skinned buttons in place and active. If you like what you see, go ahead and publish your SWF and you're good to go.

So now you know how to bend the FLVPlayback component to your will. But if every Flash video project were as simple as dropping a component onto the Stage, we'd all be out sailing the Caribbean, now wouldn't we? What happens when your client wants to integrate the player into a larger application structure, when you need to have sophisticated playlists, or when you just need a smaller file size or more control over your video object? Well, you do what any creative, industrious developer would do—you write your own!

Takin' It to the Big Screen

As you may know, in the Flash 8 Player and above, it's possible for an entire SWF to enter full-screen mode. But, did you know that in Flash 9 Player and above, it's possible for the FLVPlayback component itself to go full-screen? Let's see how it's done.

1. First, drag an FLVPlayback component onto the Stage.

2. In the parameters, set the align property to center and the scaleMode to maintainAspectRatio. Or, alternatively, in ActionScript:

   ```
   scaleMode = VideoScaleMode.MAINTAIN_ASPECT_RATIO;
   align = VideoAlign.CENTER;
   ```

3. Choose a skin that has a full-screen toggle button (e.g., SkinOverAll or SkinUnderAll) and specify your source video.

4. In your document publish settings (File > Publish Settings), click the HTML tab. Choose Flash with Full Screen Support from the Template dropdown menu. This will create the external JavaScript file and add required tags to your HTML document.

5. Publish your SWF and click on the full-screen toggle button to view your video on the big screen.

When the Stage enters full-screen mode, the FLVPlayback component covers the other content in the SWF and takes over the whole screen. When the viewer hits the Escape button to exit full-screen mode, the SWF returns to its normal layout.

Roll Your Own: Creating a Custom Player

Most video projects will require custom functionality that can't be provided by prepackaged players or components. Creating these custom players can be a challenge (which likely influenced your decision to buy this book). Considering buffering, sequencing, playlists, connectivity, error handling, data parsing, and navigation issues that come with sophisticated video players can be daunting. And although each video project has different requirements, you'll quickly find that they have many of these same issues in common. This is why we suggest developing a solid framework for your video application that is flexible enough to build on and customize for each new project—which means you won't have to reinvent the wheel with each new video project. In fact, we'll lay out one such framework for you in this section.

FLV 101: *NetStream* and *NetConnection*

In all this excitement to create a Flash video player, it's easy to gloss over the basics. Before we go any further, let's do a little recap of two basic objects that we need in our video applications and explain exactly what they do. You'll use the code examples we provide when you're creating your own player as opposed to using the FLVPlayback component. (In that case, they are still used, but they are encapsulated in the parameters of the component so you wouldn't instantiate them in ActionScript.)

What Is a *NetConnection*?

A NetConnection is used for both streaming and progressive video delivery. It lets Flash know whether you're using progressive download or streaming, and if it's streaming, it specifies where your Flash Media Server is and what application to connect to. For example, for progressive, your NetConnection code would look like this:

```
var nc:NetConnection = new NetConnection();
nc.connect(null);
```

See, if you pass null as the argument, Flash delivers your FLV as progressive download. If you're streaming your video, your NetConnection code would look like this:

```
var nc:NetConnection = new NetConnection();
nc.connect("rtmp://yourFMSserver.com/yourAppName/yourInstanceName");
```

Here you're specifying that Flash should connect via RTMP protocol to a Flash Media Server. You need to specify the host name that FMS is running on, the application you wish to connect to, and the instance name that your FLV files are associated with. (Don't worry about the details of that; we'll cover FMS in depth in Chapter 11.) That's basically all the NetConnection does. By itself, it doesn't play videos—you'll need to bring in a NetStream for that.

What Is a *NetStream*?

The NetStream class gives you the power to play FLV files from the local file system, from a web address, or streaming from FMS. The NetStream plays the FLV through the NetConnection object. You'd instantiate it like this:

```
var ns = new NetStream(nc);
myVideo.attachVideo(ns);
ns.play("yourVideo.flv");
```

Continues

FLV 101: *NetStream* and *NetConnection* (Continued)

In this example, nc is our NetConnection object, and myVideo is a video object that you want to display your FLV. This would be the same for progressive or streaming. The NetStream class gives you methods and properties you can use to control playback, track the video's progress, and more. The properties of a NetStream that you can read are:

bufferLength The number of seconds of video data currently in the buffer

bufferTime The number of seconds assigned to the buffer by NetStream.setBufferTime();

bytesLoaded The number of bytes of data currently loaded in the player

bytesTotal The total size in bytes of the video being loaded in the player

currentFps The number of frames per second currently being displayed

time The position of the playhead, in seconds

There are also three events that can be listened for on a NetStream object:

onCuePoint Triggered when an embedded cue point is reached while playing an FLV file.

onMetaData Triggered when the Flash Player receives metadata embedded in the FLV file being played. The metadata contents can vary depending on the encoding method, but usually include information such as duration, creation date, and data rate. (See Chapter 8 for more on the power of metadata.)

onStatus Triggered whenever a status change or error occurs with the NetStream object.

The NetStream has five handy methods that you can invoke:

close Stops playing all data on the stream, resets the NetStream.time property to 0, and frees up the NetStream for another use.

pause Boolean. Pauses or resumes playback of a stream.

play Begins playback of an external FLV file.

seek Accepts a number of seconds as an offset parameter. Jumps to the keyframe closest to the specified offset from the beginning of the stream.

setBufferTime Specifies how long to buffer data before starting to play the stream.

So, that's it—that's all there is to NetStreams and NetConnections. Well, that's a good overview, anyway. There is a bit more to consider when streaming through FMS, which we'll immerse you in later—in Chapter 11, when we give you an FMS crash course.

Our Player Structure

This sample player application is based on the Model-View-Controller design pattern (as discussed in Chapter 4). Figure 5.3 is a diagram of the overall structure; it's not a formal UML diagram, but simply maps out the classes and their packages so you can get a clear overview.

What we're providing you with here is a flexible basic framework for an FLV player. We'll be showing you how to extend it with features such as XML playlists and cue point captions in later chapters. It is easily skinnable as well. To use it, you'll just need to understand how it's constructed. So let's take a look. We've got a few basic packages here:

core All classes extend core. Inside the core folder is the core class:

> **Core.as** Any methods that need to be global can be added here. We don't have any in this basic application, but the aim of this framework is to make it customizable and expandable for your video apps, so we've extended core.

pattern.mvc A core MVC package (that can be used to make any sort of MVC application). Inside this folder you'll find:

> **Controller.as** Stores references to the Model and View.
>
> **Model.as** Stores a reference to the View.
>
> **View.as** Stores references to the Model and the Controller, and sets up the container, which will be the scope in which our View will be built. Also implements the ICoordinateSpace interface in addition to IView.
>
> **MVCApplication.as** Brings our MVC player together, referencing the Model, View, and Controller and the container.

ui.component.mediaPlayer The video-specific package that extends and implements the core MVC classes. This package contains:

> **MediaPlayerController.as** Controls playback with play, playMedia, pause, stop, get/setMediaPosition, get/setVolume, playNext, and playPrevious methods, which in turn call those methods on the MediaPlayerModel.
>
> **MediaPlayerModel.as** Handles data and events with get/setConnection, get/setStream, play, playMedia, pause, stop, get/setMediaPosition, get/setVolume, get/setPlaylist, playNext, playPrevious, handleOnMetaData, and handleOnStatus methods.
>
> **MediaPlayerView.as** Sets up/updates the user interface and passes events to the Model through get/setVideoInstance, onMetaData, onStatus, onPlay, onPlayMedia, onPause, onStop, onSetMediaPosition, and onSetVolume methods.
>
> **MVCMediaPlayer.as** Brings the Model, View and Controller together, creating an instance of each and initializing them.

MediaPlayer.as Our main class, this creates an instance of the MVCMediaPlayer and passes in all the parameters needed to build your specific video application, including its coordinates and playlist (in this simple example, an array), and initiating the building of the View.

NetStreamExt.as Instantiates a NetStream instance, connecting to the NetConnection that's passed in as a parameter.

ui.component.mediaPlayer.playlist A package that contains the classes needed for working with playlists. This package contains:

Playlist.as Basic class to manage playlists. Sets up get/setList, getIndex, getItemAt, getCurrentItem, hasNext, hasPrevious, getNext, getPrevious, atEnd, atStart, addItem, addUniqueItem, addItemAt, removeItem, removeItemAt, replaceItem, and replaceItemAt methods.

PlaylistUtils.as Utility methods for working with playlists. Used by Playlist.as.

ui.util Here we have a utility class needed by the MVC player:

CoordinateSpace.as A utility class that defines a global coordinate space without a movie clip. Provides methods for changing x, y, width, and height.

util A package to hold extra classes we'll need.

Proxy.as This is a utility class that acts like the Delegate class, allowing you to access instances and methods outside of the local scope. The benefit to using Proxy is the ability to send parameters along with method calls.

This very simple implementation of our video player allows you to play, pause, and stop. Although we're not diving into playlists just yet, the player structure is set up to read a simple array and play next and previous clips in the list. We will be building on that functionality when we discuss playlists in depth in Chapter 7.

You'll also notice that all packages have an associated ifc folder, or Interface package. Interfaces describe all the public methods and arguments of a class. They are essential to framework development, assuring that all implementations of the Interface will contain certain methods. So you'll notice that many of our player's classes will have an associated Interface file inside an ifc folder. It may seem like a bit of overkill to some developers to see so many interfaces in this relatively simple application. We've built them in, however, because we'd like this framework to be a starting point for readers to develop more complex applications. They are there if you need them. (You'll see more detailed examples of the usefulness of this approach in case studies at the end of this book.)

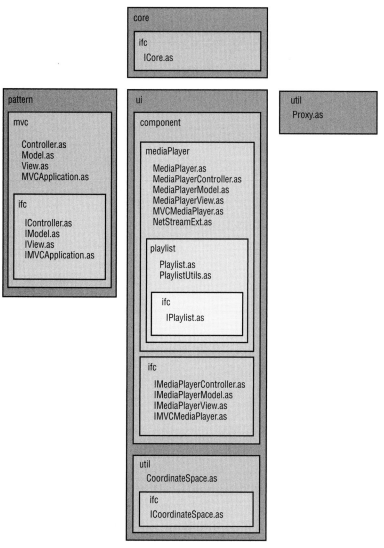

core
ifc
ICore.as

pattern

mvc
Controller.as
Model.as
View.as
MVCApplication.as

ifc
IController.as
IModel.as
IView.as
IMVCApplication.as

ui

component

mediaPlayer
MediaPlayer.as
MediaPlayerController.as
MediaPlayerModel.as
MediaPlayerView.as
MVCMediaPlayer.as
NetStreamExt.as

playlist
Playlist.as
PlaylistUtils.as

ifc
IPlaylist.as

ifc
IMediaPlayerController.as
IMediaPlayerModel.as
IMediaPlayerView.as
IMVCMediaPlayer.as

util
CoordinateSpace.as

ifc
ICoordinateSpace.as

util
Proxy.as

Figure 5.3 Overall class structure of our basic video player

Note: If you're not familiar with interfaces, don't freak out. They're just an easy way to keep consistency in an application framework. An interface is just a class that describes what its instances will do. Each class that implements a specific interface will contain all of the methods included in the Interface class. For example, we have a Dog class. This Dog class implements the IDog interface, which constructs the methods bark(), sitUp(), and scratch(). All Dog classes will be required to have all three of these methods. You can have each Dog class do whatever you want within the methods, but the methods must be present. Examining an application's interfaces can give you a nice overview of the application's structure.

You should now be getting a clearer view of what's happening inside the application. (Figure 5.4 illustrates the structure and flow, adapted from the generic MVC structure diagram from Chapter 4.)

Don't be overwhelmed. In practice, you may never need to crack open most of these classes when using this player framework in simple video projects. It's actually designed to be customizable with only limited changes to the structure—the beauty of the MVC pattern. It is important, however, that you understand the framework's structure so you can fully utilize it in your applications. Just implementing code that works, but that you don't fully understand, can turn into a real headache when you try to add features or make changes. So we've broken it down for you in a few ways to help you get your head around it. See Figure 5.5 for an example sequence: what happens when the application loads and plays the first video.

Dissecting the Code

Now let's dig into the ActionScript a bit, so you can see what's going on inside the application.

Refer to Figure 5.6 to see the player in action. Then take a look at our main class, MediaPlayer.as, in the AS2 below.

Note: The AS2 and AS3 versions of this player share the same basic MVC structure. There are of course some syntax differences in AS3, but that's about it. The only difference you may notice is the use of a Main class to instantiate the player. Otherwise, the framework is basically the same, so we just show the AS2 version in the code examples here. Both AS2 and AS3 versions are available for download from www.sybex.com/go/flashvideo.

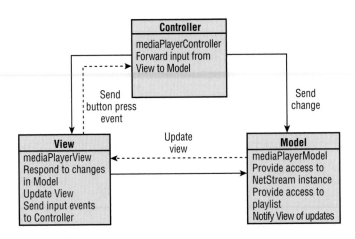

Figure 5.4 Structure diagram of basic MVC video player application

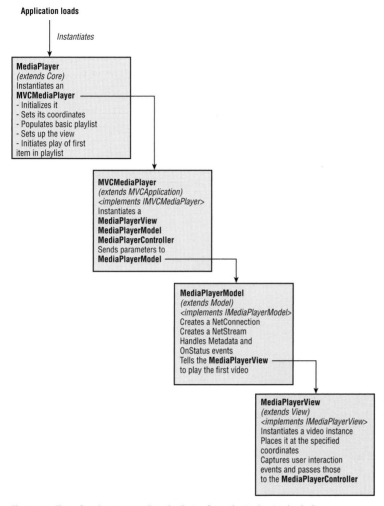

Figure 5.5 Flow of application upon launch; playing first video in the simple playlist

Figure 5.6 Sample video application preview in Flash 8

MediaPlayer.as in ActionScript2

This class begins the setup of the application when it's instantiated:

```
import com.flashconnections.core.Core;
import com.flashconnections.ui.component.mediaPlayer.ifc.IMVCMediaPlayer;
import com.flashconnections.ui.component.mediaPlayer.MediaPlayerView;
import com.flashconnections.ui.component.mediaPlayer.MVCMediaPlayer;


class com.flashconnections.ui.component.mediaPlayer.
➡ MVCMediaPlayer

extends Core
{
```

This code imports the MVCMediaPlayer interface, MVCMediaPlayer, MediaPlayerView, and of course Core.

Next we set up the MVCMediaPlayer instance (player), calling its init functions, populating the playlist, and calling the layout() method on the View to build the user interface. Finally, we call the method to initiate playback of the first video in the playlist.

```
private var player:MVCMediaPlayer;

public static function main():Void {
    var a:MediaPlayer = new MediaPlayer (_root);
}
public function MediaPlayer(mc:MovieClip) {
    player = new MVCMediaPlayer();
    player.init(mc);
    player.initCoordinates(40, 60, 320, 240);
    player.populatePlaylist(["sl_lg.flv", "med_lg.flv", "fast_lg.flv"]);
    player.getView().layout();

    player.playMedia(String(player.getPlaylist().getItemAt(0)));
    }
}
```

Note that the playlist here is just a simple array. As we mentioned earlier in this section, this list can be pulled from any number of sources in your custom video application. This could be populated from XML, culled from a database, or even created by reading the contents of a streams directory in FMS. For now, we're just going to hard-code the filenames here in a simple array. We call the initCoordinates method to specify the placement of the player on the Stage, as well as the video size.

Besides customizing these basic parameters, something else you'll likely need to do when reusing this code from project to project is change the skin or the UI behavior. Conveniently, these elements are isolated to the MediaPlayerView, so you can create a new View for each project and have a custom application, just like that!

In the MediaPlayerView.as class, you can customize what happens when the MediaPlayerView receives notification of certain changes, such as when the video is paused, the buffer is full, or the video has changed to the next in the playlist. Let's walk through the code and examine what's going on.

MediaPlayerView.as in ActionScript 2

First we import the classes needed to instantiate the MVC objects, then begin our constructor.

```
import com.flashconnections.pattern.mvc.Controller;
import com.flashconnections.pattern.mvc.Model;
import com.flashconnections.pattern.mvc.View;
import com.flashconnections.ui.component.mediaPlayer.ifc.IMediaPlayerView;
import com.flashconnections.ui.component.mediaPlayer.MediaPlayerController;
import com.flashconnections.ui.component.mediaPlayer.MediaPlayerModel;
import com.flashconnections.util.Proxy;


class com.flashconnections.ui.component.mediaPlayer.MediaPlayerView


extends View


implements IMediaPlayerView


{
```

The MediaPlayerView extends our basic pattern class View and implements the IMediaPlayerView interface. Then we create a video object instance:

```
    private static var VIDEO_CONTAINER:String = "videoContainer";
    private static var NESTED_VIDEO_INSTANCE:String = "videoInstance";


    private var __videoInstance:Video;


    public function MediaPlayerView(model:Model, cntrl:Controller,
➥ cont:MovieClip) {
        super(model, cntrl, cont);
    }
```

Next, we create an init function that sets up our content container, places a video object on the stage, and gets the current stream from the Model:

```
public function init():Void {
    var depth:Number;
    mpModel = MediaPlayerModel(getModel());
    mpController = MediaPlayerController(getController())
    depth = getContainer().getNextHighestDepth();
    setContent(getContainer().attachMovie(VIDEO_CONTAINER,
➡ VIDEO_CONTAINER + depth, depth));
    setVideoInstance(getContent()[NESTED_VIDEO_INSTANCE]);
    getVideoInstance().attachVideo(getMPModel().getStream());
}
```

Then we get into our public methods that set up the UI and link up our classes:

```
public function initCoordinates(x:Number, y:Number, w:Number,
➡ h:Number):Void {
        getContent()._x = x;
        getContent()._y = y;
        getContent()._width = w;
        getContent()._height = h;
    }
    public function setVideoInstance(val:Video):Void {
            __videoInstance = val;
    }
    public function getVideoInstance():Video {
        return __videoInstance;
    }
    public function layout():Void {

        var cont:MovieClip = getContainer();
        var cntrl:MediaPlayerController =
➡ MediaPlayerController(getController());
        cont.playButton.onRelease = Proxy.create(cntrl, cntrl.play);
        cont.pauseButton.onRelease = Proxy.create(cntrl,
➡ cntrl.pause);
        cont.stopButton.onRelease = Proxy.create(cntrl, cntrl.stop);
        cont.nextButton.onRelease = Proxy.create(cntrl, cntrl.playNext);
        cont.prevButton.onRelease = Proxy.create(cntrl,
➡ cntrl.playPrevious);
    }
```

These next public functions are where the fun can happen. Right now, we have just included traces to let you know the methods are being fired, but you add whatever functionality you need inside. For example, for onPause, you may want to have text come up over the video saying "Paused..." and have a tint of gray over the image. Or upon reading captions in as metadata, you may want to display the text in a text box next to the video. All of this functionality can be added within these methods:

```
public function onMetaData(val:Object):Void {
    trace("MediaPlayerView.onMetaData" + " " + val.code);
}
public function onStatus(val:Object):Void {
    trace("MediaPlayerView.onStatus" + " " + val.code);
}
public function onPlay():Void {
    trace("MediaPlayerView.onPlay");
}
public function onPlayMedia(path:String):Void {
    trace("MediaPlayerView.onPlayMedia" + " " + path);
}
public function onPause():Void {
    trace("MediaPlayerView.onPause");
}
public function onStop():Void {
    trace("MediaPlayerView.onStop");
}
public function onSetMediaPosition(val:Number):Void {
    trace("MediaPlayerView.onSetMediaPosition" + " " + val);
}
public function onSetVolume(val:Number):Void {
    trace("MediaPlayerView.onSetVolume" + " " + val);
}


public function toString() : String {
    return "com.flashconnections.ui.component.mediaPlayer.
➡ MediaPlayerView";
}
}
```

So, your next question undoubtedly is "How can I change how the player looks? My client has a brand to consider, you know!" No worries; you can skin this player to your heart's content. Let's take a look at how it's done.

Skin It!

In our example, the UI is constructed with movieclips on the stage in Flash. You can open the MediaPlayer.fla file and directly edit the basic buttons we have there, or you can create your own with the same instance names as shown in Table 5.2.

▶ **Table 5.2** Instance Names for the MVC Player Buttons

Play	playButton
Pause	pauseButton
Stop	stopButton
Next	nextButton
Previous	previousButton

You can create any sort of buttons you like, and as long as they have those instance names, they'll work with this framework (see Figure 5.7 for a basic example). If you want to add additional buttons and functionality, you can use these as a starting point to set up your methods.

Figure 5.7 Sample skinned video player application

In upcoming chapters, we'll explore how to extend the functionality of this basic flexible structure to add captions, video bookmarks, dynamic playlists with thumbnails, and more. Also, to further bridge the gap between concept and application, we provide a case study at the end of the book that takes this MVC framework and applies it to a real-world client project. Seeing it in action should prove helpful in understanding how to extend it.

Summary

In this chapter you learned about the various options for creating and skinning video players—from the most basic using components and video objects, to a more complex player application framework.

You should now understand:

- What each approach offers you, and which is most appropriate for your project
- How and when to use the Flash CS3 FLVPlayback component
- What UI components are available to use in video players and how to customize them
- How to create and deploy a custom-skinned SWF
- The basic structure of our Model-View-Controller–based video player example
- When to utilize this class structure and how it can be a basis for all of your video projects to speed development

Next, we'll take a step back from the player structure and look ahead to a solid final product—examining testing methods, bandwidth issues, and the client review process. It may seem like we're getting ahead of ourselves, but we've found that taking the whole process into account at the beginning of a project is essential to its success (and saves a lot of pain, to boot).

Getting It Out There: Test, Optimize, and Deploy

OK, so you've got that kickin' video application planned and your basic video player developed. Now you're ready to build in features like playback controls, dynamic playlists, preroll and postroll clips, cue point bookmarks...wait! Did you properly test that video player before you started adding those bells and whistles? Are you sure it can react appropriately to clogged connections, overtaxed servers, or slow computers? How large should your video buffer be? Will the XML data parse before the playlist is rendered? If you're not sure, and you don't pause to test, you may end up with a very unprofessional-looking application, or one that doesn't work at all.

Chapter Contents

Test It, Then Test It Again. Repeat.
Nobody Likes to Wait: Bandwidth Considerations
3, 2, 1... Ready to Launch!
But Wait, There's More: Project Wrap-up

But we're here to save you from all of that. How? First, by giving you solid code examples; second, by providing advice on testing procedures; and third, by outlining a smooth client approval process. Then we'll give you tips on dealing with client feedback and expectations. By the end of this chapter, you'll have the tools you need to ensure that your video apps truly rock—not sink like a stone.

Test It, Then Test It Again. Repeat.

Testing is an often-overlooked step in web development. Workflow commonly consists of coding for a while, compiling and viewing in a browser, debugging, coding some more, compiling again, beating head against keyboard, a bit more debugging, then sending to the client for review. The process then starts over again, continuing until launch.

There is a better way! Well, it still consists of coding and debugging, then coding and debugging again, but it can eliminate the part where you beat your head against the keyboard. By implementing a standardized testing procedure, you streamline the development process and end up with a much more robust application, tested from the inside out.

Two schools of thought regarding testing are test-driven development (officially known as TDD) and the more informal approach of testing code as it's being written. Though this section can apply to all of your Flash development work, we include it here because testing is so crucial to professional Flash video applications. The formal testing frameworks we discuss may seem a bit daunting to incorporate into your workflow right away—but we encourage you to adopt some sort of testing, even if it's very basic. So, that being said, let's take a look at the ways some developers handle testing.

Test-Driven Development vs. Testing While Coding

The basic tenet of test-driven development is the assertion that you shouldn't begin by writing classes to perform the functions of your application; you begin by writing a test. Next, you write a class that fails that test. Then you rewrite that class to pass the test. (This effectively tests both the class and the test itself.) Only then do you integrate the class into the application framework. This TDD procedure is referred to as *red/green/refactor*. It can yield the cleanest and most concise code, but of course requires you to write lots and lots of tests. Strict implementations of TDD require that test files accompany the class files when submitted to the project manager (as proof that they have been tested) before they can be added to the project.

Note: If you are interested in applying the TDD approach to your application development workflow, we suggest you investigate the concept of extreme programming (XP). Some books to get you started: *eXtreme Programming in Action: Practical Experiences from Real World Projects* by Martin Lippert, Stephen Roock, and Henning Wolf (Wiley, 2002); or *Agile Modeling: Effective Practices for eXtreme Programming and the Unified Process* by Scott Ambler and Ron Jeffries (Wiley, 2001).

The basic principle behind a "testing while coding" approach is unit testing. Unit testing consists of writing test cases for every class. (This is slightly different from a strict TDD approach, as the tests are written *after* the class is written.) The unit test cases in this approach demonstrate how to interact with the unit, or class, and what data to expect to be returned. After writing your code, you'd write a "test case" or scenario that describes something a user would need your application to do. This could be as simple as "Drag progress bar to the middle of the progressive video before the video has completed loading" or "Record video from webcam and save to FMS server, adding the filename to the list of available videos." These test cases could include one class or numerous classes, but each class would have to be tested individually before testing how they work together in accomplishing the proposed task.

So you can get an idea of how this works, here's a (very) simple class, in psuedocode:

```
class Multiplication {
    public function Multiplication() {
        var calculation = 2 * 2;
        return calculation;
    }
}

class TestMultiplication {
    assertEquals("Multiplication", 4);
}
```

Assert statements are the core of unit testing. They allow you to test different conditions, such as assertFalse, assertEquals, assertNotNull, assertNull, assertNotUndefined, or assertUndefined. Conveniently, when using a testing framework such as AsUnit, the test class will be discovered automatically, provided you follow the proper naming convention (e.g., TestMultiplication is the test for the Multiplication class).

Both of the testing styles we've covered can be appropriate, depending on the complexity of your application, your deadline, and the number of members in your development team. Both incorporate the concept of unit testing: breaking down an application into its smallest parts (in ActionScript, its classes) and testing each part individually before integrating with the rest of the application. In TDD you write the tests first, then the class; in testing during development you write the class first, then the test. In most smaller-scale applications it's perfectly fine to forego a strict TDD approach (provided you create a system for actually testing consistently throughout the project).

 Note: Some recommended tools to help you standardize your unit testing:
AS2: Use AsUnit (supports Flash 6,7,8, and 9)
AS3 and Flex: Use FlexUnit or AsUnit

Caveat

Though unit testing is invaluable in professional applications, there are certain things that it won't do. It won't help you find errors in application architecture or logic. It doesn't know a thing about aesthetics. Does that menu open smoothly or just snap open? You know that the preload graphic loads when it's supposed to, but does it indicate when the video might start exactly? We ran into one of these instances while working on a recent project. Our client called us and said they were having trouble viewing the videos in our most recently staged proof. We knew they had a slow connection, but we had a bandwidth check in place, so they were to receive the low bit rate video. When we checked this ourselves, we got a smooth video, but the quality wasn't what we had expected. After some sleuthing, we found that the source videos had been incorrectly named; the low bit rate and high bit rate filenames were transposed. We had no errors in our tests; the videos were there and were played. Only by having a human test the application did it become apparent there had been a mistake.

In addition, local unit testing doesn't alert you to performance problems or bandwidth issues that you might run into in real-world deployment. Let's examine some of those potential problems and how to guard against them.

Tests, Tests, and More Tests

You will need to perform a number of other checks on your video application, both during the coding process and into the proofing stages.

Quality assurance (QA) is one of the first things to get nixed as the project deadline appears to be getting closer. A word to the wise: If it's ignored, the illusory gain in productivity will inevitably backfire. All major projects should also have their final review stage. You wouldn't update your XML file for your video playlist and not test it to be sure you have no typos (would you?). All major operations include a quality control stage. For example, Ben and Jerry's cuts pints of Chunky Monkey into quarters to make sure that the chocolaty chunks and walnuts are evenly distributed. You should never have an application "go live" without making sure every part of it works properly, from data loading, to video buffering, to video quality. The QA plan you decide on is largely determined by the complexity of the project and the budget. Making QA a policy, not an afterthought, will keep you in business—and sane.

We'll talk about potential issues to address during final deployment next, but here are some steps you can insert into your workflow to avoid mishaps in your final application.

Save Versions of All Working Files

Implement a procedure to keep track of changes that allows you to roll back to a previous version (the one before you added that cool extra feature that disabled your navigation, for example). This system can be as simple as saving copies of the application in different folders named using a date notation (e.g., 20070402_videoplayer, 207070403_videoplayer, etc.) or as robust as a full version control system such as SVN or Subversion. The more people you have involved in the project, the more important version control is. Initial setup of a professional version control utility is often a bit of a headache, but not nearly as painful as sorting through numerous versions of the same class file or FLA trying to find the most recent file. Deploying the wrong version for client approval can be costly in credibility as well as time, and this occurs all too often.

Test on Multiple Browsers and Platforms

This can reveal problems with Player embed scripts, Flash-browser communication (JavaScript or other variable-passing methods), and relative URLs, for example. Don't skip this step. Set up a testing suite (with both Mac and PC computers, and Linux if applicable) with shortcuts to all the browsers on the desktop of each. Have a procedure set up so you don't have to think about it each time you test. Refer back to your project specs and be sure you don't forget to test to the target user specs you had agreed upon with your client up front.

Note: When your SWF and HTML files are not deployed in the same location, you may have trouble with relative links from within Flash. If when you test your movie in the wild your external links aren't working or imported content isn't loading, specifying a base URL in your <OBJECT> and <EMBED> tags may solve the issue:

<param name="base" value="http://www.example.com/relative_path/">

The base attribute specifies the base directory used to resolve all relative path statements in your SWF. We mention this here because it's common to have video files and player SWFs in different locations, so this issue has plagued many a video project.

Note: If you have an old, slow machine kicking around the office, dust it off and set it up as a "lo-fi" testing station. If it works on Bessie, it should work on the PC over in your client's accounting department. (And if you want to be really sure, test it on the PC over in your client's accounting department.) You'll find that slow processors can get bogged down with high frame-rate VP6 video. Even if the computer has a fast Internet connection, decompressing a 30fps VP6 FLV can easily choke an older computer.

Test on Various Flash Player Versions

This step is mostly to reveal operator error; it's easy to accidentally compile for Flash Player 9 when you meant to deploy to Flash Player 8. This also can ferret out problems with Player version–detection scripts and Express Install implementations. Often developers have the most recent Player build installed on their own machines, so they never notice there's an issue with the Player version until the first round of client testing. Don't let your clients find your mistakes before you do!

Note: An easy way to switch between Flash Player versions is by using the free Flash Switcher extension available for Firefox: http://www.sephiroth.it/weblog/archives/2006/10/flash_switcher_for_firefox.php. It's available for both Mac and PC and allows you to switch between any Flash Player versions on the fly, and even remove a version (to test Express Install, for example).

Test Over Various Connection Speeds

This step can unveil hidden problems such as slow-loading dynamic data, attempts to invoke methods or otherwise access objects before they've been initialized, attempts to access timeline frames that haven't loaded yet, or asynchronous operations that are executed in a different order than expected. Then, of course, there are the pervasive video buffering issues, which we'll address in more detail in the next section of this chapter.

As a preliminary test of connection speeds, use the Simulate Download feature in Flash. Test with this tool early, especially when adding data access methods or loading external assets such as FLVs and SWFs. It's great for initial testing as you build, but don't rely on it entirely—always test on various real connections before deployment.

One good practice is to rely on callbacks from methods and event handlers, such as onLoadComplete or onStatus, to sequence the operations of your application. For example, if you are streaming video, use the built-in NetConnection information objects to keep you from trying to access properties that may not have initialized yet. Here's an example in ActionScript 2, so you can see what we're talking about:

```
nc = new NetConnection();
nc.onStatus = function(info){
    if (info.code == "NetConnection.Connect.Success") {
        readSharedObjects();
    } else {
        if (! nc.isConnected){
        showError("NetConnection Failed.");
        }
    }
};
```

First, the new NetConnection is instantiated. The onStatus event handler can then let you know if the connection was successful, and if so, fire additional events that use the NetConnection.

Note: Charles is an invaluable utility for debugging Flash, giving you the ability to preview the contents of LoadVariables, LoadMovie, XML loads, and Flash Remoting calls. And most remarkably, it simulates modem speeds by actually throttling your bandwidth—so you can experience your application just as a visitor with a slow connection would. It's available at http://www.xk72.com/charles/.

Make a Plan to Squash Bugs

While testing, record any bugs and print out error statements. Assign each bug a priority level so the most critical can be addressed first. Also, be sure to note if the bug can be reproduced and, if it can, list the steps to do so. You can make a simple spreadsheet or checklist to keep your testing organized. Then use this testing log, along with the error printouts, to track the completion of bug testing. There are also tools out there such as Bugzilla to help find and record bugs. Regardless of how you keep track of them, having a system to track and squash bugs will be necessary whether you're working by yourself or in a team.

Here are some other tools for debugging and testing:

Flash Debugger A general debugger built into the Flash IDE; lets you set break points in scripts.

NetConnection Debugger Also built into the Flash IDE; shows you information flowing between the Flash client and a server (such as Flash Media Server or Flash Remoting).

Flex Client ActionScript Debugger and Flash Debug Player External to the Flash IDE; lets you diagnose various problems and provides more feedback than the standard player. (Note: You may have to uninstall your standard player before installing the debug player. Available to download for free at Adobe.com.)

Ready for Soft Launch

Put all the files on the client server as early on in the development process as possible. Your testing won't be accurate until you're in this real-world scenario.

We've run into issues with our clients' server configuration on a few occasions, with differing levels of distress. In the worst of these examples, our client insisted there were no special considerations to deploying Flash within their large commercial site. Then, when it came time to load the final application into their content management system, it was "discovered" that they had a distributed delivery system to load-balance their servers. This meant that external assets we were loading into the application wouldn't necessarily be located in the path our parent SWF expected. In fact, they might be on another server altogether. We had to change the design of the application to be one encapsulated file, which took extra time and pushed back the delivery date.

Don't Forget Usability Testing

Even if there's no budget for formal usability testing, you can and should still test. One way to do this is to have some individuals use the application and see how they attempt to navigate. Notice if they can find what they are looking for, how long it takes them to get to that content, and what their frustration level is. Be sure to ask people who reflect the target audience. (You can refer back to Chapter 2 for more about usability testing.)

You've Passed Your Tests. What's Next?

Now you know your video application is solid. It runs on all browsers and platforms, it is optimized for the target Flash Player version, you've documented and eliminated all bugs, and you've launched a preliminary proof on the client server. You've encoded the best optimized video following the advice in Chapter 2. Now, how do you make sure that all viewers, regardless of their Internet connection speed, get the best video possible? The answer lies in good bandwidth management.

Nobody Likes to Wait: Bandwidth Considerations

Someday, in the not-so-distant future, we will have so much available bandwidth that streaming high-definition video over the Internet will be a smooth and seamless experience. We'll be able to download the latest Mel Gibson epic, while simultaneously watching him get arrested live on CNN! But, alas, that glorious day has not yet arrived. Though broadband connections have brought us closer, we still need to deal with preloading and buffering issues in Flash, especially in Flash video applications.

Video Buffering: Not If, but How Much

You need to strike a balance between long buffering times (a long wait for the video to start) and shorter buffering times (the buffer may empty too soon and the video will stutter or pause while rebuffering). You'll need to know two key variables: *user connection speed* and *video bit rate*. Once you determine these values, you can then calculate the buffer time required for the video to play back smoothly. This is accomplished in different ways depending on your method of delivery, as discussed in the next section.

The following ActionScript 2 code sets the buffer time to 15 seconds on the NetStream instance `ns`:

```
ns.setBufferTime(15);
```

And here it is for ActionScript 3:

```
ns.bufferTime = 15;
```

Just arbitrarily picking a number and using it as your standard isn't a good solution, of course. Each video application will likely have a slightly different target audience and video quality baseline, and more importantly, each of your viewers will have a different connection speed. So, with all that in mind, how do you determine the best buffer time? Well, if you have a tech-savvy audience, you could have them choose it from a dropdown box. A better solution in most cases, however, is to detect it automatically (we'll show you how to do that next).

Once you have determined an appropriate buffer time through user choice or detection, you have two choices:

- Deliver an FLV with the appropriate bit rate to each viewer, depending on their bandwidth. This will require you to encode several versions of each video, but will ensure a more consistent loading/playback experience for all viewers.
- Set a buffer time variable value based on connection speed (a higher number for low bandwidth, a lower number for higher bandwidth). This will serve the same video to all viewers, with an appropriate buffer time for their connection.

So, assuming that you'll want to detect connection speed within your application rather than letting the user choose, let's take a closer look at how that's done.

Bandwidth Detection: How Much Can We Push Through That Pipe?

Though there is nothing built into the Flash Player to detect bandwidth, you can write a script that downloads a small file to the viewer (100k or larger, for a good sample), measures how long it takes them to receive it, then calculates their bandwidth from there. This works for progressive or streaming video delivery, but you have additional options available if you're streaming through FMS2. FMS2 has built-in bandwidth detection, and it also allows you to swap out clips with differing bit rates on the fly to accommodate fluctuations in connection speed. We'll talk about those specifics in Chapter 11. The following code examples will deal with a progressive video implementation (but you could always use it for streaming as well, if you don't want to code for FMS).

The example presented here illustrates how to deliver an FLV optimized to the viewer's connection speed (the first option listed earlier). Then, if you want to have variable buffer time instead, we'll talk about how you'd edit this code to do so.

Note: Avoid running bandwidth detection tests at the same time you're trying to load other assets. This will give you a bandwidth calculation that's lower than the actual speed, since the other items are loading at the same time. It's recommended that you present the main elements of your SWF first, run the bandwidth test, and then present the video elements.

Let's take a look at the specifics of bandwidth detection, in both AS2 and AS3, for progressive video delivery.

ActionScript 2 Bandwidth Check Example

Let's start with ActionScript 2:

```
import mx.utils.Delegate;
```

We need to import just one class, Delegate. Then on to the constructor:

```
class FLVPlayerBasicBwCheck {

    private var ns:NetStream;
    private var nc:NetConnection;
    private var myVid:Video;
    private var vidname:String;
    private var timeStart:Number;
    private var fileSize:Number;
    private var kbps:Number;
    private var mcl:MovieClipLoader;
    private var mclListener:Object;
    private var loader_mc:MovieClip;

    public function FLVPlayerBasicBwCheck(targetclip:MovieClip,
    ➡videoobject:Video){
      myVid = videoobject;
      testConnection(targetclip);
    }
```

We pass one variable to the constructor: the instance name of the video object that we've placed on the Stage. Then we go ahead and fire the testConnection method:

```
    private function testConnection(targetclip:MovieClip):Void {
      loader_mc = targetclip.createEmptyMovieClip("bandwidthtester_mc",
    ➡targetclip.getNextHighestDepth());
      mcl = new MovieClipLoader();
      mclListener = new Object();
      mclListener.onLoadStart = Delegate.create(this, onLoadStart);
      mclListener.onLoadComplete = Delegate.create(this, onLoadDone);
      mcl.addListener(mclListener);
      mcl.loadClip("http://www.flashconnections.com/flash-video-
    ➡pro/ch06/bw_testing.jpg?"+getTimer(), loader_mc);
    }
```

OK, let's get this connection test started. First, we create a new movie clip. Then we create a new MovieClipLoader and attach a listener to it. We listen for two events: onLoadStart and onLoadComplete. Finally, we load a remote file into the MovieClipLoader. (This is important; even though you may be testing locally, you'll want to grab a file that's located out on the Internet to get a valid test result.) Now, you may be wondering why we included that extra code at the end of the URL. Why would we need to get the time at that point? This is a way to create a unique URL each time a test is performed. (You may want to run it more than once to get an average speed.) By grabbing the amount of time passed since the Flash Player started running and appending that to your filename as a query string, you trick the browser into thinking it's a new file, and not the one that's cached. You could also use a random number, the current time of day, or if you prefer the more geeky approach, the number of milliseconds since the Unix Epoch (January 1, 1970) using Date.valueOf().

Next, we define the methods being triggered by the events we're listening for:

```
private function onLoadStart():Void {
    timeStart = getTimer();
    // Hide the test JPG
    loader_mc._visible = false;
}
```

Here we're starting the timer as the file begins to load and assigning the value to the variable timeStart. Then we hide the graphic that's loading. (No need to see it; we just want to see how long it takes to download it!) Then on to the second event:

```
private function onLoadDone(target) : Void {
    var timeTotal:Number = getTimer() - timeStart;
    trace("timeTotal "+timeTotal);
    var seconds:Number = timeTotal / 1000;
    var fileSize:Number = target.getBytesTotal();
    var kb:Number = fileSize * 8 / 1000;
    var kbps:Number = kb / seconds;
    trace ("kbps"+kbps);
```

A lot's happening in this method. Note that we've left in some helpful trace statements; these are optional, of course. The first operation is to capture the current timestamp and subtract the time the download started; the result is the amount of time, in milliseconds, that the file took to download (timeTotal). Then, we convert that number from milliseconds to seconds. Next, we determine the file size of the downloaded JPEG file through the getBytesTotal() function, and then convert that number from bytes to kilobits. Finally, we determine the kilobits per second by dividing our total kbps by the number of seconds elapsed. Whew! Now, let's see what we can do with that number:

```
// Determining the appropriate clip to play
  if(kbps <= 80) {
    playVideo("video/myvideo_56.flv");
    trace("play low");
  }
  else if(kbps <= 310) {
    playVideo("video/myvideo_256.flv");
    trace("play medium");
  }
  else {
    playVideo("video/myvideo_512.flv");
    trace("play high");
  }
}
```

We've now determined our viewer's connection speed. Just what do we do with that information? In this example, we feed them a different clip depending on their speed. The conditional statement fires the **playVideo** method, sending the video filename as an argument. (Note that we're taking into account some bandwidth overhead, such as audio and bandwidth fluctuations, when choosing 80 and 310 as parameters in this example.)

```
public function playVideo(vidname:String):Void {
  // Create the NetConnection and connect
  nc = new NetConnection();
  nc.connect(null);

  // Construct NetStream and connect to flow through NetConnection
  ns = new NetStream(nc);

  // Set buffer time
  ns.setBufferTime(5);

  // Trace NetStream events
  ns.onStatus = function(infoObj:Object){
  for (var prop in infoObj) {
    trace("\t"+prop+":\t"+infoObj[prop]);
    }
  };
```

```
// Attach NetStream to video object on the stage
myVid.attachVideo(ns);

// Tell the NetStream which FLV to play
ns.play(vidname);

trace("myVid:"+myVid);
  }
}
```

This method should look familiar; it configures a very basic player for the video. If you needed to present the same video to everyone, you could have passed the variable for buffer time as an argument here instead of passing different filenames.

Finally, we have to open Flash 8 or Flash CS3 and create a new ActionScript 2 Flash file. We create a new Video object by clicking on the menu at the top right of the Library panel and choosing New Video (ActionScript-controlled). Then we drag this new object from the Library to the Stage and give it an instance name of myVid. We click on the first frame of the timeline and enter the following code:

```
import FLVPlayerBasicBwCheck;
// Instantiate an instance of the FLVPlayerBasic class,
// passing in your parameters
var FLVPlayer:FLVPlayerBasicBwCheck = new FLVPlayerBasicBwCheck(this,
myVid);
```

We save the file in the same folder as the FLVPlayerBasicBwCheck.as file. (In our example setup, this would be inside Eclipse's working folder.) Then, we publish the file. At this point, we'll see our bandwidth measurement, in kbps, in the Output window. Depending on the location of the file you choose to use as a test, you may want to upload this SWF to a web server to test remotely, adding a text field that displays the value of kbps.

ActionScript 3 Bandwidth Check Example

First, we import the classes we'll be using:

```
package {
    import flash.display.Sprite;
    import flash.net.NetConnection;
    import flash.net.NetStream;
    import flash.media.Video;
    import flash.display.MovieClip;
    import flash.net.URLLoader;
```

```
import flash.net.URLRequest;
import flash.utils.getTimer;
import flash.events.Event;
```

The imported classes to note here are URLLoader, URLRequest, getTimer, and Event. We'll be using them in a moment to load a JPEG and calculate the time it took to receive it.

```
public class FLVPlayerBasicBwCheck extends Sprite {
    private var testLoader:URLLoader;
    private var timeStart:Number;
```

Next, we initialize the testLoader and timeStart variables; we'll use them in our testing methods later:

```
public function FLVPlayerBasicBwCheck() {
    testConnection();
}
private function onMetaData(data:Object):void {
}
private function testConnection():void {
    testLoader = new URLLoader();
    var request:URLRequest = new
URLRequest("http://www.flashconnections.com/flash-video-
    ➡ pro/ch06/bw_testing.jpg?"+getTimer());
    trace(request.url);
    testLoader.load(request);
    testLoader.addEventListener(Event.OPEN, onLoadStart);
    testLoader.addEventListener(Event.COMPLETE, onLoadComplete);
}
```

OK, here's where we get down to business. We've added a testConnection() method, which is called right away. Inside this method, we create a new URLLoader instance, called testLoader. Then we instantiate a new URLRequest, and include the URL to a JPEG on a remote server as an argument. (This is important; even though you may be testing locally, you'll want to grab a file that's located out on the Internet to get a valid test result.) We've included an argument at the end of the string to create a unique URL each time a test is performed. (You may want to run it more than once to get an average speed.) By grabbing the amount of time passed since the Flash Player started running and appending that to our filename as a query string, we trick the browser into thinking it's a new file and not one that's cached. (As mentioned before, you could also use a random number, or the current time of day if you prefer.)

We then add event listeners to the testLoader object, prompting methods to run when the URLRequest is started (OPEN) and when it's finished (COMPLETE). Next, we create those methods:

```
private function onLoadStart(event:Event):void {
    // Start the timer
    timeStart = getTimer();
}
```

The onLoadStart method fires when the bw_testing.jpg file begins downloading. Here we start the timer and assign the timestamp to the variable timeStart, which we declared earlier:

```
private function onLoadComplete(event:Event):void {
    var timeTotal:Number = getTimer() - timeStart;
    // Convert milliseconds to seconds
    var seconds:Number = timeTotal / 1000;
    // Get size of file downloaded
    var fileSize:uint = testLoader.bytesTotal;
    // Convert file size (bytes) to kilobits
    var kb:Number = fileSize * 8 / 1000;
    // Determine kilobits per second
    var kbps:Number = kb / seconds;
    trace("kbps "+kbps);
```

The onLoadComplete method is where we do the real work. (We've left the traces in that we found helpful during development.) The first order of business is to grab the current timestamp and subtract the time the download started; the result is the amount of time, in milliseconds, that the file took to download (timeTotal). Then, we convert that number from milliseconds to seconds. Next, we determine the file size of bw_testing.jpg by accessing the bytesTotal property of testLoader and convert that number from bytes to kilobits. Finally, we determine the kilobits per second by dividing our total kbps by the number of seconds elapsed. Now, let's play a video:

```
// Determining the appropriate clip to play
if(kbps <= 80) {
    playVideo("video/myvideo_56.flv");
    trace("play low");
}
else if(kbps <= 310) {
    playVideo("video/myvideo_256.flv");
    trace("play medium");
}
```

```
        else {
            playVideo("video/myvideo_512.flv");
            trace("play high");
        }
    }
}
```

Now that we know the viewer's connection speed, we can make some decisions. In our example, we feed the viewer a different clip depending on their speed. (Note that we've left some bandwidth breathing room here for audio and connection speed fluctuations). The conditional statement fires the playVideo method, sending the video filename as an argument. (Note that you could choose to set the NetStream bufferTime property to different durations here instead, if your client wanted to serve a video of the same quality to everyone.)

Note: When encoding your video, append your filename with the bit rate of the file. Using this as a standard naming convention helps you keep track of your FLVs, and lets all team members know the bit rate of a particular file at a glance.

```
private function playVideo(vidName:String):void {
    // Construct NetConnection
    var nc:NetConnection = new NetConnection();
    nc.connect(null);

    // Flash is looking for an onMetaData method,
    //route all calls to an object
    var metaObject:Object = new Object();
    metaObject.onMetaData = onMetaData;

    // Construct NetStream and connect to flow through NetConnection
    var ns:NetStream = new NetStream(nc);
    ns.bufferTime = 15;
    ns.play(vidName);
    // Route all onMetaData calls on NetStream to the metaObject
    ns.client = metaObject;

    // Construct video object with dimensions
    var video:Video = new Video(160, 120);
```

```
            // Attach video to the NetStream, and add to the display list
            video.attachNetStream(ns);
            addChild(video);
        }
    }
}
```

You should be familiar with this method by now; it sets up a very basic player for the video, playing the file with the appropriate bit rate.

Note: As we've discussed, bandwidth fluctuates often. You may want to consider checking the viewer's bandwidth more than once and then calculating an average. We suggest doing this only if the viewer has a high initial bandwidth reading, however. If they have a connection speed of over 256 kbps, for example, you could run the test three or four times to get a more accurate number without slowing down the load time more than a few seconds. You can then be more confident that you're feeding the viewer the correct video for their connection.

Keep in mind that even this detection solution isn't perfect. Bandwidth tends to fluctuate depending on many factors, such as increases in server load, simultaneous downloads/uploads on the client's machine, or your neighbor deciding to download the entire first season of *Battlestar Galactica* while you're trying to test your application. (I hate when that happens.) Streaming via FMS2 can give you more tools to compensate for these fluctuations, but of course this can be more costly to deploy.

Now that you've got bandwidth detection conquered, let's review the steps involved in getting your Flash video project off the ground.

3, 2, 1... Ready to Launch!

One of the very last tasks left to do (see the next section for others that you may have glossed over) is to actually launch the site. It will likely be hosted either on your client's in-house server or with a hosting company they have an account with. You may be sending files via FTP and configuring the site for them, or they may have their IT department handle the deployment. Or maybe the client has contracted you to handle hosting. No matter what the deployment plan, you'll want to document the installation of the site carefully, so that the file structure is very clear to both you and anyone else who may be involved down the road. Let's look at a typical deployment for both progressive and streaming video applications.

Progressive Deployment

Progressive deployment is generally very straightforward; you just upload your FLVs, SWFs, and other associated assets to a standard web server. Your directory structure might look something like Figure 6.1.

Figure 6.1 Typical server directory structure for progressive video

The FLVs are stored and referenced just like any other content. However, when you need to accommodate large amounts of traffic, load balancing and server bandwidth considerations will come into play. If this is the case, you'll likely want to use a content delivery network (CDN), as we discussed back in Chapter 3. Although you'll find that each CDN will have a unique account interface, upload utilities, and server setup, we'll walk you through a typical site configuration here. We're using NaviSite in this example.

1. Log in to the system, then choose Add New Stream (Figure 6.2).

2. Select a file and upload it to NaviSite (Figure 6.3).

3. You'll be taken to a screen that previews your video and prompts you to "HotRoute" a video. (HotRouting is NaviSite's file hosting technology, which serves the video file from the server that is physically closest to the viewer.) Select the environment to deploy to. Choose NaviSite Shared Flash Server and click HotRoute Now (Figure 6.4).

The file location information for your account will be provided to you by Navi-Site when you sign up. You'll use that URL in your video filename paths, and NaviSite will determine how to best deliver the file to your viewer behind the scenes.

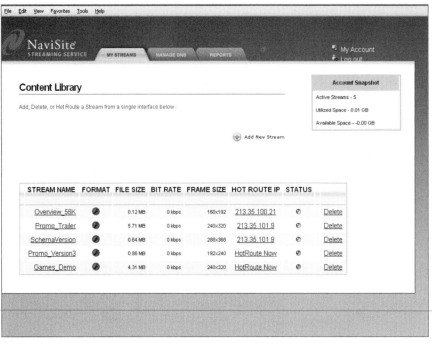

Figure 6.2 Add a new video file to the NaviSite Content Delivery Network

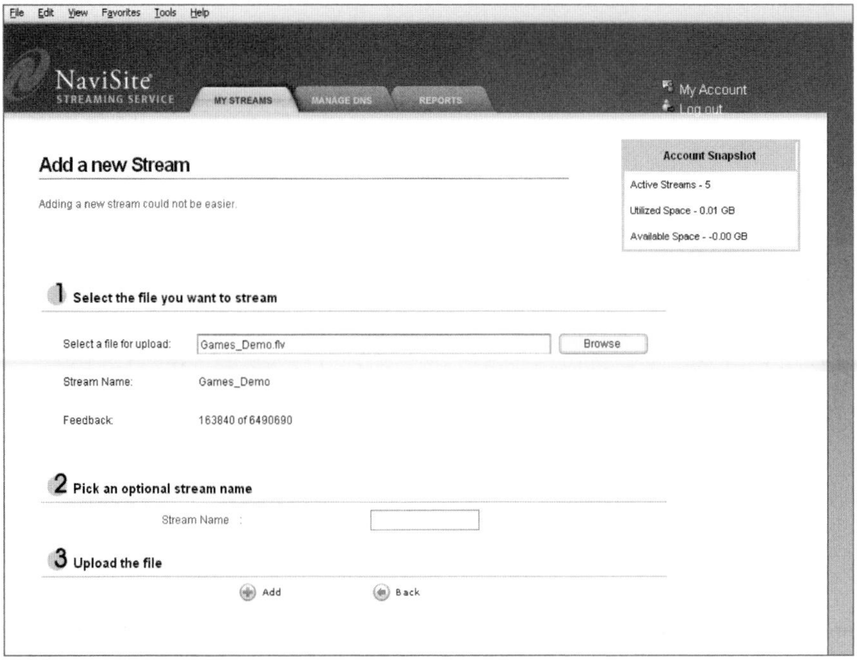

Figure 6.3 Upload your video file to the NaviSite servers.

Figure 6.4 Preview the video and choose a server to deploy to.

Streaming Deployment

Deploying a streaming video application will likely involve a Flash Media Streaming Service (FMSS) or other CDN, as outlined in Chapter 3. Each CDN will have its own interface for adding video to its system for streaming. We use Influxis, so we'll show it as an example. (If you developed this streaming app on a local development server, you should recognize the file structure here. It's the same, but within a web interface.)

> **Note:** If you do plan to deploy the site on your own Flash Media Server, you'll want to be sure you have vigilant tech support, because if the server goes down and the videos don't play, it's your neck on the line. You'll have to be available 24/7 for tech support. We have our own FMS license running on a dedicated server, but use it only for experimentation and prelaunch testing.

1. Go to File Manager.
2. Click the Add New Application button and give your new application a name. We're calling ours flashvideopro.
3. If you don't have any server-side code (you likely wouldn't for a straightforward streaming video player), choose Include the Standard main.asc File. Click Continue (Figure 6.5).

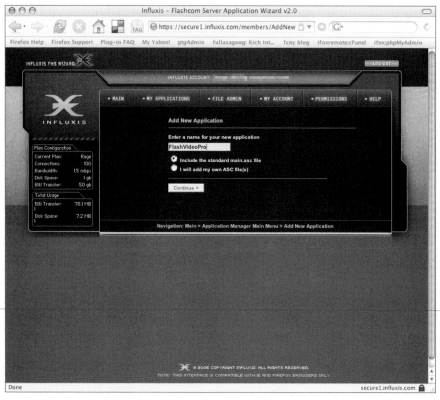

Figure 6.5 Influxis New Application window

4. You'll get a confirmation screen (Figure 6.6) giving you the connection string that you'll need to enter as your NetConnection URI. Click Go to File Manager.

5. Here's where you add your FLVs (Figure 6.7). Click on the new application (FlashVideoPro in this example), choose New Directory, and call it **streams** (all lowercase, as shown).

6. Select the newly created streams folder and make another new directory inside called _definst_; this will be your default streams folder for your application.

7. Choose this folder and click Upload File. Upload all of your FLVs into this folder so they can be accessed for playback using the NetConnection URI for the application (Figure 6.8).

Note that this is where you'll put the FLVs you wish to stream; your SWFs and other assets will reside on a standard web server, and will just use the NetStream URI provided by your CDN (Influxis, in this case) to connect and present the video.

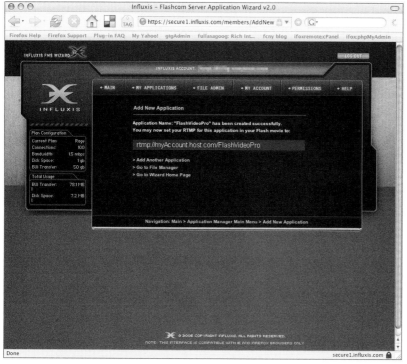

Figure 6.6 Influxis NetConnection URI

Figure 6.7 Creating a streams directory for your streaming application

Figure 6.8 Adding FLV files to your streaming application via the Influxis web interface

Figure 6.9 shows the final file structure. In this example, you'd use the following strings (for both ActionScript 2 and 3) in the NetConnection and NetStream.play code to link to this uploaded video:

```
nc.connect("rtmp://myAccount.host.com/flashvideopro");
ns.play("acct_mike_01");
```

 Note: When specifying the video filename, leave off the .flv extension!

But Wait, There's More: Project Wrap-up

Now that you've completed the functional testing, administered the soft launch, optimized your application for various connection speeds, and uploaded your files to a web server, you're finally ready to move on to the last steps.

Figure 6.9 Final directory structure with uploaded video (note the added feature of video preview!)

Note: It may seem strange that we are addressing final steps before you even get to the middle of this book. We're including this here because it's important that you keep these things in mind throughout the development process. This will save you much grief at the end of the project—so read on!

Revisiting the Spec Sheet

We hope you've been referring to the spec sheet all along, but in the event that it got buried in a pile of paperwork, dig it out. This is the time to reassess your project. This time, instead of defining the project, you refer to the spec sheet (which you created in Chapter 2) to verify that you've accomplished the project goals successfully. At this point, your application is likely working fine, but there may be a detail that you missed.

Final Walkthrough

Send the working URL for review to everyone who contributed. (You may want to get clearance to do so by your main client contact first.) Be sure that all content creators and developers get an opportunity to review the application for errors. This includes designers, copywriters, content creators, and clients. Only they will recognize if their work is appearing correctly or the way they intended it to. With multiple people working on projects there are many opportunities for errors to occur.

Launching

Publishing, or "going live," means that all of your testing and fixes have been completed. Once you've launched, you may feel a great sense of relief. Your work here is finally done. And by this time, you're likely fired up to get started on the next project you have lined up—or maybe you are excited that you will be able to leave your computer for an afternoon. Not so fast. You still have one stage left: the project wrap-up.

Today, everyone is happy. Come tomorrow, your phone will be ringing. What could they possibly want? Well...answers to endless questions and loose ends. Providing documentation will bridge the gap between your work and the ongoing questions from the maintenance team. Once you've reached the time allotted for the back and forth (calculated for in your original proposal—see Chapter 1), you'll need to renegotiate billable hours beyond that if further time is needed. Otherwise, you will become ongoing pro bono tech support.

Deliverables: Documentation and Asset Files

Oh yeah, that. Provide ample documentation that pertains to your application, such as video specs, content update instructions, and class specifications if you're turning over source files. (You may want to try JavaDocs, a great utility that automatically produces code documentation for you.) Send an e-mail to your client in advance confirming the materials you will be including. Have them confirm these deliverables, and then send them off. Final project assets often consist of the following:

- Art, including layered files and fonts
- Usage rights waivers
- FLA files
- Class files
- Source video
- Documentation
- Any other files needed for deployment

Schedule a Meeting

Be sure to schedule a meeting with your client at the end of the project. This gives everyone involved a chance to address any problems or steps moving forward. Even with the smallest projects you'll want to administer the handoff in this way. Chances are, most of your interaction has been completed by e-mail and phone. You may not have had any face time up to this point except for the initial meeting. So if it's possible to have an in-person meeting, this is the time make that happen. Don't underestimate the power of face time.

Archiving

File all hard copies along with your digital storage in a place where you can retrieve them easily if need be. Be sure to include any important e-mails, the original proposal, change orders, project plans and site maps, your creative brief, as well as any time and project logs.

Client Separation Anxiety

Inevitably, at the end of the project your client will keep having "just one last thing" for you to complete before you hand it off completely, or rather, before you submit the final invoice. This home stretch is usually met with apprehension from your client. You can refer to your original contract that states the deliverables to use as a benchmark. Treat additional last-minute requests with a change order and follow your contract as closely as possible, within reason.

Project Wrap-up Checklist:

- Did you perform at least two complete run-throughs of formal or informal functional testing to test and fix bugs?

- Did you test on various browsers?

- Did you test various connection speeds, both simulated and actual?

- Did you test on various versions of the Flash Player, confirming that the version detection is effective?

- Have you administered a soft launch and ensured that there are no server-specific bugs?

- Have you conducted usability testing?

Continues

Project Wrap-up Checklist: *(Continued)*

- Does the final project satisfy the spec sheet, keeping in mind the initial creative brief and proposal?

- Did you receive the final review and sign off from all parties who contributed to the project?

- Did you compile the documentation and asset files together in an organized method and provide everything to the client?

- Did you archive the complete project, both hard copies and files?

- Did you create a maintenance plan for moving forward to keep the site updated?

- Did you schedule and have a meeting with your client to wrap up the details and review the project highlights?

Summary

In this chapter we gave you some testing strategies, optimization procedures, and methods for deployment as well as some client tips. You now know:

- The importance of testing and some formal and informal approaches

- Why you should torture test on multiple browsers, platforms, player versions, and connection speeds

- Troubleshooting procedures to squash bugs

- How to detect viewers' bandwidth and what to do with that information

- How to send both progressive and streaming projects into the wild

- What you need to do to wrap it up—the final handoff client checklist

Now that you get the big picture of the project from start to finish, you can get back to the business of coding. In Chapter 7 we'll expand the basic player we created in Chapter 5 to allow for dynamic updates to the video content.

Dynamic Playlists

More than likely, you're not creating a video application that just plays one specific video. You're going to want your player to be flexible, with the ability to play any FLV you throw at it. And it seems every video application these days requires some sort of playlist. Clients want easily reusable applications (and you should too)! With a well-constructed dynamic video application, clients can maintain their own video content— and you can be free to move on to your next groundbreaking project.

This chapter will outline what constitutes a well-constructed dynamic video application, and will walk you through creating editable playlists from simple to complex.

7

Chapter Contents

When Clients Attack: Handling Content Updates
Playlists in the Wild: Your Options
Mixing It Up: Sequential and Shuffle Playback
Integrating an XML Playlist into the MVC Player

Giving clients the power to edit their own content really is essential. You do need to be careful when you give your clients free reign to edit their content, however, so we'll note some pitfalls that can occur with client updates and how you can avoid them. (We've had our share, so learn from our ordeals.) Let's start our journey into the wild world of dynamic playlists!

When Clients Attack: Handling Content Updates

Unless you're just implementing a simple talking head or alpha channel video with a single play and a single purpose, you're going to want to be able to easily update your video content and provide some way to add new videos to the application. Likely, you're not going to be the one adding that content; someone on the client's side will be. It may be the person you're dealing with on the project, or it may be an editorial assistant months later who has to figure out how it's done.

So, when considering the various dynamic updating options we discuss in this chapter, keep in mind the following questions:

What level of technical knowledge will my client need to have? Can they edit a simple XML document without freaking out, or do they need a web interface (which in turn writes the XML for them, or adds the items to a database)?

If the client introduces an error in the data, will the player still function? Is there an automatic backup of the previous data that they can easily revert to?

Will all future content have the same dimensions, or does the application need to autodetect the size of the video and resize the player? It's never safe to assume that videos will always be a certain size. You should plan for some variation (say, in aspect ratio) unless a certain consistent dimension is given in the project spec.

Will more information be needed, now or in the future, such as captions or other metadata? Will this be included in the XML or database, or will it be injected into the FLV? (You'll learn more about metadata in Chapter 8.)

Your answers to these questions will determine the amount of time and energy you need to devote to your playlist and what form it should take. Your choices will become clearer when you get into the specifics of each approach in this chapter.

Along with any application, you'll want to include detailed instructions that any future content manager can follow to easily perform updates. We advise that you spend the time to do this up front to avoid inevitable support requests months later. In most of our applications, having the client edit a simple XML document works out well. It's straightforward, though not entirely foolproof. We provide detailed instructions and a sample file, and always keep a backup file in the application folder that they can revert to if need be. We also advise clients to always work on a copy, then upload and test—only deleting the original after everything checks out.

If your client is especially non-tech-savvy, you may want to create an interface for them to update the XML through a web form that can check the data as it's being entered and automatically create the XML to spec. This can be done in any language you choose; PHP, Java, ColdFusion, ASP, and Ruby are a few of the favorites. Though creating this interface is beyond the scope of this book, spending the time to create it would help streamline your application for clients who break into hives at the site of XML code.

Playlists in the Wild: Your Options

The steps to implementing any playlist are:

1. Load data into Flash.

2. Display data and make each item selectable.

3. Play FLV when selected.

You can load FLV data in a number of ways. For example:

- Read from a hard-coded array.

- Read in and parse an XML or RSS file.

- Retrieve data from a database.

- Read filenames from a directory.

- Parse a text document.

Each of these options offers a different degree of flexibility. For example, the simplest approach would be to feed the player a hard-coded array of FLV filenames, which then get added to the playlist. This is the implementation we have in our basic MVC video player in Chapter 5. This works fine if you very rarely, if ever, need to swap out the FLVs.

If you need more automation and not much file information, reading filenames from a directory or a text file may be a good solution. Using server-side language such as PHP, ColdFusion, Ruby, or ASP, you can read the contents of a directory, load the filename data into Flash, and then add those files to your playlist. In this approach, though, you wouldn't have any other information associated with the video (unless you read in some metadata that's embedded inside the FLV).

Reading in the data from XML or a database offers you the most flexibility. You can include all sorts of associated data with each FLV, such as title, synopsis, external links, thumbnail images—whatever you like.

Next, you need to decide how you're going to display your playlist data in Flash. There are lots of options here as well (see Figures 7.1 and 7.2 for examples):

List Component This is a straightforward and common solution, providing you with a full-featured list box that automatically adds a scroll bar as more content is added. You can even extend the List component to include thumbnails if you like.

ComboBox Component Adding the filenames or titles to a ComboBox component (drop-down menu) is another common solution.

Accordion Component (ActionScript 2) You'd likely only use this approach for very specialized applications, but it can be a nice effect if you have distinct video "sections" or "channels" that you want to expand when selected.

Radio Button Group You can dynamically create radio buttons and assign an FLV to each. This works well when you don't have a lot of data to accompany the video names or descriptions.

Menu Component (ActionScript 2) Another drop-down solution; this can be a good way to display video titles or filenames in limited space.

Clickable Thumbnails A more custom solution; you could grab thumbnails either through ActionScript (see Chapter 10) or as specified in the XML or database and place them in a row on the Stage. This would be a good solution for playlists with a set number of videos. If you have many videos or need to accommodate an unknown number of videos, you'd probably want to use the List component or create your own custom scrolling playlist movieclip.

Simple Buttons Assigning links to buttons on the Stage through ActionScript is also an option, though, as with the clickable thumbnails, you'd want to control the number of videos you have in your list so you don't run out of space on the Stage for all of your buttons.

Other Custom Display Maybe none of these solutions is right for your application. Perhaps you want a 3-D playlist that scrolls backward and forward in space, or one where the video thumbnails increase in size when selected. There are a myriad of options that can be applied to the basic playlist principles we'll be outlining in this chapter. Our advice: start with a basic display, and build from there.

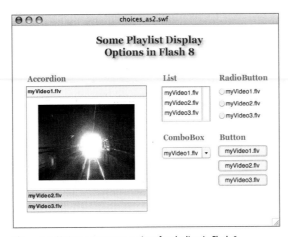

Figure 7.1 Various component options for playlists in Flash 8

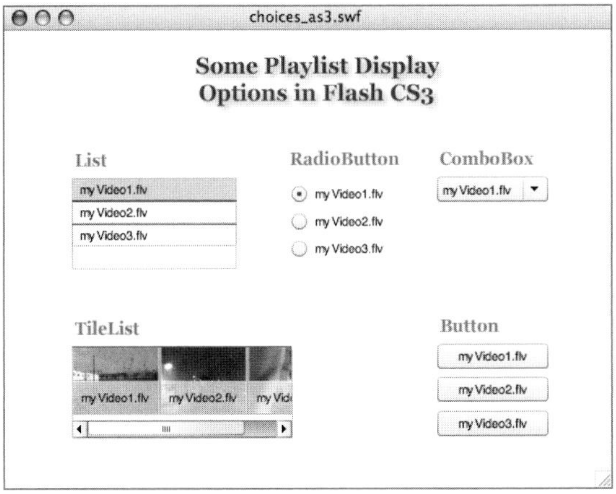

Figure 7.2 Various component options for playlists in Flash CS3

Interactive Video: From Couch Potato to Mouse Potato

Generally, watching a movie is a passive experience. Sure, DVDs offer you the chance to navigate scenes and access additional meta content such as subtitles or commentary, but for the most part we just sit and watch.

The Internet offers a more active, nonlinear experience. Keeping our interest for long periods of time is more difficult. For this reason, video on the Web is either edited down to snippets or produced as short-form features. This is true not only of video, but even text articles. Due to the active nature of the Internet—clicking around, multitasking with e-mail, and multiple browser windows open at any given time—we are conditioned to digest short bits of information. This creates a challenge for us as web developers. Video is traditionally experienced in a passive manner and can be too long—so how do we present it in a meaningful way? How do we keep the viewers' attention and give them the information, or entertainment, they're dropping by to see?

Currently, the big pitfalls in online video include:

- Difficulty searching from search engines
- Lack of searchability within a video for desired content
- Absence of feedback, sharing user reactions, or discussion of content
- Inability to have clickable content or internal links

Flash video applications, of course, can handle some of these issues when designed well, but it takes some forethought and creativity to really make video applications engaging.

Continues

Interactive Video: From Couch Potato to Mouse Potato *(Continued)*

TiVo is probably the first model developed where you can "interact" with your video. However, this is still based on the TV-set/remote control model, not monitor/mouse. So in order to make the experience of video more Internet-friendly (and more useful or digestible), we need to find ways to get the user more involved and ultimately give them control.

So what's out there now? One notable example, Veotag (shown in graphic below), allows you to bookmark or add chapters to your video content so you can easily jump around to individual segments. Using cuepoints as bookmarks, their application allows you to upload your video and set the cuepoints in their web interface. "Veotagging" also makes it possible for search engines to search your video content, cataloging the tags and generating links to that specific content. This service is well suited to educational content, the breaking up of long-form content, and general video sharing.

Another innovator, Click.TV (shown in the graphic below), allows users and content producers to add comments to specific points inside a video. A visual representation of comments appears over the video itself, and a box below lists the comments. You can jump to those points in the video as well as search the comments.

Interactive Video: From Couch Potato to Mouse Potato *(Continued)*

Then there are the sites that offer video "mashups." One great example of this is Jumpcut (shown in the graphic on the next page), an online video editing program that allows you to edit your clips (or other users' clips) into a movie. You can compile video, audio, and photos together to make your final "remixed" movie and then share it. With the power Flash technology brings to online video, we're seeing more and more of these "mashup" applications. The website Eyespot.com offers an application similar to Jumpcut, with the ability to download the mix as a video file.

Continues

Interactive Video: From Couch Potato to Mouse Potato *(Continued)*

In the Web 2.0 world, many innovative approaches are being developed to make video interactive and useful. Currently, most of the best cutting-edge interactive video applications are Flash based. What we've seen so far is only the beginning. Over the next couple of years many startups and software companies will improve and experiment in the manipulation and use of video. Behavior marketing specialists will spend countless hours analyzing the data around this topic to advise sales and marketing teams where to spend their dollars. Social networking sites, education, workshops, conferencing, and user-generated content sites will all continue to utilize and grow their video capabilities. What will some of these delivery methods look like? How will they be achieved? Armed with the tools that Flash video provides, *you* could create the next innovation in video interaction!

Here are some relevant links for more insight into the unique challenges of web video:

"Making videos work the way the web works," by Mike Lanza, Founder and CEO, Click.TV (http://www.adobe.com/devnet/flashmediaserver/articles/clicktv_web_video.html)

Business of Video blog (http://blog.streamingmedia.com)

PlaylistListBox.fla: Simple Array into a ListBox

We'll follow our own advice here and start out with a very simple example. These first examples will be coded in the Flash IDE instead of being class based, so you get a clear picture of how each method works. In our last example, we'll show you a class-based implementation so you can take the concepts further and implement them into your larger application. (We'll plug our example into the MVC player from Chapter 5.) Let's begin by walking through the code that loads a hard-coded playlist array into a List component. See Figure 7.3 for a screenshot of the final application.

1. Drag an FLVPlayback component near the top of the Stage in Flash and give it an instance name of **myFLVPlybk**. (See Figure 7.3 for placement.) Resize it to 320 pixels wide by 240 pixels high.

2. Grab a List component and drop it on the Stage. Give it an instance name of **myList**. Resize it to 350 pixels wide by 100 pixels high and place it under your FLVPlayback component.

3. Enter the following code on the first frame of the FLA, using the appropriate syntax for your version of ActionScript:

ActionScript 2 code:

```
var myArray:Array = ["videos/fast_lg.flv",
                     "videos/train_med_lg.flv",
                     "videos/sl_lg.flv"];


// Populate the list box
for(var i:Number=0; i<myArray.length; i++) {
    myList.addItem({label:myArray[i]});[
}


// Add a listener to detect when
// new video is selected and play it
var listListener:Object = new Object();
listListener.change = function(evt:Object) {
    myFLVPlybk.play(evt.target.value);
}
myList.addEventListener("change", listListener);


// Automatically play the first video
myFLVPlybk.play(myArray[0]);
// And select the first video
myList.selectedIndex = 0;
```

Or, in ActionScript 3:

```
var myArray:Array = ["videos/fast_lg.flv",
                     "videos/train_med_lg.flv",
                     "videos/sl_lg.flv"];


// Populate the list box
for(var i:Number=0; i<myArray.length; i++) {
    myList.addItem({label:myArray[i]});
}


// Add a listener to detect when
// new video is selected and play it
function listListener(event:Event) {
    myFLVPlybk.play(event.target.selectedItem.label);
}
myList.addEventListener(Event.CHANGE, listListener);


// Automatically play the first video
myFLVPlybk.play(myArray[0]);
// And select the first video
myList.selectedIndex = 0;
```

4. Make sure you change the video paths in the array to your own, or use the samples we provide with the exercise files. Now save your file as **PlaylistListBox.fla**, compile your SWF, and voilá! You have a selectable playlist of videos populated with your array of FLV filenames (see Figure 7.3).

Next, let's keep the List component, but this time load in some XML as the source.

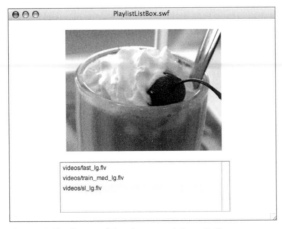

Figure 7.3 Simple array of three items populating a ListBox

PlaylistListBox_XML.fla: XML Data into a ListBox

In this example we also load the FLV filenames into a list box, but instead of the hard-coded array, we parse in the playlist data from an XML file. It's much simpler than it sounds; let's give it a go.

1. Save a copy of the FLA used in the previous example and name it **PlaylistListBox_XML.fla**; then replace the ActionScript code with the following, depending on your version (see Figure 7.4):

   ActionScript 2:

```
// Create a new XML object
var playlistXML:XML = new XML();
// Ignore whitespace in XML doc
playlistXML.ignoreWhite = true;

// After XML is loaded, populate the listbox
playlistXML.onLoad = function() {
    var nodes = this.firstChild.childNodes;
    for(i=0; i<nodes.length; i++) {
        myList.addItem(nodes[i].attributes.desc,
nodes[i].attributes.flvurl);
        trace(nodes[i].attributes.desc+" :
"+nodes[i].attributes.flvurl);
    }
    // Automatically play the first video and select it

    myList.selectedIndex = 0;
      myFLVPlybk.play(myList.value);
}

// Load the XML document
playlistXML.load("playlistXML.xml");
// Add a listener to detect when
// new video is selected and play it
var listListener:Object = new Object();
listListener.change = function(evt:Object) {
    myFLVPlybk.play(evt.target.value);
}
myList.addEventListener("change", listListener);
```

Or, ActionScript 3:

```actionscript
var xmlLoader:URLLoader = new URLLoader();
xmlLoader.addEventListener(Event.COMPLETE, xmlLoaded);
xmlLoader.load(new URLRequest("playlistXML.xml"));

function xmlLoaded(event:Event):void {
    var playlistXML:XML = new XML(event.target.data);
    var item:XML;
    for each(item in playlistXML.videoname) {
        trace("item: "+item.attribute("flvurl").toXMLString());
        myList.addItem({label:item.attribute("desc").toXMLString(),
        ➥ data:item.attribute("flvurl").toXMLString()});
    }
    // Select the first video
    myList.selectedIndex = 0;
    // And automatically play it
    myFLVPlybk.play(myList.selectedItem.data);
}


// Add a listener to detect when
// new video is selected and play it
function listListener(event:Event) {

    myFLVPlybk.play(event.target.selectedItem.data);
}
myList.addEventListener(Event.CHANGE, listListener);
```

2. Create your XML file in Dreamweaver, Flash, or any text editor. Use the format shown here, and save it as **playlistXML.xml** in the same directory as your FLA.

```xml
<?xml version="1.0" encoding="iso-8859-1"?>
<playlist>
<videoname
    flvurl="videos/fast_lg.flv"
    desc="Surfer Shots" />
<videoname
    flvurl="videos/train_med_lg.flv"
    desc="Into the Light" />
<videoname
    flvurl="videos/sl_lg.flv"
```

```
                desc="Ruby's Diner" />
        <videoname
            flvurl="videos/med_lg.flv"
            desc="Circle Line" />
        <videoname
            flvurl="videos/wiper_fast_lg.flv"
            desc="Subway Car Wash" />
        </playlist>
```

Make sure you either change the flvurl paths to your own videos or download our samples from the book's website.

3. Now, switch back to Flash and publish your SWF. Your XML data will be read in and your list box will be populated with the description of each FLV, each linking to its appropriate FLV file (see Figure 7.4).

You could, of course, add even more data into the XML that would be passed in to Flash, such as author, extended description, video size, or any other custom data you may need.

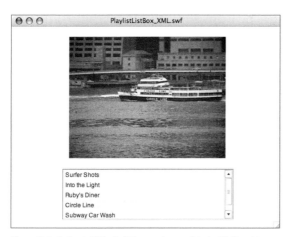

Figure 7.4 A simple XML playlist example, populated with five videos

Note: Though database integration is outside of our scope here, you could adapt the XML code relatively easily to integrate with a database. You'd have to have an intermediary script, such as PHP, ASP, Ruby, or ColdFusion, to make the calls to the database, then read the data into Flash using loadVariables (AS2) or URLVariables (AS3).

Automagically Playing an FLV from a Directory

Here's a tricky solution that can be very handy for clients who don't ever want to touch code. You can read an FLV filename from the file system, pass the name into Flash, and play it automatically in an FLVPlayback component—no XML parsing, no hard-coded filenames. In this example, we use PHP to read the directory contents, and then pass the filename into Flash using the loadVariables method.

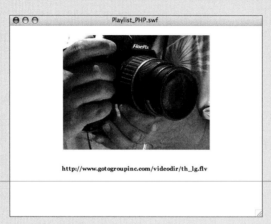

Reading a video filename into Flash using PHP, then displaying the file path and playing the FLV

The following is a simple PHP script that will read the contents of any directory whose name is passed to it and return the filename to Flash as a string. If you'd like to try this example, you'll need access to a web server (either running on your local computer or a web host). OK, let's get started.

1. Enter the following code into a new document in Dreamweaver, or a text editor, and save it as **read_dir_contents.php**. (See the graphic at the end of this sidebar to see how to set up the directory structure for this example.)

```php
<?php
// grab directory name (Note: Make sure to look for
// variables in the right place. Not all servers have global
// variables turned on by default. For more info:
// http://www.php.net/manual/en/security.globals.php
$dir = $_REQUEST['dir'];
// open specified directory and grab the filename
if (is_dir($dir)) {
    if ($dh = opendir($dir)) {
        while (($filename = readdir($dh)) !== false) {
            if (($filename != ".") && ($filename != "..")) {
```

```
                        // print the filename so Flash
                        // can retrieve it
                        print "videoName=" . $dir . "/" . $filename;
                }
        }
        // close the directory
        closedir($dh);
    }
}
?>
```

2. In Flash, open a new document and call it **Playlist_PHP.fla**. (This example is in ActionScript 2.)
    Create a new layer, call it **Actions**, and enter the following code on the first frame:

```
// Pass in the target directory name in the url
loadVariables("read_dir_contents.php?dir=videodir",
➡ this, "GET");

function checkDataLoaded() {
    if (videoName == undefined) {
        trace("still loading");
    } else {
        trace("got it");
        clearInterval(data_interval);
        videoName = videoName;
        trace(videoName);
        myFLVPlybk.play(videoName);
    }
}
var data_interval:Number = setInterval(checkDataLoaded, 100);
```

3. Great. You've got the code handled. Now drag an FLVPlayback component onto the Stage and
    give it an instance name of **myFLVPlybk**.

4. Create a dynamic text field beneath the FLVPlayback component and assign it a variable
    name of **videoName** in the Properties panel. This will just show you the value that was
    passed in to Flash for the FLV filename. Save the file.

Continues

Automagically Playing an FLV from a Directory *(Continued)*

5. Set up the directory structure so the script can find your video. To do this, create a folder called **videodir** in the same directory where your SWF will reside. Place an FLV file inside that you'd like to play. (See graphic below for reference.)

6. Finally, test your SWF. It will take a couple of seconds to read the directory contents, then the text box will be populated with the filename and the video will play. If you replace the FLV file in the videodir directory, the new FLV will be discovered and played. Easy as pie!

This example demonstrates how to pass in a single simple value to Flash. To read in more than one filename as an array, you'd need to serialize (process) this more complex data using a utility such as Flash Remoting, which is a bit beyond our scope here. Alternatively, if you just need to read in a specific number of videos, you could assign their names to individual variables (e.g., filenameOne, filenameTwo, filenameThree, etc.) and pass them into a playlist after you get them into Flash.

The directory structure for the PHP
filename-to-Flash example

Mixing It Up: Sequential and Shuffle Playback

Sometimes you'll want a playlist that just plays the whole list of videos automatically. The quick and easy way to implement this is to use the FLVPlayback component. Built into the component is a complete event, which you can listen for and then trigger the next video to play. You can set up your script to play the videos in succession, or even play a random video, much like the shuffle feature in iTunes.

Basically, here's what's happening:

1. You set the initial contentPath property to the first video you want to play.

2. When that video finishes playing, a complete event is fired. Listen for this event.

3. When you receive the complete event notification, call the play method to play the next video (either the next in sequence, or the next random video).

Let's take a closer look at how it's done, using a simple array as our playlist source.

PlayListAutoPlay.fla: Sequential Playback

To re-create this example:

1. Drop an FLVPlayback component on the Stage in Flash and give it an instance name of **myFLVPlybk**.

2. Enter the following code on the first frame of the FLA, using the appropriate syntax for your version of ActionScript:

ActionScript 2:

```actionscript
var myArray:Array = ["videos/fast_lg.flv",
                     "videos/train_med_lg.flv",
                     "videos/sl_lg.flv"];
myFLVPlybk.bufferTime = 3;
var vidNum:Number = 0;
myFLVPlybk.contentPath = myArray[vidNum];
var vidNumMax:Number = myArray.length - 1;
myFLVPlybk.addEventListener("complete", vidCompleted);
// Listen for complete event; then play next FLV
function vidCompleted(eventObj:Object):Void {
    if (vidNum < vidNumMax) {
        vidNum++;
        trace(vidNum);
        myFLVPlybk.play(myArray[vidNum]);
    }
    else {
        trace("end of playlist reached");
        return;
    }
};
```

Or, in **ActionScript 3**:

```actionscript
import fl.video.*;
var myArray:Array = ["videos/fast_lg.flv",
                     "videos/train_med_lg.flv",
                     "videos/sl_lg.flv"];
var vidNum:Number = 0;
myFLVPlybk.source = myArray[vidNum];
var vidNumMax:Number = myArray.length - 1;
myFLVPlybk.addEventListener("complete", vidCompleted);
// Listen for complete event; then play next FLV
function vidCompleted(eventObj:Object):void {
```

```
        if (vidNum < vidNumMax) {
            vidNum++;
            trace(vidNum);
            myFLVPlybk.play(myArray[vidNum]);
        }
        else {
            trace("end of playlist reached");
            return;
        }
    };
```

3. Save the file and then export the SWF. The first video will play, followed by the next in the array, and then the third. When the end of the array is reached, the playback will stop and you'll see an "end of playlist reached" message in the Output window if you're testing in Flash.

Note: It should be noted here that the FLVPlayback component has a built-in "behavior" that you can access in the Flash IDE that allows you to add up to seven videos to a list, which will play sequentially and even loop if needed. We decided to show you how to do it strictly in code here instead, because it's much more flexible. Just thought you should know.

PlaylistShuffle.fla: Playing Random Videos from Your Playlist

Changing this code to play a random video is pretty easy.

1. Begin by saving a copy of the FLA used in the above example; call it **Playlist-Shuffle.fla**. We'll just replace the ActionScript with the code in this section.

2. Instead of incrementing the vidNum on the complete event to step through the video list, you'll just choose a random number between 0 and the vidNumMax, then play the FLV file that is at that random position in the Array, like so:

ActionScript 2:
```
var myArray:Array = ["videos/fast_lg.flv",
                     "videos/train_med_lg.flv",
                     "videos/sl_lg.flv"];
myFLVPlybk.contentPath = getRandomVideo();
myFLVPlybk.addEventListener("complete", vidCompleted);
// Listen for complete event; then play next FLV
```

```
function vidCompleted(eventObj:Object):Void {
    myFLVPlybk.stop();

    if(myArray.length>0) {
        myFLVPlybk.contentPath = getRandomVideo();
    } else {
        trace("end of playlist reached");
    }
};


function getRandomVideo() {
    return myArray.splice(random(myArray.length), 1)[0];
}
```

And in ActionScript3:

```
var myArray:Array = ["videos/fast_lg.flv",
                     "videos/train_med_lg.flv",
                     "videos/sl_lg.flv"];
myFLVPlybk.source = getRandomVideo();
myFLVPlybk.addEventListener("complete", vidCompleted);
// Listen for complete event; then play next FLV
function vidCompleted(eventObj:Object):void {
    if(myArray.length>0)
        myFLVPlybk.source = getRandomVideo();
    else {
        trace("end of playlist reached");
    }
};
function getRandomVideo() {
    return myArray.splice(Math.floor(Math.random()*myArray.length),
    ➟ 1)[0];
}
```

When you test this SWF, the first random video will play automatically; then the next video will be another random one from your array. Of course, this works best when you have a large number of videos in your playlist. The videos will continue until the end of the last video is played.

So, now you're thinking, "This is all well and good, but how do I actually add this playlist to my video application?" Well, we've expanded the MVC player example that we introduced back in Chapter 5 to include a playlist that reads from an XML file. Let's take a closer look at how it's implemented.

Integrating an XML Playlist into the MVC Player

In our example Model-View-Controller–based player covered back in Chapter 5, we had an array of FLV filenames as a source for our playlist. As you may have noticed, that was a pretty bare-bones implementation without much flexibility. A few changes are needed to adapt the original player framework to use an XML source for the playlist, but not as many as you might think. We were already using an array, so the simplest way to change over to XML would be to turn XML into an array, right? Well, using a handy little utility open source class called XMLSA, we can do exactly that. (XMLSA can be downloaded at http://proto.layer51.com/d.aspx?f=957.)

 Note: An alternative to the XMLSA utility in Flash 8 is the built-in XPathAPI.

Here's an overview of the changes to this version of the application:

• Added util.XMLSA

• Added a folder called playlist inside the deploy folder, with a sample XML file: test_playlist.xml

• Edited MediaPlayerModel to detect when it reached the beginning or end of the playlist, and changed syntax to deal with an XMLSA array

• Changed the main MediaPlayer class so the first thing it does is load an XMLSA object

As you know if you've been working with this player framework, the model holds an instance of our playlist. The playlist object itself is constructed in the Playlist class (ui/component/mediaPlayer/playlist/Playlist.as). To parse the XML source in this class, we use the XMLSA class (util/XMLSA.as), which converts the XML into an object with properties we can access, instead of forcing us to climb around in the XML tree.

So, ultimately, all you need to do to implement your own XML playlist in this version of the application framework is to edit a copy of the test_playlist.xml file and then specify that file in the MediaPlayer.as class. When you instantiate this class in your application, the XML will be parsed into an object which will ultimately populate your view.

test_playlist.xml

Let's start by taking a look at the structure of the XML file example:

```
<playlist>

    <item>
      <path>test_01.flv</path>
```

```
        <title>test 01</title>
        <description>description here</description>
    </item>
    <item>
        <path>test_02.flv</path>
        <title>test 02</title>
        <description>description here</description>
    </item>
    <item>
        <path>test_03.flv</path>
        <title>test 03</title>
        <description>description here</description>
    </item>

</playlist>
```

In this example, we just have a file path, title, and description for each video, or item. You could, of course, have whatever additional information you like here for each. We'll show you how to access that data in a minute, when we walk through the MediaPlayerModel. Next, though, let's look at what's going on in our main class, MediaPlayer, in ActionScript 2.

AS2: *MediaPlayer.as*

This is the main class that you'll instantiate in the first frame of your Flash document, just as you did back in Chapter 5. You'll notice that we've got a new class here that we're importing, XMLSA:

```
import com.flashconnections.core.Core;
import com.flashconnections.ui.component.mediaPlayer.
➠ ifc.IMVCMediaPlayer;
import com.flashconnections.ui.component.mediaPlayer.MVCMediaPlayer;
import com.flashconnections.util.Proxy;
import com.flashconnections.util.XMLSA;


class com.flashconnections.ui.component.mediaPlayer.MediaPlayer

extends Core {

    private static var TEST_PLAYLIST_PATH:String =
➠ "playlist/test_playlist.xml";


    private var player:IMVCMediaPlayer;
```

```
        private var xObject:XMLSA;

        public function MediaPlayer(mc:MovieClip) {
            xObject = new XMLSA();
            xObject.onLoad = Proxy.create(this, initMediaPlayer, mc);
            xObject.load(mc.playlistPath != undefined ?
➠ mc.playlistPath : TEST_PLAYLIST_PATH);
        }


        public static function main(mc:MovieClip):Void {
            var a:MediaPlayer = new MediaPlayer(mc);
        }
```

OK, you've probably spotted a few changes here. Notice a new private static variable, TEST_PLAYLIST_PATH. Here's where you specify your playlist file. This can be a full HTTP address or a relative file path. (But don't forget Flash's security sandbox issues; if you are loading in a file from a different domain, you'll need to deal with cross-domain security.) Then, right away we instantiate an XMLSA object, xObject, and load our playlist path into it. The xObject will give us an array of the child nodes.

```
        private function initMediaPlayer(bool:Boolean,
➠ mc:MovieClip):Void {
            player = new MVCMediaPlayer();
            player.init(mc);
            player.initCoordinates(40, 60, 320, 240);
            player.populatePlaylist(xObject.item);
            player.getView().layout();

            player.playMedia(String(player.getPlaylist().
➠ getItemAt(0).path.getValue()));
        }
    }
```

Now, when we initialize our MediaPlayer object, we send our xObject.item child nodes as a parameter to the populatePlaylist method instead of the hard-coded array we had earlier. The Playlist object is still expecting an array, and it's still getting one, so we shouldn't have to alter too much of our other code. There are some syntax changes that need to be made to drill down into the XMLSA object once it's passed, though. Let's take a look at how that's handled next.

AS2: *MediaPlayerModel.as* Changes

Not a lot has changed in this class, so let's just focus in on the two methods that we updated, playNext and playPrevious. Here's the code we had for dealing with a standard array:

```
// standard implementation...
public function playNext():Void {
    if (getPlaylist().hasNext())
➠    playMedia(String(getPlaylist().getNext()));
}
public function playPrevious():Void {
    if (getPlaylist().hasPrevious())
➠    playMedia(String(getPlaylist().getPrevious()));
}
```

Now, here's the new code that reads the XMLSA object:

```
// XMLSA implementation...
public function playNext():Void {
    if (getPlaylist().hasNext())
➠    playMedia(String(getPlaylist().getNext().path.getValue()));
}
public function playPrevious():Void {
    if (getPlaylist().hasPrevious())
➠    playMedia(String(getPlaylist().getPrevious().path.getValue()));
}
```

Note the highlighted code above, where our syntax has changed. The part that changed is (with casting removed):

```
getPlaylist().getNext().path.getValue();
```

In this code, .path.getValue() drills into the XMLSA node retrieved by getPlaylist(). getNext() and grabs the value of the path object. (See the corresponding path nodes in test_playlist.as.) XMLSA is a timesaver, but in a way, it hard-codes things that shouldn't be hard-coded. Now our model requires us to use the nodeName path in our code. This is not so great, but the alternative would require us to write a lot more code. So, for that benefit, we can live with it.

From here, if you wanted to update your display with other information from the current playlist item, you could do so in the MediaPlayerView.onPlayMedia method. For example, to retrieve a title, inside that method you could say something like:

```
var title:String =
➠ getMPModel().getPlaylist().getCurrentItem().title.getValue()
myField.text = title;
```

and so on.

AS3: *Main.as*

Converting the ActionScript 3 MVC video player to implement an XML playlist is even more straightforward. Due to the significant improvements in the handling and parsing of XML in AS3, we only need to make changes to two classes, Main.as and MediaPlayerModel.as. (The changes from the simple array example from Chapter 5 are highlighted in the code that follows.)

```
package
{
    import flash.display.MovieClip;

    import flash.display.StageAlign;
    import flash.display.StageScaleMode;

    import com.flashconnections.core.Core;
    import
    com.flashconnections.ui.component.mediaPlayer.ifc.IMVCMediaPlayer;
    import
    com.flashconnections.ui.component.mediaPlayer.MediaPlayerView;
    import com.flashconnections.ui.component.mediaPlayer.MVCMediaPlayer;

    import flash.xml.*;

    import flash.net.URLLoader;
    import flash.net.URLRequest;
    import flash.events.Event;

    public class Main extends MovieClip
    {
        private var _player: MVCMediaPlayer;
        private var urlLoader:URLLoader;

        public function Main ():void
        {
            stage.scaleMode = StageScaleMode.NO_SCALE;
            stage.align = StageAlign.TOP_LEFT;
            // Load the Playlist file, and when complete,
            // initialize the media player
            urlLoader = new URLLoader();
```

```
        urlLoader.addEventListener(Event.COMPLETE, initMediaPlayer);
        urlLoader.load(new URLRequest("playlist/test_playlist.xml"));


    }

    public function initMediaPlayer(event:Event):void
    {
        var myXML:XML = new XML(urlLoader.data);
        player = new MVCMediaPlayer();
        player.init(this);
        player.initCoordinates(40, 60, 320, 240);


        player.populatePlaylist(myXML.item);


        player.getView().layout();
        player.playMedia
➡ (String(player.getPlaylist().getItemAt(0).path));
    }
    }
}
```

In this code, we just import some classes to process the XML file, and then specify
the URL of the file to be loaded. Otherwise, the parsed XML is handled just like the
array that we had in our previous simplified example.

AS3: *MediaPlayerModel.as* Changes

Now, we just need to make a tiny change to our last two methods in the MediaPlayer-
Model.as class. Changes are highlighted in the following code:

```
    public function playNext():void {
        playMedia(String(getPlaylist().getNext().path));
        MediaPlayerView(getView()).onPlay();
    }
    public function playPrevious():void {
        playMedia(String(getPlaylist().getPrevious().path));
        MediaPlayerView(getView()).onPlay();
    }
```

All we changed here was the way the FLV path is being sent to the playMedia
method. Because we are not just sending an element in an array but are sending an
object from the XML, we added .path to the command.

So, as you can see, this approach gives you lots of flexibility when creating dynamic playlists. You can read in any sort of data you need for each video, and create useful, dynamic, elegant, and—most important to your bottom line—easily reusable video applications.

 Note: If you'd like a more robust and detailed analysis of the MVC player and how to extend it in AS2, we've included an in-depth case study in the Appendix of this book.

Summary

Playlist data can come from a myriad of sources: an array, a database, an XML file, user input, or even the contents of a directory. In this chapter you discovered ways to integrate your applications with each of these sources. We discussed linear versus non-linear video experiences, and why video on the Web is a different animal. You also learned how to:

- Deal with client updates, and common pitfalls to avoid
- Use various types of common playlist interfaces
- Read a simple array into a playlist
- Parse XML data into a playlist
- Play back contents of a playlist randomly and in sequence
- Integrate an XML playlist source into our MVC video player framework
- Extend the sample XML version of the framework to include custom data

We covered a lot in this chapter. You should have a clear understanding of playlists now, whether you plan to create your own or extend our MVC player. Next, we'll get into the magical world of metadata and explore how it can give you even more power to navigate not just *between* videos, but *within* a video.

Demystifying Metadata and Cue Points

Inside each FLV lurks hidden information: tags like video duration, dimensions, author credits, even markers that you can use to trigger events at certain times during playback. How do you crack open an FLV and get this valuable information, you ask? Don't fret; read on, and all will be revealed.

Simply put, metadata is data that is embedded into an FLV file. You can access this information when you load in the FLV, and then use it to customize your application. In this chapter, we'll outline the variety of information you can embed—and show you how to access it. One particularly useful application we'll cover ticks away the time left in a video, using duration metadata. You should walk away from this chapter with a solid understanding of metadata, how to grab it, and what you can do with it.

Chapter Contents

Metadata Magic

Cue Point Power

Progressive Sleight-of-Hand: Scripted Pseudo-Streaming

Cue points can also be embedded into an FLV file, but unlike metadata, they can also be added using ActionScript. We'll outline the different kinds of cue points available in Flash and how you'd use each. In real-world applications, captions and subtitles are a common use for cue points. We'll show you how to add them to your player, along with embedding and linking to "chapters" within the video. Through this variety of examples, you'll become familiar with the possibilities these handy little tags can open up for your video applications.

We'll also clue you in on some killer utilities for dealing with cue points and metadata, and introduce you to a clever way to make progressive video act like streaming video.

That's a lot of ground to cover—so grab your flashlight and let's begin our adventure into the inner world of the FLV!

Metadata Magic

You've likely heard talk of metadata—that mysterious information embedded inside video files—but what exactly is it? What kind of data is in there? How do you extract it, and what can you do with it?

The short answer is, you can embed almost any data you like, such as captions, subtitles, credits, or file statistics. It can provide invaluable information for tracking legacy video files, or can at least give you the duration, width, and height of an FLV that you can then use to customize your display.

The traditional use of metadata is to assist in indexing and cataloging vast quantities of assets or information. This is why search engines use metadata—it's the condensed, meaningful information that can be sorted and searched. Of course, FLV metadata can be quite useful—necessary in fact—to optimize playback and provide context. But since it's only read in at runtime, it's generally not used to catalog or index video in Flash applications. Theoretically, you could read in the FLV and then write that information to a database somewhere to keep a record of it, but generally most Flash video applications don't require use of metadata in that way.

Depending on what software you use to encode your FLVs, the default metadata properties will differ. Let's take a look at some of the differences between encoding tools, and see what types of metadata properties are available.

 Note: Cue points are actually metadata. They are just passed as an array, rather than a single property, and can be read using either the onCue point or onMetaData handler. We'll cover this topic in-depth in the next section.

Four common properties are expected in any FLV:

- duration
- width
- height
- framerate

You should expect these four properties to be in any FLV that was encoded using professional software. Each encoding tool has its own additional default properties as well. In On2 Flix Pro 8.51, for example, these default values are automatically encoded into your FLV:

- creationdate
- canSeekToEnd
- audiocodecid
- audiodelay
- audiodatarate
- videocodecid
- framerate
- videodatarate
- height
- width
- duration

Sorenson Squeeze 4.5.5 gives you many more options for customizing metadata. There are three levels: file properties, persistent metadata, and nonpersistent (optional) metadata:

- File properties
  - audiocodecid
  - videocodecid
  - framerate
  - audiodatarate
  - videodatarate
  - duration
  - width
  - height
- Persistent properties
  - Encoded_With
  - Encoded_By

- Nonpersistent (optional) properties
  - dc_title
  - dc_rights
  - dc_source
  - dc_creator
  - dc_publisher
  - dc_contributor
  - dc_date
  - Resource_Genre
  - dc_identifier
  - dc_subject
  - dc_description
  - dc_language
  - dc_relation
  - dc_coverage

In Squeeze-encoded FLVs, file properties are always included, with differing values from video to video. Persistent properties are included, with values specific to your individual software. Nonpersistent properties are completely optional and editable.

If you need more details on encoder-specific metadata properties, check the software help files and read up on their common usages. For example, if you are encoding a huge catalog of videos that need to have permanent data attached, leveraging some of the specialized fields in Squeeze may come in handy.

Refer to Tables 8.1–8.3 for details about the standard metadata info objects that are retrievable via the onMetadata handler. Remember, you can read in any and all existing metadata properties (custom or standard) into Flash and display their values at runtime.

▶ **Table 8.1** Standard Metadata Retrievable by the *onMetadata* Handler

Parameters	Description
audiocodecid	A number that specifies which audio codec was encoded. (See Table 8.2 for details.)
audiodatarate	The data rate used to encode the audio, in kilobits per second.
audiodelay	The amount of delay between the video and audio. (The audio needs to be slightly ahead of the video to properly synchronize.)
canSeekToEnd	A Boolean value. canSeekToEnd is set to true if the FLV was encoded with the last frame as a keyframe; this allows seeking to the end if the data is being served via progressive download. canSeekToEnd is set to false if the last frame is not a keyframe.

Parameters	Description
cuePoints	An array of objects. Each object is a cue point. If there are no cue points in the file, cuePoints returns undefined. (We'll deal with the specifics of cue points in the next section.)
duration	The duration of the FLV file, in seconds.
framerate	The encoded frame rate of the FLV file.
height	The height of the FLV file, in pixels.
videocodecid	A number that specifies the codec version used to encode the video. (See Table 8.3 for details.)
videodatarate	The encoded video data rate of the FLV file, in kilobits per second.
width	The width of the FLV file, in pixels.

► **Table 8.2** Possible Values for the *audiocodecid* Parameter

audiocodecid	Codec Name
0	Uncompressed
1	ADPCM
2	MP3
5	Nellymoser 8 kHz mono
6	Nellymoser

What's with the missing numbers? Your guess is as good as ours...must be top-secret Adobe codecs!

► **Table 8.3** Possible Values for the *videocodecid* Parameter

videocodecid	Codec Name
2	Sorenson H.263
3	Screen video (Flash 7 and later only)
4	VP6 (Flash 8 and later only)
5	VP6 video with alpha channel (Flash 8 and later only)

Reading Metadata

When you want to access metadata in a given FLV, you'll of course need to wait for that data to be received by Flash. Luckily, ActionScript gives us a handy onMetadata event handler to let us know when the metadata's arrived. This method is fired after the NetStream.play method but before the video actually begins to play. Here's the basic code for cycling through all of the metadata properties in a given FLV, and tracing them to the Output window in Flash:

ActionScript 2

```
var nc:NetConnection = new NetConnection();
nc.connect(null);
var ns:NetStream = new NetStream(nc);


ns.onMetaData = function(infoObject:Object) {
    for (var propName:String in infoObject) {
        trace(propName + " = " + infoObject
   ➠ [propName]);
  }
};


ns.play("videos/med_lg.flv");
```

ActionScript 3

```
var nc:NetConnection = new NetConnection();
nc.connect(null);

var ns:NetStream = new NetStream(nc);
// Specify that callbacks should be made to this instance
ns.client = this;

function onMetaData(infoObject:Object):void {
    var propName:String;
    for (propName in infoObject) {
        trace(propName + ": " + infoObject
   ➠ [propName]);
    }
}
ns.play("videos/med_lg.flv");
```

In this example, we don't actually *display* the video (to do so you have to attach the NetStream to a video object on the Stage), but you can see all the metadata that's inside—traced to the Output panel (Figures 8.1 and 8.2). You'll notice that there are slight differences between the AS2 and AS3 output. You'll need to keep that in mind when you're working with data in each version or trying to port an old AS2 application into AS3.

OK, now that you know how to grab metadata, let's do something a bit more constructive with it.

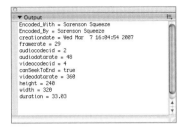

Figure 8.1 The Output panel in Flash 8, showing metadata values traced in ActionScript 2

Figure 8.2 The Output panel in Flash CS3, showing metadata values traced in ActionScript 3

How Long Is This Video?

Sometimes it can be handy to know the length of a video. Viewers often like to know what kind of time commitment a video will require before they start to watch. Getting this information from metadata and displaying it is pretty easy. Let's walk through a simple script that grabs the total duration of an FLV and then ticks down the time elapsed as the movie plays (Figure 8.3).

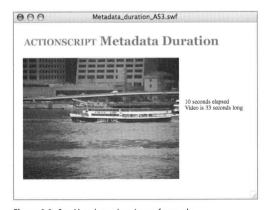

Figure 8.3 Our *Metadata_duration.swf* example

ActionScript 2: *Metadata_duration.swf*

Let's start with an ActionScript 2 example:

1. Open Flash 8 and create a new Flash file. Set the Stage size to 500 × 350, and save it as **Metadata_duration.fla**.

2. In the Library drop-down menu, choose New Video (ActionScript controlled). Drag that video onto the Stage and give it the coordinates x = 182 and y = 193. Give it an instance name of **myVid**.

3. Add a title on the top if you like, as shown in Figure 8.3.

4. Using the Text tool, create a new text box to the right of the video, approximately 145 wide × 65 high. In the Parameters panel, choose Multiline, Dynamic Text and give it an instance name of **ticker**. Change the point size to 11. We used Georgia for the font; you can choose whatever font you prefer.

5. On the main timeline, add a new layer and call it **Actions**. Select the first frame and enter the following script:

```
var duration:Number;

ticker.text = "** loading **";

var nc:NetConnection = new NetConnection();
nc.connect(null);
var ns:NetStream = new NetStream(nc);
myVid.attachVideo(ns);

function updateDuration() {
        if(duration > 0 && ns.time > 0) {
                ticker.text = Math.round(ns.time) + "
➡ seconds elapsed\n" +
                "Video is " + Math.round(duration) +
                " seconds long";
        }
}

ns.onMetaData = function(infoObject:Object) {
        duration = infoObject.duration;
};

setInterval(updateDuration, 12);

ns.play("videos/med_lg.flv");
```

6. Change the video name in the last line to your one of your own videos, and compile your SWF. Your video will start. The total duration of the clip will be displayed as the elapsed time ticks by.

ActionScript 3: *Metadata_duration.swf*

The setup for AS3 is a bit easier, as we dynamically create some of our assets.

1. Open Flash CS3 and create a new AS3 document. Set the Stage size to 500×350, and save the file as **Metadata_duration_AS3.fla**.

2. Add a headline as shown in Figure 8.3, if you like.

3. On the main timeline, create a new layer and name it **Actions**. Choose the first frame of that layer and enter the following script:

```
var ns:NetStream;
var myVid:Video;
var ticker:TextField;
var duration:uint;

myVid = new Video(320, 240);
ticker = new TextField( );
ticker.autoSize = TextFieldAutoSize.LEFT;
myVid.x = 20;
myVid.y = 70;
ticker.y = 150;
ticker.x = 350;
ticker.text = "** loading **";
duration = 0;
var nc:NetConnection = new NetConnection( );
nc.connect(null);
ns = new NetStream(nc);

var client:Object = new Object( );
client.onMetaData = onMetaData;
ns.client = client;
myVid.attachNetStream(ns);
addChild(myVid);
addChild(ticker);

function updateDuration(event:Event):void {
        if(duration > 0 && ns.time > 0) {
```

```
            ticker.text = Math.round(ns.time) +
    ➡ " seconds elapsed\n" +
            "Video is " + Math.round(duration) +
            " seconds long";
        }
    }

    var myTimer:Timer = new Timer(0, 0);
    myTimer.addEventListener("timer", updateDuration);
    myTimer.start();

    function onMetaData(infoObj:Object):void {
        duration = infoObj.duration;
    }

    ns.play("videos/med_lg.flv");
```

4. Compile your SWF, and the video will play. The time elapsed will tick by, and the total duration of the clip, in seconds, will be displayed as well.

Though the syntax is a bit different between versions, both the AS2 and AS3 versions are performing basically the same sequence of actions. First, we establish the NetConnection and NetStream and attach the NetStream to a video object. We have an onMetaData method, which grabs the duration property of the metadata and assigns it to a variable, duration. Then we set up an onEnterFrame function that checks every frame for an update to the ns.time property. (ns.time returns the time in seconds where the playhead is in the FLV.) If the duration is greater than 0 (the property exists) and the NetStream is streaming a video (the ns.time property is greater than 0), then we update the dynamic text box with the current information. Whew! It's pretty straightforward once you get through it, and you can grab any metadata property you like using this simple method.

 Note: Sometimes the embedded duration value isn't always correct. It's close, but could be off by a second or so, especially if you're rounding the number as we do in the previous example. Just keep that detail in mind when planning video applications that rely on precise duration values.

Now you should understand the basics of metadata and can use it for a myriad of applications, from playback status to film credits. Let's now delve a bit deeper into the mysterious inner world of FLVs—ever-useful cue points.

Cue Point Power

As hyped as they may be, cue points are remarkably useful in rich video applications, and definitely worth spending some time to fully understand.

Basically, cue points are a form of metadata (meaning they are data embedded inside an FLV). However, instead of just containing a single value (as standard metadata does) cue points are objects, held in an associative array, that are tied to a specific point in time in a video. This means that each cue point can contain a nugget of data that will specify a timecode along with any other relevant data you choose to associate with it.

A cue point is a time value, in seconds, and should be assigned a unique name. From there, it's up to you. You can assign a movieclip linkage ID, a caption string, or even an external SWF filename. It all depends on what you want to do when that cue point (time) is reached.

Why Would You Want to Use Cue Points?

There are many reasons you'd want to add cue points to your videos. Some common uses include:

- Long-form video content
- Conference presentations, board meetings, symposia, classes—any event where you may fall asleep at some point while watching
- Coordinated media
- To sync video with slides, audio, captions, links, or other dynamic content
- Logging

You can use cue point data to keep track of playback statistics, such as advertising views, or along with other metadata, create a list of videos watched. The possibilities are only limited to your imagination and the task at hand.

What Data Does a Cue Point Contain?

A cue point will always have the following properties:

Time The timecode (HH:MM:SS.mmm) when the onCuePoint handler will be triggered for this cue point

Name The name you assign the cue point

Type Either *navigation* or *event* (details on the differences appear later in this section)

Parameters Any optional parameters you choose to associate with the cue point

Now That You Want to Use Cue Points, How Do You Add Them?

Ultimately, cue points are either embedded directly into the FLV or added using Action-Script. Any professional encoding tool, such as the Flash Video Encoder, Sorenson Squeeze, or On2 Flix, will give you the ability to encode this information into your FLV file. You can add cue points by:

Embedding during FLV Encoding Embedded cue points are permanently hard-coded into the FLV file. You can't move or change these in any way.

Injecting Them into the FLV after Encoding Utilities are available (only for Windows at this time, regrettably) that allow you to add custom cue points after the FLV has been encoded. See the sidebar "Third-Party FLV Metadata Tools" later in this chapter for some tips.

Editing the Cue Point Parameter in the FLVPlayback Component Properties These are still editable, but they are not dynamic. If you add cue points with this method, you can only edit them in the Parameters panel in the Flash IDE.

Using ActionScript In both AS2 and AS3, you can dynamically add and delete cue points. You then add code to listen for and respond to them. Note, however, that you *must use the FLVPlayback component to utilize the ActionScript methods for working with dynamic cue points*. The methods available for this approach are explained in Table 8.4.

▶ **Table 8.4** Cue Point Management Methods for Use with the FLVPlayback Component

Method	Description
addASCuePoint()	Adds an ActionScript cue point. Has the same effect as adding the cue point as a parameter in the Flash IDE, but can be dynamically added at runtime.
removeASCuePoint()	Removes an ActionScript cue point. Uses name and time properties to specify the *cue point* to be removed.
setFLVCuePointEnabled()	Enables or disables cue points, specifying whether or not they should be recognized for events and navigation.
seekToPrevNavCuePoint()	Seeks to the previous navigation cue point encountered.
seekToNextNavCuePoint()	Seeks to the next navigation cue point encountered.
seekToNavCuePoint()	Seeks to a cue point specified (by name or time).
findNextCuePointWith Name()	Finds the next cue point that matches the name passed to the method.
findNearestCuePoint()	Finds a cue point of the specified type that matches (or is earlier than) the time specified in the method call. If none are found, returns null.
findCuePoint()	Finds the cue point of the specified type that matches the time or name (or both) that is passed to the method call. Note that this search includes disabled cue points.

Note: Using the FLVPlayback component gives you much more built-in control over dynamic cue points than you would have with just a video object. FLVPlayback provides a number of methods to control these cue points that, unfortunately, are not available if you just use a video object to play back your video. You can view and react to embedded cue points using your own custom NetStream/video object, but to add or edit them on the fly using the built-in methods, you'll need to use the component.

Note: So, if you're not using the FLVPlayback component, you have two choices. Either the cue points must be embedded in the FLV or you need to develop your own framework for checking the current playback time and comparing it to your array of external cue point data. That's a bit too involved for this chapter, so when we deal with AS cue points in examples here, we'll use them with the component.

What Are the Three Types of Cue Points Used For?

There are three types of cue points: navigation, event, and ActionScript. Which one you choose depends on your application. Let's compare:

Navigation These are embedded into the FLV file when you encode it, letting viewers jump to a specific point in the video. A keyframe is added at this point in the encoding. Navigation cue points are recognized automatically by the FLVPlayback component, and most of the supplied skins will give you the ability to jump forward and backward between navigation cue points.

Event Also embedded during encoding, event cue points can be added into the video at specific points. You can then write code to handle the events. (These are not recognized as navigation controls to the FLVPlayback component, but can be accessed via event handlers you write in ActionScript.)

ActionScript These cue points are created in ActionScript, and are external to the FLV file. You then write code to handle what happens when each cue point is reached. These can be added either through the FLVPlayback.addASCuePoint() method or in the Parameters panel of the FLVPlayback component. (Cue points that are added in the Parameters panel are still considered ActionScript cue points, as they aren't actually embedded in the FLV file.) You can use ActionScript to add and remove AS cue points, find cue points, seek to a navigation cue point, enable and disable cue points, and listen for cue point events (see Table 8.4).

Note: Don't be confused by Sorenson Squeeze—navigation cue points are referred to as "chapter markers" and event cue points are "keyframe markers." Same difference.

One note about navigation cue points: If you are planning to use them to jump to a specific point in the video, you may want to embed them in the file when encoding. When you do this, a keyframe is created at that point, allowing you to jump directly to that frame. Also remember that if you're planning to use progressive video delivery, you won't be able to jump forward in the video until the file is downloaded to that selected point. If you want to be able to jump around willy-nilly within a video, you should use streaming delivery. (Caveat: See the upcoming section "Progressive Sleight-of-Hand: Scripted Psuedo-Streaming.")

How to Read Cue Points on a *NetStream*

So, you understand that cue points are read in as an array of metadata, but just how do you access them? Again, we've got a handy-dandy handler that fires whenever cue point data is received on a stream: onCuePoint. This handler can be attached directly to a NetStream instance or to an FLVPlayback component. The syntax is slightly different for each implementation, as you'll see in the following examples. Let's start out by simply tracing any cue point data to the Output panel in Flash. The properties of each cue point will be traced as the video plays. In this example, you can use the sample video we provide in the exercise files, or you can use one of your own FLVs that has embedded cue points.

ActionScript 2: *CuePoint_trace.swf*

We'll start with the AS2 example:

1. Open Flash 8 and create a new Flash file. Save it as **CuePoint_trace.fla**.

2. Add a title on the top if you like.

3. In the Library drop-down menu, choose New Video (ActionScript controlled). Drag that video onto the Stage and assign it the coordinates x = 182 and y = 193. Give it an instance name of **myVid**.

4. On the main timeline, add a new layer and call it **Actions**. Select the first frame and enter the following script:

```
var nc:NetConnection = new NetConnection();
nc.connect(null);

var ns:NetStream = new NetStream(nc);

ns.onCuePoint = function(cpObj:Object):Void {
    for (var propName:String in cpObj) {
            trace(propName + " = " +
➡ cpObj[propName]);
```

```
            }
        trace("*******");
    };


    myVid.attachVideo(ns);
    ns.play("videos/libertybbVP6_512K_gtg_.flv");
```

5.   Compile the SWF. As the video plays, the cue point data will trace into the Output panel in Flash.

    Next, let's see how it's done in AS3.

ActionScript 3: *CuePoint_trace_AS3.swf*

Like the metadata example earlier in the chapter, the setup for our example in AS3 is a bit easier, as we dynamically create some of our assets.

1.   Open Flash CS3 and create a new AS3 document. Save the file as **CuePoint_trace_AS3.fla**.

2.   Add a headline, if you like.

3.   On the main timeline, create a new layer and name it **Actions**. Choose the first frame of that layer and enter the following script:

```
    var nc:NetConnection;
    var ns:NetStream;
    var myVid:Video;


    myVid = new Video(320, 240);
    myVid.x = 20;
    myVid.y = 70;


    nc = new NetConnection();
    nc.connect(null);
    ns = new NetStream(nc);


    // make main timeline the client
    ns.client = this;


    myVid.attachNetStream(ns);
    addChild(myVid);


    function onCuePoint(cpObj:Object):void {
        for (var propName:String in cpObj) {
```

```
                    trace(propName + " = " + cpObj
➧ [propName]);
      }
      trace("*******");
}


      ns.play("videos/libertybbVP6_512K_gtg_.flv");
```

4. Compile your SWF. You'll see the cue point data traced into the Output panel in Flash CS3. We'll bet you never knew all that information could be hidden inside an innocent-looking little FLV!

Now, we mentioned that you could add cue points dynamically using Action-Script. It's pretty easy to do, so let's give it a go.

Note: If you try to load video with cue point data in ActionScript 3 and don't specify an onCuePoint or onMetaData callback method, you'll encounter the nasty AsyncErrorEvent. You may want to keep this in mind when constructing your application and build in an AsyncErrorEvent handler, like so:

```
myNetStream.addEventListener(AsyncErrorEvent.ASYNC_ERROR,
➧ asyncErrorHandler);
function asyncErrorHandler(event:AsyncErrorEvent):void {
    trace(event.text);
}
```

This code will handle the exception and trace out the specifics. Of course, you can always just include an onMetaData handler to avoid the error altogether. Your call.

Adding Dynamic ActionScript Cue Points

In this example, we use the FLVPlayback component so we can add cue points via ActionScript. Note that there is now a listener object assigned to the FLVPlayback component that triggers the cue point handler. Remember, these cue points are external—not embedded in the FLV. (This means that if you want to create an interface that lets viewers set their own cue points, you'll have to store that data somehow.) Here we just arbitrarily set a hard-coded cue point at 1.5 seconds, with the name timecode.

CuePoint_trace_comp.swf

The instructions for both AS2 and AS3 versions are pretty much the same:

1. Create a new document in either Flash 8 or Flash CS3, and call it **CuePoint_ trace_comp.fla.**

2. From the Components panel, drag an instance of the FLVPlayback component to the Stage and give it an instance name of **myFLVPlybk.**

3. On the main timeline, create a new layer and name it **Actions.** Choose the first frame of that layer and enter the appropriate code as shown here, depending on your AS version:

ActionScript 2:

```
myFLVPlybk.contentPath = "videos/med_lg.flv";
// create cue point object
var cpObj:Object = new Object();


//create the dynamic cue point
//using time and name parameters
//attached to the FLVPlayback component
myFLVPlybk.addASCuePoint(1.5, "timecode");


var listenerObject:Object = new Object();


listenerObject.cuePoint = function(cpObj:Object)
➥ :Void {
        trace("Cue Point triggered at: " +
➥ cpObj.info.time +
            "\nName: " + cpObj.info.name +
            "\ntype: " + cpObj.info.type +
            "\n*******");
}
myFLVPlybk.addEventListener("cuePoint",
➥ listenerObject);
```

ActionScript 3:

```
myFLVPlybk.bufferTime = 3;
myFLVPlybk.source = "videos/med_lg.flv";


//create the dynamic cue point
//using time and name parameters
```

```
//attached to the FLVPlayback component
myFLVPlybk.addASCuePoint(1.5, "timecode");

function onCuePoint(cpObj:Object):void {
    trace("Cue Point triggered at: " + cpObj.
➥ info.time +
                "\nName: " + cpObj.info.name +
                "\ntype: " + cpObj.info.type +
                "\n*******");
}

myFLVPlybk.addEventListener("cuePoint",
➥ onCuePoint);
```

4. Compile your SWF. Here's what you'll see traced to the Output panel in Flash (also see Figure 8.4):

```
Cue Point triggered at: 1.5
Name: timecode
type: actionscript
*******
```


Pretty simple, eh? Now that you understand how to trace out the cue point data on both a NetStream and an FLVPlayback component, let's take it to the next step: adding captions. We'll show you how it's done using both approaches.

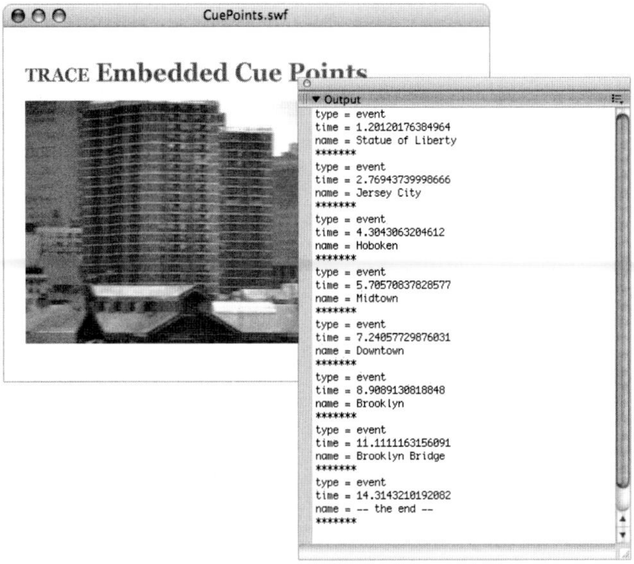

Figure 8.4 Trace of an FLV's embedded cue points

Adding Captions

OK, enough of this tracing business—now we're getting to the juicy part. Let's do something useful with all this embedded data: captions!

Here's how you can easily make simple text captions appear at various points in your video. We'll start with an example using a video object in both AS2 and AS3, and then show you how it's done with the FLVPlayback component.

ActionScript 2 with *NetStream* + Video Object: *CuePoints_ns_captions.swf*

Let's get started with the example using a video object, in AS2.

1. Open Flash 8 and create a new Flash file. Save it as **CuePoint_ns_captions.fla**.

2. In the Library drop-down menu, choose New Video (ActionScript controlled). Drag that video onto the Stage and assign it the coordinates x = 182 and y = 193. Give it an instance name of **myVid**.

3. Add a dynamic text field on top of the video, and give it an instance name of **place_txt**. Set the font color to white, Verdana Bold, at a size of 22, aligned center. For added readability, click the Filters tab and add a drop shadow. The default settings should be fine.

4. Add a title on the top if you like, as shown in Figure 8.5.

5. On the main timeline, add a new layer and call it **Actions**. Select the first frame and enter the following code:

```
var nc:NetConnection = new NetConnection();
nc.connect(null);

var ns:NetStream = new NetStream(nc);

ns.onCuePoint = function(cpObj:Object):Void {
    for (var propName:String in cpObj) {
        place_txt.text = cpObj[propName];
    }
};

myVid.attachVideo(ns);
ns.play("videos/libertybbVP6_512K_gtg_.flv");
```

6. Compile your SWF. If you used our sample video, you'll see something like Figure 8.5, with the captions appearing on top of the video at the appropriate time in the clip.

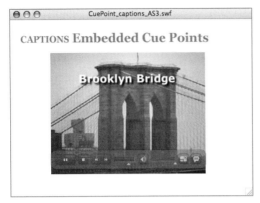

Figure 8.5 Video in FLVPlayback component with overlaid cue point captions.

ActionScript 3 with *NetStream* + Video Object: *CuePoints_ns_captions_AS3.swf*

Let's do the same thing now in AS3.

1. Open Flash CS3 and create a new AS3 Flash file. Save it as **CuePoint_ns_captions_AS3.fla.**

2. Add a dynamic text field 300 pixels wide by 31 pixels high. Place it at x = 95 and y = 100, and give it an instance name of **place_txt**. Set the font to Verdana Bold, color to white, at a size of 22, aligned center. For added readability, click the Filters tab and add a drop shadow.

3. Add a title on the top if you like, as shown in Figure 8.5.

4. On the main timeline, add a new layer and call it **Actions**. Select the first frame and enter the following code:

```
var nc:NetConnection;
var ns:NetStream;
var myVid:Video;

myVid = new Video(320, 240);
myVid.x = 80;
myVid.y = 70;

nc = new NetConnection();
nc.connect(null);
ns = new NetStream(nc);

var client:Object = new Object();
ns.client = client;
```

```
client.onCuePoint = onCuePoint;
myVid.attachNetStream(ns);
addChild(myVid);
addChild(place_txt);

function onCuePoint(cpObj:Object):void {
    for (var propName:String in cpObj) {
            place_txt.text = cpObj[propName];
    }
}
ns.addEventListener(AsyncErrorEvent.ASYNC_ERROR,
➡ asyncErrorHandler);
function asyncErrorHandler(event:AsyncErrorEvent)
➡ :void {
    trace(event.text);
}
ns.play("videos/libertybbVP6_512K_gtg_.flv");
```

5. Compile your SWF, and you'll see the captions appear on top of your video as it plays. If you used our sample video, you'll get a whirlwind view of Manhattan, complete with city markers. Just don't blink or you'll miss the tour!

ActionScript 2 with FLVPlayback Component: *CuePoints_captions.swf*

Now let's try it in AS2 using an FLVPlayback component instead of a video object:

1. Open the previous caption example that we created using a video object, and save it as **CuePoints_captions.fla**.

2. Delete the video object and replace it with an FLVPlayback component. Give the component an instance name of **myFLVPlybk**.

3. Click on the first frame of the Actions layer. Replace the code there with this:

```
myFLVPlybk.contentPath = "videos/libertybbVP6_512K_gtg_.flv";

var listenerObject:Object = new Object();

listenerObject.cuePoint = function(cpObj:Object):Void {
        place_txt.text = cpObj.info.name;
}
myFLVPlybk.addEventListener("cuePoint", listenerObject);
```

4. Compile your SWF. Again, you'll see the captions, but this time with all the controls of an FLVPlayback component.

ActionScript 3 with FLVPlayback Component: *CuePoints_captions_AS3.swf*

And now, let's look at the FLVPlayback component example, in AS3:

1. Open the previous caption example that we created using a video object, and save it as **CuePoints_captions_AS3.fla**.

2. Place an FLVPlayback component in the center of the Stage. Give the component an instance name of **myFLVPlybk**.

3. Click on the first frame of the Actions layer. Replace the code there with this:

```
myFLVPlybk.source = "videos/libertybbVP6_512K_gtg_.flv";


function onCuePoint(cpObj:Object):void {
    place_txt.text = cpObj.info.name;
}


myFLVPlybk.addEventListener("cuePoint", onCuePoint);
```

4. Compile the SWF. Captions will appear on top of your video as it plays.

We're certain you can think of a ton of cool uses for cue point captions: subtitles, product links, credits—all sorts of "extra" data that can make your video content more meaningful and the viewer experience richer. This, of course, is the real beauty of video in Flash.

Next, let's take a look at a basic example that reads cue point data into a list, presenting viewers with chapter links that jump to specific points in the video.

Note: Another option for captioning, if you're using the FLVPlayback component and ActionScript 3, is to use the FLVPlaybackCaptioning component built into Flash CS3. This new component enables captioning within the FLVPlayback component. It works by importing a specially formatted type of XML file called a Timed Text (TT) file. For more information, consult the Flash CS3 documentation.

Bookmark It!

If you use AS-scripted cue points, you can add them dynamically—say, when a viewer wants to mark an especially interesting point in a video while watching it. The code for this application is a bit involved, so it's beyond our scope here, but we can give you a basic overview of how you'd do it.

Bookmark It! *(Continued)*

A dynamic cue point set by the viewer would, of course, not be hard-coded into the video, so we'd have to figure out a way to capture it. Then, to use that cue point data (timecode) as a bookmark, we'd have to pass its time parameter to the SWF as a parameter in a URL:

1. The user clicks the Bookmark button, which assigns cue point data to a variable.

2. This action constructs a link that includes this variable in a query string (e.g., http://www. domain.com/FLVPlayer.html?link=cuepointdatavalue/) and displays it for the user to copy and share.

3. When someone then goes to that URL, the query string would be read back into Flash using loadVars. Using that cue point timecode information, the application would then jump to that point in the video.

We recommend using SWFObject to pass variables into Flash, but you could also use a server-side language such as PHP, ASP, or Ruby.

Adding Chapter Links

Often you'll want to read in cue points and use them as chapter markers, like you see on DVDs. Particularly if you anticipate your application having long videos (even 3 minutes can be considered long in the web video world), you'll want to have a way for viewers to get right to the content that interests them.

One thing to remember about chapter links, though—you'll only want to use them with streaming video. Streaming video allows you to jump around within a video at will; progressive delivery requires that the FLV file be downloaded up to the point that you jump to. If it's not, the playback will fail.

> **Note:** If you don't have access to a streaming server and want to test this example, you can link to a video that's on your local hard drive and let it play through once. It'll be cached, so you can jump around pretty smoothly.

You can follow along in the comments within the code to see just what's going on here. Basically, we grab the cue point data right away when the video loads, through the onMetaData handler, so we don't have to wait for each cue point to fire before it gets added to the list (which is what we'd have to do if we had used the onCuePoint handler). Then we do some fancy footwork to drill down into the cue point data to get the time property. We then add that to the list, and can seek right to that point in our video when the chapter is selected.

Let's take a closer look.

ActionScript 2: *CuePoints_playlist.swf*

Let's start with the AS2 example:

1. Open Flash 8 and create a new Flash file. Save it as **CuePoints_playlist.fla**.

2. In the Library drop-down menu, choose New Video (ActionScript controlled). Drag that video onto the Stage and assign it the coordinates x = 182 and y = 193. Give it an instance name of **myVid**.

3. From the Components Library, drag a List box to the Stage. Position it at x = 420, y = 140, with a width of 130 pixels and a height of 130 pixels. Give it an instance name of **myList**.

4. Add a title on the top if you like, as shown in Figure 8.6.

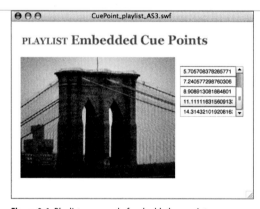

Figure 8.6 Playlist composed of embedded cue points

5. On the main timeline, add a new layer and call it **Actions**. Select the first frame and enter the following code:

```
var nc:NetConnection = new NetConnection();
nc.connect(null);

var ns:NetStream = new NetStream(nc);
myVid.attachVideo(ns);

//cycle through the metadata object
//to retrieve the data inside the cue point object
```

```
//We do this here, so we get all the data
//at once, and don't have to wait for each cue point
ns.onMetaData = function(infoObject:Object) {
    var propName:String;

    for (propName in infoObject) {
        if (propName == "cuePoints") {
            // cycle through all cue points
            for(var cp in infoObject[propName]) {
                traceObject(infoObject[propName][cp]);
            }

            myList.sortItems(sortValues);
        }
    }
};


function sortValues(a:Object, b:Object):Boolean {
    return (a.value > b.value);
}
//function to further drill down into the cuePoint data
//and add to the list box
function traceObject(obj:Object):Void {
    var listObj = new Object();

    for (var prop:String in obj) {
        var val = obj[prop];

        if (prop == "time")     {
            listObj.value = val;
        }
        if (prop == "name") {
            listObj.label = val;
        }
    }

    myList.addItem(listObj);
}
```

```
// Add a listener to detect when
// new video is selected and play it
var listListener:Object = new Object();
listListener.change = function() {
    ns.seek(myList.selectedItem.value);
};

myList.addEventListener("change", listListener);
ns.play("videos/libertybbVP6_512K_gtg_.flv");
```

6. Compile the SWF. Your list box should be populated with the chapters pulled from the cue point data (Figure 8.6). You can click on any of the items in the list and seek to that point in the video.

ActionScript 3: *CuePoints_playlist_AS3.swf*

Let's see how it's done in AS3:

1. Open Flash CS3 and create a new AS3 Flash file. Save it as CuePoint_playlist_AS3.fla.

2. From the Components Library, drag a List box to the Stage. Position it at x = 420, y = 140, with a width of 130 pixels and a height of 130 pixels. Give it an instance name of **myList**.

3. Add a title on the top if you like, as shown in Figure 8.6.

4. On the main timeline, add a new layer and call it **Actions**. Select the first frame and enter the following code:
```
var nc:NetConnection;
var ns:NetStream;
var myVid:Video;

myVid = new Video(320, 240);
myVid.x = 20;
myVid.y = 70;

nc = new NetConnection();
nc.connect(null);
ns = new NetStream(nc);
ns.client = this;

//cycle through the metadata object
//to retrieve the data inside the cue point object
```

```
//We do this here, so we get all the data
//at once, and don't have to wait for each cue point
function onMetaData(infoObject:Object):void {
    var propName:String;
    for (propName in infoObject) {
        if (propName == "cuePoints") {
            // cycle through all cue points
            // and add them to the list box
            for (var cp in infoObject[propName]) {
                traceObject(infoObject[propName][cp]);
            }

            myList.sortItems(sortData);
        }
    }
}


myVid.attachNetStream(ns);
addChild(myVid);

//function to further drill down into the cuePoint data
//and add to the list box
function traceObject(obj:Object):void {
    var listObj:Object = new Object();

    for (var prop:String in obj) {
        var val = obj[prop];

        if (prop == "time") {
            listObj.data = val;
        }
        if (prop == "name") {
            listObj.label = val;
        }
    }

    myList.addItem(listObj);
}
```

```
function sortData(a:Object, b:Object):Boolean {
    return (a.data > b.data);
}


// Add a listener to detect when
// new video is selected and play it
function listListener(event:Event) {
    ns.seek(event.target.selectedItem.data);
}


myList.addEventListener(Event.CHANGE, listListener);
ns.play("videos/libertybbVP6_512K_gtg_.flv");
```

5. Compile your SWF. You should see the time properties of any embedded cue points displayed in the List box. Click on one to seek to that point in the video.

As you can see, there are lots of possibilities for making this feature even richer. For example, since you can embed any information you like into cue points, you could add a JPG filename and display a thumbnail that associated with that chapter link. Or, although it may be considered a bit rude, you could even trigger a function on a cue point that opens a new web page with content related to that part of the video. Another common use for event cue points is to trigger movie clips or SWFs to load next to the movie, such as presentation slides.

Note: onMetaData versus onCuePoint event handlers: You may have noticed that both methods read metadata embedded in an FLV file. What's the difference? We had the same question when we started working with cue point data. Here's the difference: onMetaData grabs all the cue point information at once when the video loads. onCuePoint gets triggered each time a cue point is reached as the video plays. Therefore, if you just want to know what the cue points are, use onMetaData. If you want to respond to them as they are reached, use onCuePoint. There. It's all clear now!

Drop It Like a Hotspot!

OK, that's probably the worst heading we've come up with yet...but it got your attention! So, what's a hotspot, exactly? It's a clickable, trackable area that follows an object or area in a video. You can then trigger actions, as you would with a button, when the hotspot is clicked. Usually this would be a web link or more information about the target item.

Drop It Like a Hotspot! *(Continued)*

Though a very specialized feature, hotspotting is something that may have great marketing potential if used judiciously. And, in the future, one of your clients may likely ask for it. For that reason alone, we found it worthy of mention here.

The quickest way to implement hotspots in your video application is to use a nifty extension called hotFlashVideo (http://www.flashloaded.com/flashcomponents/hotflashvideo/). Compatible with Flash MX 2004, 7, or 8, hotFlashVideo uses JavaScript Flash (JSFL) to automate the creation of interactive hotspots within the authoring environment that follow areas in an FLV during playback.

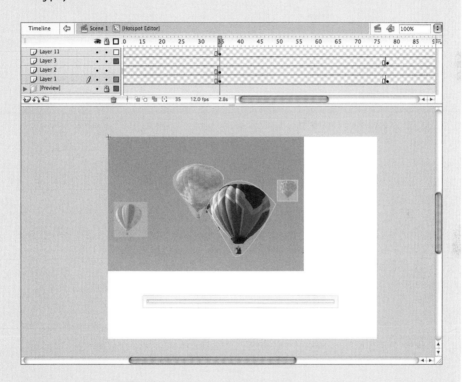

These hotspots are included in an overlay, not actually embedded in the FLV. Basically, the workflow goes like this:

1. You create the hotspots using the drawing tools in Flash, so they can be any shape you like.

2. After customizing a few variables, you import your FLV (for reference only; you link to the FLV file for your final deployment) and draw hotspots over your target areas on keyframes along the timeline.

3. Once you're finished, the extension does the rest.

Continues

Drop It Like a Hotspot! *(Continued)*

The downside to using the extension is that everything's done on the timeline, which can be quite a hassle, not to mention poor OOP structure. The upside is that you have precise control over the placement of the overlays as the movie plays, and all logic is handled for you by the extension.

An alternative is to create a framework that writes out all the hotspot placements to an XML file, which is then parsed and used to animate hotspot objects, synchronized with keyframes or timecodes in the video. That's entirely possible, but for 60 bucks and a couple of un-OOP elements, the hotFlashVideo component may very well be your best solution.

Progressive Sleight-of-Hand: Scripted Psuedo-Streaming

Ever wonder how, though you know darn well they're serving progressive video, Yahoo!'s video player allows you to jump forward in a video right away, even if you haven't downloaded that far yet? Well, that's because they're working some server-side magic, a technique we like to call scripted pseudo-streaming (SPS).

SPS is a technique that enhances progressive download by providing server-side seek capabilities. Its development was a group effort, mostly fueled by a blog post by Stefan Richter, enhanced by Rick Flomag, then ported to ColdFusion by Steve Savage.

Traditional Progressive Download

As Figure 8.7 illustrates, traditional progressive download restricts users from scrubbing beyond the range of the progressive download. Users must wait until the portion of the video they would like to seek to has been downloaded.

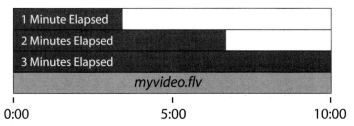

Figure 8.7 Traditional progressive download

Scripted Pseudo-Streaming

This technique enables users to seek beyond the barrier of the progressively download-ing FLV. Instead of relying on the NetStream stream object for seeking, this technique calls the seek command on a server-side PHP script. When the PHP script receives the seek command, it will load the FLV file into RAM, locate the seek time, and begin send-ing the FLV data from that point forward. End result: The user is able seek to any posi-tion in a given FLV without having to wait for the progressive download to complete.

Figure 8.8 depicts a user jumping 6 minutes into an FLV file. The dark gray area shows the part of the FLV file that will be loaded after the seek command is issued.

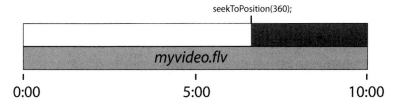

Figure 8.8 Seeking forward in a progressive file using SPS

Here are the steps to implementing SPS:

1. Download the example files from http://www.sybex.com/flashvideo/.
2. Encode the video using your favorite FLV encoder.
3. Add keyframe metadata to FLV using Burak's FLV MetaData Injector (Windows only; refer to the sidebar "Third-Party FLV Metadata Tools" later in this chapter), as shown in Figure 8.9. Do the following in this window:
   A. Select the input FLV.
   B. Select the output FLV.
   C. Check the Include Keyframes Object check box.
   D. Click the Run FLVMDI button.

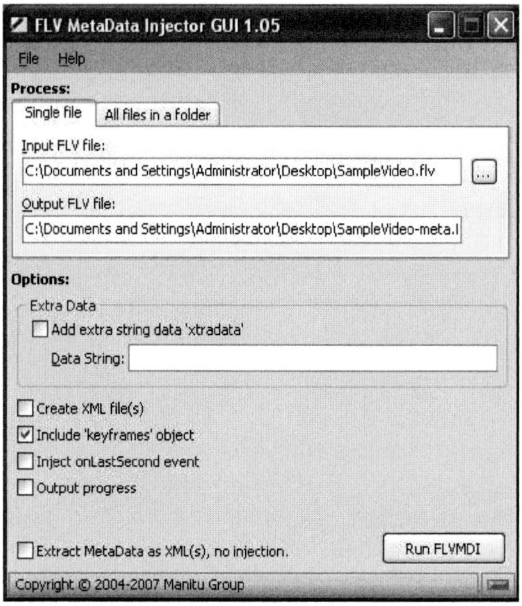

Figure 8.9 Injecting metadata into an FLV using Burak's FLV MetaData Injector (FLVMDI)

4. Open the example FLA and change the _vidName variable to the name of your newly injected video. Compile the SWF.

5. Upload the updated FLV and PHP script (or alternative CFM script) and player SWF to your web server.

6. Test the video application, and jump around to your heart's content.

Pros and Cons

The benefits to this approach are:

- Avoiding the expense of Flash Media Server.

- Simpler server deployment (single PHP script vs. full streaming media server).

- The potential to save server bandwidth, when compared with progressive download.

But of course, there are a few catches to this approach:

- It uses more server-side CPU power compared to progressive download.

- FLV file size may be constrained by the amount of memory available to PHP.

- More tinkering is necessary to get it to work.

- Stock Adobe components do not work.

You can see a sample of this technique on our blog: http://www.flashconnections.com/flash-video-pro/

More Information

For more information on pseudo-streaming, check out these resources:

Original Discussion of PHP Streaming Approach http://www.flashcomguru.com/index.cfm/2005/11/2/Streaming-flv-video-via-PHP-take-two

Best PHP Source Code Available at Time of Printing http://socios.smo.org.mx/videos/flashphpstream.tar.bz2

Metadata Injector http://www.buraks.com/flvmdi/

Note: This section was written by Lou Klepner of klepner.com.

Third-Party FLV Metadata Tools

There are three main tools for manipulating FLV metadata: Burak's FLV MetaData Injector (FLVMDI), Burak's Captionate, and Inlet Media's FLVTool2.

FLV MetaData Injector (FLVMDI)

This free, closed source, Microsoft Windows application (http://www.buraks.com/flvmdi/) adds onMetaData Action Message Format (AMF) data to FLV files through a command-line interface or optional graphical user interface. For the first few years, FLV encoders injected little or no metadata in their output. At this time, Burak's FLV MetaData Injector was an indispensable tool, embedding the critical height, width, and duration data. Modern FLV encoders (2005 and later) provide this information by default but still fall short of providing all the metadata possible. One of FLVMDI's handiest features is the ability to inject a list of all keyframes, which can be used for intelligent keyframe-based seeking and streaming applications.

FLVTool2

FLVTool2 is a cross-platform, open source metadata injector (http://inlet-media.de/flvtool2/). In addition to FLVMDI's capabilities, FLVTool2 provides the ability to inject onCuePoint tags from external XML files, add custom key-value pairs, and cut FLV files into pieces. FLVTool2 must be used from the command line, it supports command chaining, and it is ideally suited for server-side processing.

Continues

Third-Party FLV Metadata Tools *(Continued)*

Captionate

Burak's Captionate tool (http://buraks.com/captionate/) is a commercial Windows application that provides all of the features of FLVMDI in addition to a host of marker, caption, and cue point capabilities (see graphics below). Captionate provides a timeline-based approach, allowing users to view the video while editing the associated metadata. As its name implies, Captionate excels at creating closed-captioning metadata, supporting multiple languages and speakers, each with their own display name, language code, and target words per minute rate. Text can be entered when the video is playing or imported from a plain text file. Sporting a simple timeline-based approach, this product makes scrubbing and setting metadata a breeze. Metadata can be injected into FLV files or exported as XML.

Captionate 2.16 supports both Sorenson Spark and On2 VP6 codecs, Flash 8 cue points, as well as Adobe FLVCoreCuePoints XML, which was recently introduced in Adobe's Soundbooth beta. Publishing of captions has been greatly simplified by the release of Michael Jordan's FLVPlayback Component skins by Adobe. MXP is available for download at http://blogs.adobe.com/accessibility/2006/10/captionskins.html.

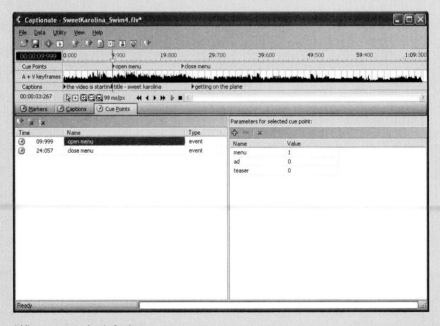

Adding event cue points in Captionate

Third-Party FLV Metadata Tools *(Continued)*

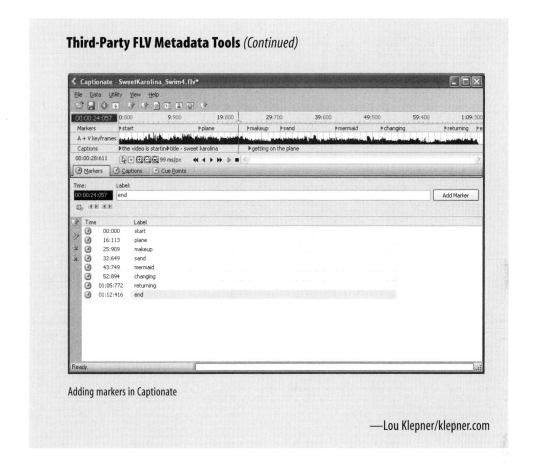

Adding markers in Captionate

—Lou Klepner/klepner.com

Now That You're Enlightened...

I'm sure the wheels are turning in your head now, thinking of all the clever uses you can come up with for cue points. Coordinating slides with video, prompting the viewer to send e-mails (populated with the viewer's info and the video they were watching at the time), and tracking viewership (making sure they watched the interspersed ads) are just a few of the wide range of uses. What will you do with them?

Summary

Metadata and cue points are powerful tools for tracking and interacting with video in Flash and a key part of Flash's domination in interactive video applications. This chapter should have cleared up any confusion you may have had about how to access and manipulate them. You learned:

- The standard metadata information you can expect to be in any FLV
- Methods for injecting custom metadata into an FLV
- How to read metadata values and use the information in your application
- What cue points are and why you'd want to add them to your video
- Methods for adding cue points, both embedded and via ActionScript
- How to display caption data coordinated with your video
- How to read in and create a list of chapter links
- What scripted pseudo-streaming is, and how it can make your progressive videos act like streaming
- What utilities are available to make working with metadata and cue points easy

In the next chapter, we'll get even trickier—exploring video effects using filters and masks. Gotta love Flash video. Let the pixel bending begin!

Bending Pixels with Filters and Masks

Now that you've had your fill of dealing with data in the previous chapter, let's get back to the visuals. In this chapter we'll show you what's possible and demonstrate some of the filters and masking effects we've found useful in video applications. If you need to create a player that doesn't look like the typical "video in a box," you're in the right place. Whether your client wants a fancy transition between videos, a custom-shaped video object, or their video tinted to match their logo color, you can do it all with ActionScript.

9

Chapter Contents

What Can I Do to My Video?
One Video, Many Masks
Alpha Channels, Revisited
Fun with Filters and Tints
Lost in Transitions

What Can I Do to My Video?

Filters, masks, transitions—oh my! Yes, video can be treated like any other object in Flash. It can be rotated, skewed, filtered, masked, and otherwise transformed. You can use bitmap effects and blend modes to increase the contrast, shift the colors, or even apply semitransparent masks. By scripting these manipulations, you can create transitions from one video to another. Dynamic masks can be added to have video "peek through" a shape.

With all of these options available to you, it's important to pause and ask these three questions:

Is this effect necessary to my viewer's experience? Maybe the effect enhances the design of the site or reinforces a brand image. If it doesn't make the video unwatchable or annoying to the viewer, then go for it.

How complex is the effect, and how much will it tax the viewer's processor? This is the second test. Flash is having to calculate image transformations on each frame of the video, which can get pretty hairy if you have a high-quality video and/or layered effects. If applying an effect slows down the video or crashes the browser, it's obviously a bit too much math for Flash to handle.

Is it possible to achieve outside of Flash, in the video-editing process (through Adobe After Effects or other postproduction software), or does it need to be interactive or dynamic? In many cases, a desired filter effect can be achieved more effectively by applying it before converting the video to FLV. If you just want to add more blue to the video overall, or add contrast and saturation to look like a 1950s Technicolor movie, it's best to do that in the video itself. Why ask Flash to do all that math if you can do it in advance? Often, though, you'll need dynamic effects—and if used with prudence, Flash can deliver.

In the following examples, we'll demonstrate some basic filters and masking that we've found useful for custom video applications. You'll likely find these effects to be pretty cool and fun to play around with (we did)—but we can't say it enough: please always keep in mind the result these effects are having on the performance, and usability, of your application.

OK, we've sufficiently warned you—now let's start by having some fun with masking!

One Video, Many Masks

When you apply a mask to an image (or in our case, a video), its shape acts as a "cookie cutter," only revealing the shape of the mask.

No mysteries here; masking video in Flash is no different than masking a movie-clip. Actually, in Flash, masks and other effects can *only* be applied to movieclips. So we'll need to nest the video object inside of a movieclip, and then apply our mask to that. But other than that, masking video is pretty straightforward.

> **Note:** Don't confuse masks with alpha transparency. Masks, though they can be animated (as you'll see in our example), are objects independent of the FLV file. In alpha channel video, the transparency data are actually encoded into the file. (We'll give you an example of alpha channel video in the next section.)

Let's take a walk through the code for dynamically adding a mask. In this first example, we'll put together a little "switcher" application to demonstrate some of the masking techniques you can use. Here we demonstrate a standard shape mask, an animated mask, and one that you can drag around. We've just applied this to a very simple video object contained within a movieclip for this example. When you use these effects in real projects, you'll likely want to add them to a more robust player structure with dynamic buffering and other features; masks can be added on to existing applications pretty easily. Though we step through the simple "switcher" demo here, you'll be happy to know that the real work is done by one line of code. In ActionScript 2, you'd use

```
video_mc.setMask(myMask_mc);
```

And in ActionScript 3 you'd use

```
video_mc.mask = myMask_mc;
```

Let's take a look at this code in action.

ActionScript 2: *FunWithMasks.as*

We start by importing the classes we'll be using. These are just standard interface classes—nothing specific to masking here.

```
import mx.utils.Delegate;
import mx.controls.RadioButtonGroup;
import mx.controls.RadioButton;

class FunWithMasks {
    var target:MovieClip;
    var video_mc:MovieClip;
    var nc:NetConnection;
    var ns:NetStream;
    var myVid:Video;
    var stroke_mc:MovieClip;
    var anim_mc:MovieClip;
    var dragme_mc:MovieClip;
```

Now let's move on to the constructor. Here we set up a simple video object. We'll create the NetConnection and NetStream, then attach a video object (myVid) embedded within a movieclip (video_mc) that we'll place on the Stage in Flash. Don't forget to change the video filename (highlighted in the following code snippet) to one of your own.

```
public function FunWithMasks(target_mc:MovieClip) {
    target = target_mc;
    //Construct NetConnection
    nc = new NetConnection();
    nc.connect(null);
    // Construct NetStream and connect to flow through
    // NetConnection
    var ns:NetStream = new NetStream(nc);
    // Attach NetStream to movieclip containing video object
    // on the stage
    target.video_mc.myVid.attachVideo(ns);
    target.video_mc.bufferTime = 3;
    // Tell the NetStream which FLV to play
    ns.play("http://www.flashconnections.com/myvideo.flv");
    // Initialize our radio buttons
    initButtons();
    // Hide masks we've placed on the stage
    resetMasks();
}
```

OK, the initial setup is done, so let's move on to our class's methods, where we begin to deal with our various masks:

```
private function resetMasks():Void {
    target.stroke_mc._visible = false;
    target.anim_mc._visible = false;
    target.dragme_mc._visible = false;
}
```

The resetMasks() function is pretty self-explanatory; it just hides the masks we aren't using when changing mask styles in our switcher app. Next are our first methods related to our specific mask types:

```
function strokeHandler(evt_obj:Object):Void {
    resetMasks();
    target.stroke_mc._visible = true;
    vidStrokeMask();
}
```

```
function animHandler(evt_obj:Object):Void {
    resetMasks();
    target.anim_mc._visible = true;
    vidAnimMask();
}

function dragMeHandler(evt_obj:Object):Void {
    resetMasks();
    target.dragme_mc._visible = true;
    vidDragMeMask();
}
```

These event handlers are called when the corresponding radio button is chosen. First, we use resetMasks() to be sure we don't see any of the other masks; then we make the correct mask movieclip visible and call the function that will apply it to the video object.

The next method

```
private function vidStrokeMask():Void {
    target.video_mc.setMask(target.stroke_mc);
}
```

is where the action is. In this one command, we are applying the mask to the video using the setMask() method, passing the mask's instance name as a parameter. This particular mask is just a shape—in this case a scribble we made with the Paintbrush in Flash, converted to a movieclip.

The next method

```
private function vidAnimMask():Void {
    target.video_mc.setMask(target.anim_mc);
}
```

applies the second mask option, an animated mask we'll create. As we mentioned before, this animation is independent of the movie, so don't expect to be able to sync it up with your video. It's got its own timeline, and will loop unless you put a stop() function on the last frame of the animated mask.

The vidDragMeMask() method

```
private function vidDragMeMask():Void {
    target.dragme_mc._visible = true;
    target.video_mc.setMask(target.dragme_mc);
    target.dragme_mc.onPress = function () {
        this.startDrag(false);
    };
```

```
            target.dragme_mc.onRelease = function () {
                this.stopDrag();
            };
        }
```

is very similar; it just adds drag functionality. In this code:

```
        private function clickHandler(evtObj:Object):Void {
            var mask = evtObj.target.selection.label;

            switch(mask) {
                case "Brushstroke Mask":
                    strokeHandler();
                    break;

                case "Animated Mask":
                    animHandler();
                    break;

                case "Drag-Me Mask":
                    dragMeHandler();
            }
        }
```

we set up the clickHandler() event handler for the radio buttons, and route the click to the appropriate method.

And finally, we set up the radio buttons:

```
        private function initButtons():Void {
            target.radioGroup.addEventListener("click",
    ➡ Delegate.create(this, clickHandler));
            // Radio button labels
            target.stroke_btn.label = "Brushstroke Mask";
            target.anim_btn.label = "Animated Mask";
            target.dragme_btn.label = "Drag-Me Mask";
        }
    }
```

Before testing, you'll need to set up an AS2 Flash document with some assets that the script is using. Refer to Figures 9.1–9.3 as you follow these steps:

1. Open Flash 8 and create a new ActionScript document.

2. Set the Stage size to 450 × 300.

3. From the Library menu, choose New Video (ActionScript controlled), and drag the video object onto the Stage. Give it the instance name myVid. Make the size 240 × 180.

4. With this video object selected, choose Modify > Convert to Symbol (movieclip). Name the instance video_mc.

5. If the Components window isn't already open, choose Window > Components. From the Components menu, grab a RadioButton from the User Interface list and drop it on the Stage. Name the instance stroke_btn.

6. Drag two more radio buttons and name one anim_btn and the other dragme_btn.

7. Next, make your masks. Create a new layer and call it mask1. Select the first frame of this layer. Then create an odd shape or scribble on the Stage with the Brush tool. Once you have a shape you're happy with, select it and choose Modify > Convert to Symbol. Give it the instance name stroke_mc. Place it on top of your video image, and lock the layer.

8. Create a new layer, call it mask2, and select the first frame of the layer. Next, draw a large circle, about 150 × 150 in diameter, on the Stage. Choose Modify > Convert to Symbol. With this symbol selected, choose Modify > Convert to Symbol again. Double-click to edit its timeline. Add a keyframe at frame 15. Then, click on frame 1 and change the size of the circle to 10 × 10 (making sure that you are resizing from the center; you may need to open the info panel and make sure the registration point is set to Center). Add a tween between frames 1 and 15, and go back to the main timeline. Place this symbol over the video object on the Stage, give it an instance name of anim_mc, and then lock the layer.

9. Create another new layer and call it mask3. Select the first frame of the layer and draw a small box, about 50 × 40, on top of the video object on the Stage. Select it and choose Modify > Convert to Symbol. Give it an instance name of dragme_mc.

10. Finally, create one more new layer and call it Actions. Open the Actions panel and enter the following ActionScript:

```
import FunWithMasks;
var myMasks:FunWithMasks = new FunWithMasks(this);
```

Save the FLA in the same folder as your class and test the movie. It should look something like Figure 9.1. The video should play automatically—toggle between the different masks as it plays. Cool, eh? Now let's try it in AS3.

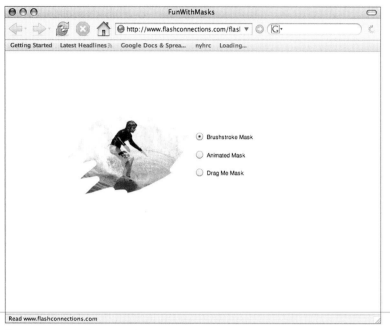

Figure 9.1 Example of a shape mask

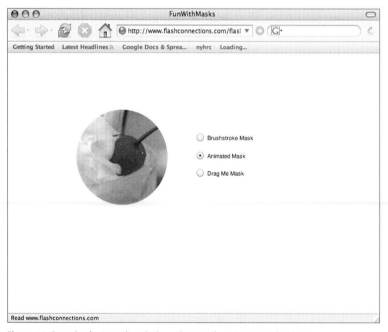

Figure 9.2 Example of animated mask; the circle grows from the center, then loops.

Figure 9.3 Example of draggable mask; the square can be dragged across the video as it plays.

ActionScript 3: *FunWithMasks.as*

In this simple AS3 example, the structure is slightly different from the AS2 version. We'll need to create some quick movieclips in Flash CS3 and import them for masks, and then create a class for each of them, in true AS3 fashion.

StrokeMask.as

First, we create the class for the stroke mask, which we'll draw on the Stage in Flash. Create a new project in Flex Builder 2 (or your AS3 editor of choice). Add a new folder in your project folder and call it FlashVideoProMasks. All your mask classes will be saved in that package. Then input the following code:

```
package FlashVideoProMasks {
    import flash.display.MovieClip;

    public class StrokeMask extends MovieClip {
        function StrokeMask(posX:Number, posY:Number) {
            this.x = posX;
            this.y = posY;
        }
    }
}
```

In this little class, we're extending the MovieClip class and placing the object on the Stage at the coordinates we'll specify in the constructor. We'll set this object up in Flash CS3 shortly, after we get our classes written. That's it for this one. Next we set up the animated mask.

AnimMask.as

Again, we set up the class in the FlashVideoProMasks package:

```
package FlashVideoProMasks {
    import flash.display.MovieClip;
    import flash.display.Sprite;
    import flash.events.Event;

    public class AnimMask extends MovieClip {
        function AnimMask(posX:Number, posY:Number) {
            this.x = posX;
            this.y = posY;
            this.addEventListener(Event.ENTER_FRAME, onEnterFrame);
        }
        public function onEnterFrame(event:Event):void {
            if(event.target.width <= 250){
                event.target.scaleX += .33;
                event.target.scaleY += .33;
            } else {
                event.target.width = 16;
                event.target.height = 16;
            }
        }
    }
}
```

Here, we import our required classes and set up a coded animation. This class will be linked to a circle that we draw on the Stage in Flash CS3. It will automatically grow from the *x* and *y* positions we specify in the constructor up to a width of 250 pixels, then back down to 16 pixels, looping continuously. That's not horribly practical, but it will give you an idea of how animated masks behave (and it will give you a teaser for our final example in this chapter, animated transitions). Next, we'll create the draggable mask.

BoxMask.as

Set this one up in the FlashVideoProMasks package as well:

```
package FlashVideoProMasks {
    import flash.display.MovieClip;
    import flash.display.Sprite;
    import flash.events.MouseEvent;

    public class BoxMask extends MovieClip {
        function BoxMask(posX:Number, posY:Number) {
            var mySprite:Sprite = new Sprite;
            mySprite.graphics.beginFill(0x555555);
            mySprite.graphics.drawRect(posX,posY,50,40);
            addChild(mySprite);
            mySprite.addEventListener(MouseEvent.MOUSE_DOWN, grab);
            mySprite.addEventListener(MouseEvent.MOUSE_UP, release);
        }
        public function grab(event:MouseEvent):void {
            event.target.startDrag();
        }
        public function release(event:MouseEvent):void {
            event.target.stopDrag();
        }
    }
}
```

Here we dynamically draw a box at the x and y coordinates specified in the constructor, then make it draggable. We could have also drawn a shape on the Stage in Flash and linked to it, as shown in the other two masks, but we thought we'd mix it up a bit.

VideoMC.as

Next, we'll create our video object:

```
package FlashVideoProMasks {
    import flash.display.MovieClip;
    import flash.display.Sprite;
    import flash.events.Event;
    import flash.net.NetConnection;
    import flash.net.NetStream;
```

```
import flash.media.Video;

public class VideoMC extends MovieClip {
    private var nc:NetConnection;
    private var ns:NetStream;
```

Everything is pretty straightforward up to this point, except you may notice here that we are extending MovieClip, not Video. This is because masks can't be applied directly to video—the video object must be inside a MovieClip, as we mentioned earlier. This is true for all the examples in this chapter.

Next, we create a Video object inside our main movieclip:

```
function VideoMC() {
    // Construct NetConnection
    var nc:NetConnection = new NetConnection();
    nc.connect(null);

    // Flash is looking for an onMetaData method,
    // route all calls to an object
    var metaObject:Object = new Object();
    metaObject.onMetaData = onMetaData;

    // Construct NetStream and connect to flow
    // through NetConnection
    var ns:NetStream;
    ns = new NetStream(nc);
    ns.bufferTime = 3;
    ns.play("video/myvideo.flv");
    // Route all onMetaData calls on NetStream
    // to the metaObject
    ns.client = metaObject;

    // Construct video object with dimensions
    var video:Video = new Video(240, 180);
    video.attachNetStream(ns);
    addChild(video);
    video.x = 100;
    video.y = 100;
}
```

```
            private function onMetaData(data:Object):void {
                // Satisfies Flash's need to send metadata with Flash Video
            }
        }
    }
```

Remember to change the video source and specify the video size, highlighted in the code.

FunWithMasks.as

Finally, we'll create our main class:

```
package {
    import flash.display.Sprite;
    import flash.net.NetConnection;
    import flash.net.NetStream;
    import flash.media.Video;
    import flash.display.MovieClip;
    import flash.events.Event;
    import FlashVideoProMasks.StrokeMask;
    import FlashVideoProMasks.BoxMask;
    import FlashVideoProMasks.AnimMask;
    import FlashVideoProMasks.VideoMC;
    import fl.controls.RadioButtonGroup;
    import fl.controls.RadioButton;
    import flash.events.MouseEvent;

    public class FunWithMasks extends Sprite {
        var anim_mc:AnimMask = new AnimMask(220,190);
        var stroke_mc:StrokeMask = new StrokeMask(90, 90);;
        var dragme_mc:BoxMask = new BoxMask(190,175);
        var video_mc:VideoMC = new VideoMC;
```

Here we import all the classes we'll need, including our newly created FlashVideoProMasks classes. Then we instantiate each one, sending the x and y parameters as required.

Next, in the constructor

```
    public function FunWithMasks() {
        var myRadioGroup:RadioButtonGroup = new
⟹ RadioButtonGroup("rbg");
        var stroke_btn:RadioButton = new RadioButton();
        var anim_btn:RadioButton = new RadioButton();
```

```
var dragme_btn:RadioButton = new RadioButton();

myRadioGroup.addEventListener(Event.CHANGE, changeHandler);

// Attach video to the NetStream,
// and add to the display list
addChild(video_mc);
addChild(stroke_mc);
addChild(dragme_mc);
addChild(anim_mc);

dragme_mc.addEventListener(MouseEvent.MOUSE_DOWN, grab);
dragme_mc.addEventListener(MouseEvent.MOUSE_UP, letgo);
dragme_mc.buttonMode = true;
}
```

We set up a new RadioButtonGroup, linking to radio buttons we'll place on the Stage, and then add an event listener to listen for changes in the radio button selection. Next, we add the objects to the display list and make the BoxMask instance draggable.

Note: In this example, we had to place RadioButton components on the Stage, specifying their parameters in Flash CS3, to have them available to the class. This was the only way to instantiate the RadioButton component code in the beta version of Flash we were working with. In subsequent versions, you should be able to instantiate with code alone.

Next, let's set up our methods:

```
private function resetMasks() {
    // Hide all masks
    stroke_mc.visible = false;
    anim_mc.visible = false;
    dragme_mc.visible = false;
}

private function strokeHandler() {
    // Make only our stroke mask visible, then apply it
    resetMasks();
    stroke_mc.visible = true;
    video_mc.mask = stroke_mc;
}
```

```
private function animHandler() {
    // Make only our animated mask visible, then apply it
    resetMasks();
    anim_mc.visible = true;
    video_mc.mask = anim_mc;
}

private function dragMeHandler() {
    // Make only our draggable mask visible, then apply it
    resetMasks();
    dragme_mc.visible = true;
    video_mc.mask = dragme_mc;
}

private function changeHandler(event:Event):void {
    var rbg:RadioButtonGroup = event.target as
RadioButtonGroup;
    switch (rbg.selection) {
        case stroke_btn:
        trace("stroke");
        strokeHandler();
        break;
    case anim_btn:
        trace("anim");
        animHandler();
        break;
    case dragme_btn:
        trace("dragme");
        dragMeHandler();
        break;
    }
}

public function grab(event:MouseEvent):void {
    event.target.startDrag();
}
```

```
        public function letgo(event:MouseEvent):void {
            event.target.stopDrag();
        }
    }
}
```

The changeHandler() method triggers the appropriate masking method, which hides all other mask instances and applies the chosen mask.

Next, we set up our assets in Flash CS3. Set up a new AS3 document and follow these steps:

1. Grab a RadioButton component from the Component Library and drag it onto the Stage. Give it the instance name stroke_btn and set the label parameter to Brushstroke Mask. Drag a second instance and name it anim_btn with a label of Animated Mask. Drag one more and give it an instance name of dragme_btn with a label of Drag Me Mask. Set the groupName parameter of each radio button to rbg.

2. Draw a scribble about the size of your video on the Stage with the Paintbrush tool. Make it a movieclip symbol and delete it from the Stage. Select it in the Library and choose Linkage from the library's dropdown menu. Select Export for ActionScript and Export in First Frame. Enter FlashVideoProMasks.StrokeMask for the class; leave flash.display.MovieClip as the base class.

3. Draw a 16 × 16 circle on the Stage and convert it to a movieclip symbol, setting its registration point to Center. Delete it from the Stage. Select it in the Library and choose Linkage. Select Export for ActionScript and Export in First Frame. Give it a class assignment of FlashVideoProMasks.AnimMask with a base class of flash.display.MovieClip.

4. On the main Stage, enter FunWithMasks as the document class in the Properties panel.

5. Save the FLA in the same folder as your main class, and test your movie. It should look something like Figures 9.1–9.3 earlier in the chapter.

Feel free to play around with masking. It can be very useful when creating custom video players and other integrated video in websites. We use it often for custom frames and even for straightforward players (Figure 9.4). Just adding rounded corners to a video can add to the design of your player. You can quickly break video out of its "box"—which, after all, is one of the strong points of Flash video. Later in this chapter, we'll show you how to use animated masks for transitions between video clips.

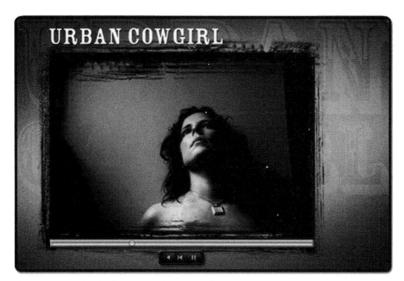

Figure 9.4 Example of a player design that uses masks

Alpha Channels, Revisited

Back in Chapter 2, we talked about how to create and encode alpha channel video. Now let's take a look at what a video with an alpha channel looks like in Flash (see Figure 9.5). You may recognize the signature "Bettina" video from Adobe's alpha channel demos. Here she's placed on a gradient background and is admiring some fine nature photography.

Figure 9.5 Video with alpha channel transparency on a gradient background

There's really no difference, from a code perspective, between a normal FLV and one with an alpha channel. In our example, the FLV is just attached to a video object on the Stage, with the other elements on layers behind it. In most cases, you'll be attaching alpha channel video to a video object rather than in an FLVPlayback component, since there's usually no need for playback controls on transparent video.

You can also add filters to alpha channel video—the drop shadow filter can be especially useful here. (See Figure 9.6 to see Bettina with a pretty realistic shadow that follows her as she walks across the scene.) This can be added in the Filters panel of the Flash IDE, or can be added through ActionScript, as you'll see in the next section. Let's bust apart another "switcher" application, one that demonstrates some cool filters you might use for video (including that nifty drop shadow).

Figure 9.6 Video with alpha channel transparency and a drop shadow filter

Fun with Filters and Tints

Filters and tints can add aesthetic value to your video, giving it a specific look and feel based on other dynamic elements in your SWF. For example, if the background color is dark brown, your video could be tinted gold, then change to dark green when the background color changes to yellow. Or maybe you need a dynamic drop shadow around the player that changes its size depending on how far it is from the background, to reinforce the appearance of depth in a 3-D scene. In one of our applications, the client wanted the colors in the video to blast out to a blue-white, then fade to black when a button on the page was clicked. This could only be achieved through scripted filters.

With both Flash 8 and Flash CS3, you have the following filters and effects available to play with:

- flash.filters.BevelFilter
- flash.filters.BlurFilter
- flash.filters.ColorMatrixFilter
- flash.filters.ConvolutionFilter
- flash.filters.DisplacementMapFilter
- flash.filters.DropShadowFilter
- flash.filters.GlowFilter

- flash.filters.GradientBevelFilter
- flash.filters.GradientGlowFilter
- flash.geom.ColorTransform

Any of these can be applied to video; however, in the interest of good taste, there are only a few that you may use often. DropShadowFilter, ColorTransform, and ColorMatrixFilter are three that we've used effectively with video. Some of the others, like BevelFilter and GradientGlowFilter, might come in handy for some specialized applications, but we haven't found any practical uses for them yet. It's just good to know they are there if you ever need to make a video appear slightly three-dimensional with a psychedelic glow around it. Hey, you never know.

Note: Each filter has parameters you can set that determine the quality and intensity of the filter. Use the lowest settings you can to achieve your desired effect. High settings will likely begin to slow down the performance of your application, as they often involve applying a transformation in several iterations.

In this example, we'll alter our "switcher" application to toggle between some different filter effects: ColorMatrixFilter, ColorTransform, BlurFilter, and DropShadowFilter (Figure 9.7). Let's step through the code so you can see how the filters are applied and what their parameters are.

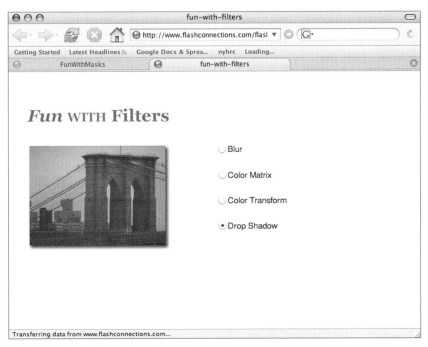

Figure 9.7 Sample application demonstrating filter effects

ActionScript 2: *FunWithFilters.as*

As always, we'll import some classes we'll need. You'll see some new ones here, from the filters and geom packages. Starting in Eclipse or your favorite ActionScript editor, create the following class:

```
import flash.filters.BlurFilter;
import flash.filters.DropShadowFilter;
import flash.filters.ColorMatrixFilter;
import flash.geom.ColorTransform;
import flash.geom.Transform;
import mx.utils.Delegate;
import mx.controls.RadioButtonGroup;
import mx.controls.RadioButton;

class FunWithFilters {
    var target:MovieClip;
    var video_mc:MovieClip;
    var nc:NetConnection;
    var ns:NetStream;
    var myVid:Video;
    var colorTransform_btn:RadioButton;
    var blur_btn:RadioButton;
    var colorMatrix_btn:RadioButton;
    var dropShadow_btn:RadioButton;
```

Here, as in the previous example, we hook up a simple video object (don't forget to change the video name to one of your own):

```
public function FunWithFilters(target_mc:MovieClip) {
    target = target_mc;
    // Construct NetConnection
    nc = new NetConnection();
    nc.connect(null);
    // Construct NetStream and connect to flow
    // through NetConnection
    var ns:NetStream = new NetStream(nc);
    // Attach NetStream to movieclip containing
    // video object on the stage
    target.video_mc.myVid.attachVideo(ns);
    target.video_mc.bufferTime = 7;
    // Tell the NetStream which FLV to play
```

```
ns.play("sl_sm.flv");

    initButtons();
}
```

Here we create a method that resets the various filter settings when toggling between filters. Each filter has different parameters, as you can see:

```
private function resetFilters():Void {
    vidColorTransform(_level0,1,1,1,1,1,1,1,1);
    var matrix:Array = new Array();
    matrix = matrix([]);
    vidColorMatrix(matrix);
    dropShadow(0,0,0,0,0,0,0,0);
    vidBlur(0,0,0);
}
```

Next are the event handlers for the radio button selections. Each one first resets the filters applied to the video to their default values, then triggers the appropriate filter method, sending it parameters that control the look of the filter. If you want to play with the filter settings you'd do that here:

```
function blurHandler(evt_obj:Object):Void {
    resetFilters();
    vidBlur(20,0,5);
}

function colorTransformHandler(evt_obj:Object):Void {
    resetFilters();
    vidColorTransform(1,1,1,1,0,0,255,0);
}

function colorMatrixHandler(evt_obj:Object):Void {
    resetFilters();
    var matrix:Array = new Array();
    matrix = matrix.concat([0, 0, 0, 3, 3]); // red
    matrix = matrix.concat([1, 1, 0, 0, 1]); // green
    matrix = matrix.concat([1, 1, 0, 0, 0]); // blue
    matrix = matrix.concat([0, 0, 0, .7, .2]); // alpha
    vidColorMatrix(matrix);
}
```

```
function dropShadowHandler(evt_obj:Object):Void {
    resetFilters();
    dropShadow(4,45,0x777777,30,5,5,1,2);
}
```

Now things get interesting. We start with the dropShadow() method:

```
private function dropShadow(distance:Number,angle:Number,
➠ color:Number, alpha:Number,blurX:Number,blurY:Number,strength:
➠ Number,quality:Number):Void {
    var myDSFilter:DropShadowFilter =
➠ new DropShadowFilter(distance,angle,color,alpha,blurX,blurY,
➠ strength, quality);
    var myDSFilterArray:Array = new Array();
    myDSFilterArray.push(myDSFilter);
    target.video_mc.filters = myDSFilterArray;
}
```

The parameters that control the appearance of the drop shadow are passed to this method: distance, angle, color, alpha, blurX, blurY, strength, and quality. (Other optional parameters for this filter are hideObject, inner, and knockout, but for the purposes of this demo, we didn't use them.) First, we instantiate a filter, passing in the parameters. Then we create an array, myDSFilterArray, to hold the parameter data. Then, this array is applied to the movieclip that holds our video object. Note that you cannot edit the filter array directly; you have to edit the filter parameters, then pass that into the array, which is then applied to the object. It's a bit convoluted, but you get the picture.

Note: If you are attempting to apply multiple filters to an object using its filter array, you'll need to track the type of filter assigned to each array index. The only way to do this is to maintain your own array of filters and use this to track the type of filter associated with each array index. Unfortunately, there's nothing built into ActionScript to do this for you. So, while it is possible to stack filters, it gets tricky if their parameters are set in the filter array for the object.

Next is the method for adding a blur:

```
private function vidBlur(x:Number,y:Number,quality:Number): Void {
    //BlurFilter(x, y, quality)
    var myFilter:BlurFilter = new BlurFilter(x,y,quality);
    var myFilterArray:Array = new Array();
    myFilterArray.push(myFilter);
    target.video_mc.filters = myFilterArray;
}
```

This is one of our favorites. You can add an overall image blur, or by just setting an x or y blur, create a motion blur. In this example, we create a horizontal motion blur. The parameters for the BlurFilter are blurX, blurY, and quality. The x and y settings control the amount of blur in each direction, from 0 to 255, with a default value of 4. The quality parameter specifies how many times to perform the blur. We recommend a quality value of 2 or 3 in most cases. If you want more blur, you're better off using a higher blur amount instead.

Note: BlurFilter x and y values that are a power of 2 (2, 4, 8, 16, 32, etc.) are optimized to render faster than other values. Always use a value that is the power of 2 for blur amounts!

Next we move on to the ColorTransform filter method:

```
    private function vidColorTransform
➟ (ax:Number,ao:Number,blue:Number,green:
➟ Number,greeno:Number,red:Number,redo:Number,rgb:Number):Void {
        var trans:Transform = new Transform(target.video_mc);
        var colorTrans:ColorTransform =
➟ newColorTransform(ax,ao,blue,green,greeno,
➟ red,redo,rgb);
        trans.colorTransform = colorTrans;
    }
```

The ColorTransform method universally adjusts the colors of the target movieclip (and the video inside). The parameters of ColorTransform are a bit complex, because they are passed in as a matrix. Explaining matrices is beyond the scope of this book, so we'll let you play with these settings on your own. If you're going to use this filter, it is well documented in the Flash help files. If you'd just like to play around with it, try changing the values being sent in to this method and see how it affects the appearance of the video.

Another filter that uses a matrix, ColorMatrixFilter, gives you even more control over the appearance of the target movieclip (or bitmap) and its contents:

```
    private function vidColorMatrix(matrix):Void {
        //create the filter
        var myCMFilter:ColorMatrixFilter = new ColorMatrixFilter(matrix);
        //apply the filter
        var myCMArray:Array = new Array();
        myCMArray.push(myCMFilter);
        target.video_mc.filters = myCMArray;
    }
```

Again using a matrix to pass in values, this filter gives you control over saturation, hue rotation, luminance, and alpha.

 Note: ColorMatrixFilter can be processor intensive, because it applies the matrix transformation to each pixel of the video and turns on cacheAsBitmap automatically when invoked (which can increase processing load significantly). Use with caution—but darn, is it cool.

```
private function clickHandler(evtObj:Object):Void {
    var effect = evtObj.target.selection.label;

    switch(effect) {
        case "Blur":
            blurHandler();
            break;

        case "Color Transform":
            colorTransformHandler();
            break;

        case "Color Matrix":
            colorMatrixHandler();
            break;

        case "Drop Shadow":
            dropShadowHandler();
    }
}
private function initButtons():Void {
    target.radioGroup.addEventListener("click",
 Delegate.create(this, clickHandler));
    // Radio button labels
    target.blur_btn.label = "Blur";
    target.colorTransform_btn.label = "Color Transform";
    target.colorMatrix_btn.label = "Color Matrix";
    target.dropShadow_btn.label = "Drop Shadow";
}
```

These last two methods just deal with the radio button selection and interface setup. Before you can test this code, you'll have to create a new Flash document with assets we'll be using:

1. Open Flash 8 and create a new ActionScript document.

2. Set the Stage size to 450 × 300.

3. From the Library menu, choose New Video (ActionScript controlled) and drag the video object onto the Stage. Give it the instance name myVid. Make the size 240 × 180.

4. With this video object selected, choose Modify > Convert to Symbol. Name the instance video_mc.

5. If the Components window isn't already open, choose Window > Components. From the Components menu, grab a RadioButton from the User Interface list and drop it on the Stage. Name the instance blur_btn.

6. Drag three more radio buttons and name one colorMatrix_btn, the second color-Transform_btn, and the third dropShadow_btn.

7. Finally, create a new layer and call it Actions. Open the Actions panel and enter the following ActionScript:

```
import FunWithFilters;
var myFilters:FunWithFilters = new FunWithFilters(this);
```

Save the FLA in the same folder as your main class and test the movie. It should look something like Figure 9.7. Like the mask example, the video should play automatically—switch between the different filters and see how it changes the look of the video. Use your imagination, play with the settings, and always be mindful of application performance.

ActionScript 3: *FunWithFilters.as*

In the AS3 example, we'll have two classes: our main FunWithFilters class and the VideoMC class. (The code is similar to the AS2 example, so refer to the notes in the previous section for more detail.)

VideoMC.as

Let's start with the video movieclip class:

```
package FlashVideoProFilters {
    import flash.display.MovieClip;
    import flash.display.Sprite;
    import flash.events.Event;
    import flash.net.NetConnection;
    import flash.net.NetStream;
```

```
import flash.media.Video;

public class VideoMC extends MovieClip {
    private var nc:NetConnection;
    private var ns:NetStream;

    function VideoMC() {
        // Construct NetConnection
        var nc:NetConnection = new NetConnection();
        nc.connect(null);

        // Flash is looking for an onMetaData method,
        // route all calls to an object
        var metaObject:Object = new Object();
        metaObject.onMetaData = onMetaData;

        // Construct NetStream and connect to
        // flow through NetConnection
        var ns:NetStream;
        ns = new NetStream(nc);
        ns.bufferTime = 3;
        ns.play("video/myvideo.flv");
        // Route all onMetaData calls on NetStream to the metaObject
        ns.client = metaObject;

        // Construct video object with dimensions
        var video:Video = new Video(240, 180);
        video.attachNetStream(ns);
        addChild(video);
        video.x = 100;
        video.y = 100;

    }
    private function onMetaData(data:Object):void {
        // Satisfies Flash's need to send metadata with Flash Video
    }
}
}
```

This class is pretty simple; we're just extending MovieClip and instantiating a video object. Don't forget to change the size and video source (highlighted in the previous code) to your own.

FunWithFilters.as

Next, let's dive into the main class:

```
package {
    import flash.display.Sprite;
    import flash.net.NetConnection;
    import flash.net.NetStream;
    import flash.media.Video;
    import flash.display.MovieClip;
    import flash.events.Event;
    import FlashVideoProFilters.VideoMC;
    import fl.controls.RadioButtonGroup;
    import fl.controls.RadioButton;
    import flash.events.MouseEvent;
    import flash.filters.BlurFilter;
    import flash.filters.DropShadowFilter;
    import flash.filters.ColorMatrixFilter;
    import flash.geom.ColorTransform;
    import flash.geom.Transform;

    public class FunWithFilters extends Sprite {
        var video_mc:VideoMC = new VideoMC;

        public function FunWithFilters() {
            var myRadioGroup:RadioButtonGroup = new
➡ RadioButtonGroup("rbg");
            var colorTransform_btn:RadioButton = new RadioButton();
            var blur_btn:RadioButton = new RadioButton();
            var colorMatrix_btn:RadioButton = new RadioButton();
            var dropShadow_btn:RadioButton = new RadioButton();

            myRadioGroup.addEventListener
➡ (Event.CHANGE, changeHandler);
            addChild(video_mc);
        }
```

First, we import the filters along with the other packages we'll be using. Then we move on to the constructor where we instantiate the video movieclip object, link to the radio buttons we'll be placing on the Stage, add an event listener, and add our video_mc to the display object. Next, we move on to the methods:

```
private function resetFilters() {
        // Reset all filters to default values
        vidColorTransform(1,1,1,1,1,1,1,1);
        var CMmatrix:Array = new Array();
        CMmatrix = [];
        vidColorMatrix(CMmatrix);
        vidDropShadow(0,0,0,0,0,0,0,0);
        vidBlur(0,0,0);
}


private function vidBlur(x:Number,y:Number,quality:Number) {
        // Instantiate filter, push into array and apply
        var myFilter:BlurFilter = new BlurFilter(x,y,quality);
        var myFilterArray:Array = new Array();
        myFilterArray.push(myFilter);
        video_mc.filters = myFilterArray;
}


private function vidColorTransform(ax:Number,ao:Number,
blue:Number,green:Number,greeno:Number,red:Number,
redo:Number,rgb:Number) {
        // Instantiate transform and filter, then apply
        var trans:Transform = new Transform(video_mc);
        var colorTrans:ColorTransform = new ColorTransform(ax,ao,
blue,green,greeno,red,redo,rgb);
        trans.colorTransform = colorTrans;
}


private function vidColorMatrix(CMmatrix:Array) {
        // Instantiate filter, push into array and apply
        var myCMFilter:ColorMatrixFilter = new
ColorMatrixFilter(CMmatrix);
        var myCMArray:Array = new Array();
        myCMArray.push(myCMFilter);
        video_mc.filters = myCMArray;
}
```

```
      private function vidDropShadow(distance:Number,angle:Number,
➡ color:Number,alpha:Number,blurX:Number,blurY:Number,
➡ strength:Number,quality:Number) {
          // Instantiate filter, push into array and apply
          var myDSFilter:DropShadowFilter = new
➡ DropShadowFilter(distance,angle,color,alpha,
➡ blurX,blurY,strength,quality);
          var myDSFilterArray:Array = new Array();
          myDSFilterArray.push(myDSFilter);
          video_mc.filters = myDSFilterArray;
      }


      // The following methods clear the current filter and
      // call selected method, passing filter parameters
      private function blurHandler() {
          resetFilters();
          vidBlur(20,0,5);
      }


      private function colorTransformHandler() {
          resetFilters();
          vidColorTransform(1,1,1,1,0,0,255,0);
      }


      private function colorMatrixHandler() {
          resetFilters();
          var CMmatrix:Array = new Array();
          CMmatrix = CMmatrix.concat([0, 0, 0, 3, 3]); // red
          CMmatrix = CMmatrix.concat([1, 1, 0, 0, 1]); // green
          CMmatrix = CMmatrix.concat([1, 1, 0, 0, 0]); // blue
          CMmatrix = CMmatrix.concat([0, 0, 0, .7, .2]); // alpha
          vidColorMatrix(CMmatrix);
      }


      private function dropShadowHandler() {
          resetFilters();
          vidDropShadow(4,45,0x777777,30,5,5,1,2);
      }


      private function changeHandler(event:Event):void {
```

```
                      var rbg:RadioButtonGroup = event.target as
➦ RadioButtonGroup;
                    switch (rbg.selection) {
                       case colorTransform_btn:
                          colorTransformHandler();
                          break;
                       case colorMatrix_btn:
                          colorMatrixHandler();
                          break;
                       case blur_btn:
                          blurHandler();
                          break;
                       case dropShadow_btn:
                          dropShadowHandler();
                          break;
                    }
                 }
              }
           }
```

The specifics of each filter function are fundamentally the same as for the AS2 version. Refer to that version for more detail about what's happening with each filter. Next, you'll need to create a Flash CS3 FLA.

1. Grab a radio button component from the Component Library and drag it onto the Stage. Give it the instance name blur_btn and make the label parameter Blur. Drag a second instance and name it colorTransform_btn, with a label of Color Transform. Drag a third and give it an instance name of colorMatrix_btn with a label of Color Matrix. Drag one more and give it an instance name of dropShadow_btn with a label of Drop Shadow. Assign a groupName value of rbg to each radio button.

2. On the main Stage, make the Document Class FunWithFilters.

Save the FLA in the same folder as your main class and test the SWF. It should look something like Figure 9.7. You can see how filters (especially the motion blur) could potentially be used in place of encoded transitions (which often don't encode well, requiring high bit rates). So, let's see how to create transitions, shall we?

Lost in Transitions

Quite often, you'll have an application that switches from one video to another. You could just change immediately from one to the next as if you were changing the channel on a TV, but what fun is that? More likely, you'll want some sort of transition from one to the other. There are numerous ways to do this, but we've chosen a simple wipe to demonstrate here (Figure 9.8).

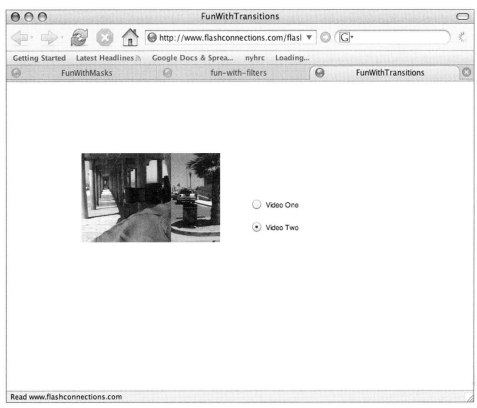

Figure 9.8 Example application with animated wipe between two videos

Let's take a look at how it's done.

ActionScript 2: *FunWithTransitions.as*

First, we import the classes we'll need—nothing too fancy here. We'll again be using radio buttons, and we'll introduce the DepthManager class to control which video is on top during our transitions. Here, we declare our variables:

```
import mx.utils.Delegate;
import mx.controls.RadioButtonGroup;
import mx.controls.RadioButton;
import mx.managers.DepthManager;

class FunWithTransitions {
```

```
var target:MovieClip;
var videoOne_mc:MovieClip;
var videoTwo_mc:MovieClip;
var nc:NetConnection;
var ns:NetStream;
var myVid:Video;

var wipe_mc:MovieClip;

var vidNameOne:String;
var vidNameTwo:String;

public function FunWithTransitions(target_mc:MovieClip):Void {
    target = target_mc;
    // Hide masks
    resetMasks();
    // Construct NetConnection
    nc = new NetConnection();
    nc.connect(null);
    // Construct NetStream and connect to
    //flow through NetConnection
    ns = new NetStream(nc);
    // Specify video filenames
    vidNameOne = "battle1.flv";
    vidNameTwo = "myvideo.flv";
    // Play first video
    vidPlay(target.videoOne_mc, vidNameOne);
    initButtons();
}
```

Then moving on to the constructor, we set up the application with a NetConnection and NetStream, and specify the video filenames. Now, on to the methods:

```
function vidOneHandler(evt_obj:Object):Void {
    vidShow(target.videoOne_mc, vidNameOne);
}

function vidTwoHandler(evt_obj:Object):Void {
    vidShowtarget.videoTwo_mc, vidNameTwo);
}
```

Here we handle the radio button click events. When you choose a video, the vidShow method is called, passing the target movieclip names and the name of the video to play. (The vidShow method doesn't actually play the video just yet, though—it triggers a "transition" wipe between the two videos.)

Next, we make sure the mask movieclip is hidden:

```
private function resetMasks():Void {
    target.wipe_mc._visible = false;
}
```

This is the method that plays the new video that's been chosen:

```
private function vidPlay(targetVid:MovieClip,
➠ vidName:String):Void {
    // Remove the old video from the video object
    targetVid.myVid.attachVideo(null);
    // Attach NetStream to movieclip containing
    // video object on the stage
    targetVid.myVid.attachVideo(ns);
    // Tell the NetStream which FLV to play
    ns.play(vidName);
}
```

First we remove the old video from the myVid video object, then attach the NetStream to the current video object, and tell the NetStream which video file to play.

Here's where our transition magic happens:

```
private function vidShow(targetVid:MovieClip,
➠ vidName:String):Void {
    // Make the new video and its wipe mask visible
    targetVid._visible = true;
    target.wipe_mc._visible = true;
    // Mask the new video, then play it
    targetVid.setMask(target.wipe_mc);
    vidPlay(targetVid, vidName);
    target.wipe_mc.gotoAndPlay(1);
    // Move the new video on top
    targetVid.setDepthTo(DepthManager.kTop);
}
```

This method is called before the vidPlay method, wiping away the old video to reveal the new one. To do this, first we make the new video and its mask visible, and then apply the mask. We start the new video playing by triggering the vidPlay method; then we play the wipe animation inside the video's mask. Finally, we make sure the new video is on top, and voilá!

These last two methods just handle the radio button functionality, allowing us to switch betwéen the two videos:

```
private function clickHandler(evtObj:Object):Void {
    if(evtObj.target.selection.label == "Video One") {
        vidOneHandler();
    }
    else {
        vidTwoHandler();
    }
}


private function initButtons():Void {
    target.radioGroup.addEventListener("click",
➡ Delegate.create(this, clickHandler));
    // Radio button labels
    target.videoOne_btn.label = "Video One";
    target.videoTwo_btn.label = "Video Two";
    // Preselect the radio button for the first video
    target.videoOne_btn.selected = true;
}
}
```

Before you can test the code, you'll need to set up a few assets in a Flash document:

1. Open Flash 8 and create a new ActionScript document.

2. Set the Stage size to 450 × 300.

3. From the Library menu, choose New Video (ActionScript controlled) and drag the video object onto the Stage. Give it the instance name myVid. Make the size 240 × 180.

4. With this video object selected, choose Modify > Convert to Symbol (movie clip). Name the instance videoOne_mc.

5. Select the movieclip you just created and choose Edit > Copy. Create a new layer on the timeline above the current one, and call it Video 2. Click on the first frame of that layer, and choose Edit > Paste in Place. Name that new instance videoTwo_mc.

6. If the Components window isn't already open, choose Window > Components. From the Components menu, grab a RadioButton from the User Interface list and drop it on the Stage. Name the instance videoOne_btn.

7. Drag another and name it videoTwo_btn.

8. Next, we'll create our wipe animation. Create a new layer and call it Mask. Select the first frame of that layer and draw a 240 × 180 box. Select it and choose Modify > Convert to Symbol (movie clip). Select it and position it directly on top of your video objects. Give it an instance name of wipe_mc. Double-click it to edit its timeline. Click on frame 15 of the timeline and choose Insert > Timeline > Keyframe. Open the Actions panel and type stop();.

9. Click on frame 1 and Shift-drag the box to the left until it is no longer covering the video objects. Select Insert > Timeline > Create Motion Tween.

10. Finally, return to your main timeline. Create a new layer and call it Actions. Open the Actions panel and enter the following ActionScript:

```
import FunWithTransitions;
var myFilters:FunWithTransitions = new FunWithTransitions(this);
```

Test your movie. The first video should play automatically. Choose Video Two and the current video will pause; then the wipe animation will play, revealing the new video. Now, let's try it in ActionScript 3.

ActionScript 3: *FunWithTransitions.as*

In our AS3 example, we'll start with the VideoMC class, to which we've made a few adjustments.

VideoMC.as

Create a new AS3 class in your favorite editor and enter the following code:

```
package FlashVideoProTrans {

    import flash.display.MovieClip;
    import flash.display.Sprite;
    import flash.events.Event;
    import flash.media.Video;
    import flash.net.NetConnection;
    import flash.net.NetStream;

    public class VideoMC extends MovieClip {
        private var vid:Video;
        private var nc:NetConnection;
        private var ns:NetStream;
        private var meta:Object;
        private var vidName:String;
```

```
public function VideoMC(vidName:String) {
    // Construct NetConnection
    nc = new NetConnection();
    nc.connect(null);
    // Flash is looking for an onMetaData method,
    //route all calls to an object
    meta = new Object();
    meta.onMetaData = onMetaData;
    // Construct NetStream and connect to
    //flow through NetConnection
    ns = new NetStream(nc);
    ns.bufferTime = 3;
    // Route all onMetaData calls on NetStream to the metaObject
    ns.client = meta;
    // Construct video object with dimensions
    vid = new Video(240, 180);
    vid.attachNetStream(ns);
    addChild(vid);
    vid.x = 100;
    vid.y = 100;
    startVideo(vidName);
}
```

Here, since we'll have more than one video in this example, we'll want to pass in a video name to our constructor as a parameter. We're still hard-coding the dimensions here, but you could of course pass those in as a parameter as well if you like. Then, we set up two methods:

```
public function stopVideo():void {
    ns.close();
}
public function startVideo(vidName):void {
    ns.play(vidName);
}
public function onMetaData(data:Object):void {
    // Satisfies Flash's need to send
    // metadata with Flash Video
}
    }
}
```

We'll want to be able to control the video from our main class, so we create methods to stop and start the video. Create a FlashVideoProTrans package folder inside your FunWithTransition project folder, and save this class inside FlashVideoProTrans. Now, on to our transition mask class.

TransitionMask.as

Here we extend MovieClip and draw a box the same size as our movie. (Don't forget to change these values if you changed the default movie size in VideoMC.) We add the box to the display list, and trigger the startWipe function to animate the transition:

```
package FlashVideoProTrans {
    import flash.display.MovieClip;
    import flash.display.Sprite;
    import flash.events.Event;

    public class TransitionMask extends MovieClip {
        var mySprite:Sprite = new Sprite;
        function TransitionMask(posX:Number, posY:Number) {
            this.x = posX;
            this.y = posY;
            mySprite.graphics.beginFill(0x555555);
            mySprite.graphics.drawRect(posX,posY,240,180);
            addChild(mySprite);
            startWipe();
        }
        public function onEnterFrame(event:Event):void {
            if(event.target.x >= -189){
                event.target.x -= 10;
            } else {
                event.target.x = -190;
                stopWipe();
            }
        }
        public function startWipe():void {
            this.x = 50;
            this.addEventListener(Event.ENTER_FRAME, onEnterFrame);
        }
        public function stopWipe():void {
            this.removeEventListener(Event.ENTER_FRAME, onEnterFrame);
        }
    }
}
```

The onEnterFrame method is set up and is turned "on" and "off" by calling the startWipe or stopWipe methods on the object, respectively. Save this file in the FlashVideoProTrans package folder.

FunWithTransitions.as

Now, let's put it all together in our main class:

```
package {
    import flash.display.Sprite;
    import flash.net.NetConnection;
    import flash.net.NetStream;
    import flash.media.Video;
    import flash.display.MovieClip;
    import flash.events.Event;
    import fl.controls.RadioButtonGroup;
    import fl.controls.RadioButton;
    import flash.events.MouseEvent;
    import FlashVideoProTrans.VideoMC;
    import FlashVideoProTrans.TransitionMask;

    public class FunWithTransitions extends Sprite {
        var wipe_mc:TransitionMask = new TransitionMask(290,50);
        var vidNameOne:String = new String;
        var vidNameTwo:String = new String;
        var videoOne_mc:VideoMC = new VideoMC(null);
        var videoTwo_mc:VideoMC = new VideoMC(null);

        public function FunWithTransitions() {
            var myRadioGroup:RadioButtonGroup = new
            RadioButtonGroup("rbg");
            var videoOne_btn:RadioButton = new RadioButton();
            var videoTwo_btn:RadioButton = new RadioButton();

            myRadioGroup.addEventListener(Event.CHANGE, changeHandler);

            // Add to the display list
            addChild(videoOne_mc);
            addChild(videoTwo_mc);
        }
```

Here we're importing our classes, and instantiating our transition mask, placing it just to the right of where our video movieclips will be, along with the other objects we'll be using. Then, in the constructor, we initialize our radio buttons, adding an event handler and adding our video movieclips to the display object. Next, we move on to where the action is—our methods:

```
        private function vidPlay(targetVid:VideoMC,
⇒ stopVid:VideoMC, vidName:String):void {
            // Play the selected video, stop the other video
            targetVid.startVideo(vidName);
            stopVid.stopVideo();
        }


        private function vidShow(targetVid:VideoMC,
⇒ stopVid:VideoMC, vidName:String):void {
            // Show the selected video
            vidPlay(targetVid, stopVid, vidName);
            // Trigger the transition animation
            wipe_mc.startWipe();
            // Move the new video to the top
            addChild(targetVid);
            addChild(wipe_mc);
            // Apply the mask
            targetVid.mask = wipe_mc;
        }
        // Radio button handlers
        private function vidOneHandler():void {
            vidShow(videoOne_mc, videoTwo_mc, "video/battle1.flv");
        }
        private function vidTwoHandler():void {
            vidShow(videoTwo_mc, videoOne_mc, "video/myvideo.flv");
        }
        private function changeHandler(event:Event):void {
            var rbg:RadioButtonGroup = event.target as RadioButtonGroup;
            switch (rbg.selection) {
                case videoOne_btn:
                vidOneHandler();
                break;
```

```
            case videoTwo_btn:
                vidTwoHandler();
                break;
            }
        }
    }
}
```

Save this file in your main FunWithTransitions project folder. Then, open Flash CS3 and follow these steps:

1. Grab a radio button component from the Component Library and drag it onto the Stage. Give it the instance name videoOne_btn and make the label parameter Video One. Drag a second instance and name it videoTwo_btn, with a label of Video Two. Give both buttons a groupName parameter of rbg.

2. On the main Stage, make the Document Class FunWithTransitions.

Save the FLA in the same folder as your main class and publish the SWF. Click the first radio button and the first video will play. Choose the second one and you'll see the wipe animation, giving you a transition from the old video to the new. This effect can be integrated into an existing player or playlist, and can be adapted to almost any kind of animation you'd like. In Chapter 11, when we talk about the bitmap object, we'll revisit this little transition script, adding a dissolve between videos.

Summary

In this chapter you learned about filters and transitions, and how they can be applied to video. We hope you had a little fun playing with the filter settings in the example apps as well. You should now understand:

- What can and can't be done to video
- When filters are appropriate, and when you should apply effects in postproduction
- Different types of masks and how to apply them
- The difference between masks and alpha channel video
- What filters are available and how to apply them
- How to create a simple transition between videos in a playlist

In the next chapter, we'll take a close look at the bitmap object and see how it can be used with video to create some innovative video applications.

Video and the BitmapData Object

Moving images are great, but sometimes you just want a still. Well, in Flash 8 and above, you can now directly access the values of displayed pixels, save them, and further manipulate the resulting image using the BitmapData *object.*

Do you ever find yourself needing a still image to use as a thumbnail preview? Or maybe you want to grab snapshots from a video as it plays. Using the BitmapData *object and its methods, you can do all this and more. Applying filters to the images you capture, you can transition from one bitmap to another using dissolves or color fills. We'll even create an application that takes snapshots from a webcam, just like an old-style photo booth. Let's take a closer look at what* BitmapData *objects are and how they can be used to enhance your Flash video applications.*

10

Chapter Contents
What Is This BitmapData Object, and Why Should I Care?
Dynamic Thumbnails: Video Snapshots
Transitions and Dissolves
The FotoBooth Application

What Is This *BitmapData* Object, and Why Should I Care?

The BitmapData object, introduced in Flash 8, is available in both AS2 and AS3. It basically allows you to take a "snapshot" of any object or area of your SWF (yes, including video!), and save it as bitmap data. This resulting bitmap object can be either opaque or transparent (containing alpha channel data), and it can be manipulated in a number of ways, including using Flash's filter effects.

Note: To be saved as bitmap data, an object must be visible.

Well, this is all good and well, you say...but we're working with video here! What can BitmapData do for you? Well, you already saw some of the possibilities back in Chapter 9, when we covered filter effects. Filter effects can be used on BitmapData in the same way, applying color tints and other transformations to a captured bitmap. And we'll be covering even more specific uses in this chapter, such as creating video transitions, capturing thumbnails—even taking snapshots from a webcam. So what exactly is a BitmapData object?

A BitmapData object is an array of pixel data. It is composed of 32-bit integers, with each one describing one pixel in the bitmap. The code for instantiating a BitmapData object in both ActionScript 2 and 3 is as follows:

```
var myBitmapData:BitmapData = new BitmapData(width:Number, height:Number,
    transparent:Boolean, fillColor:Number);
```

The only difference between AS2 and AS3 implementation is the fillColor data type: it's Number in AS2 and uint in AS3.

Note: The maximum width or height of a BitmapData object is 2880. Also worth noting: Once you create an opaque bitmap, you're committed—you can't change it to transparent, or vice versa.

There are different ways to proceed from here, depending on your ActionScript version. In AS2, to display the BitmapData object on the Stage you can attach it to a MovieClip object by using the MovieClip.attachBitmap() method. Or, if you just want to fill an area in a MovieClip, you can use the MovieClip.beginBitmapFill() method. In AS3, the technique is slightly different—you need to assign the BitmapData object to a Bitmap object, either in its constructor or by assigning it to the Bitmap object's bitmapData property. Then, of course, you'll have to add the Bitmap instance to the display list to show it on the Stage.

So, in AS2, the following code would create a new BitmapData object called myBitmapData that is 100 pixels wide by 80 pixels high, is opaque with a background color of red, and is attached to a MovieClip object called mySnapshot:

```
import flash.display.BitmapData;
var myBitmapData:BitmapData = new BitmapData(100, 80, false, 0xFF0000);
var mySnapshot:MovieClip = this.createEmptyMovieClip("mySnapshot",
➡ this.getNextHighestDepth());
mySnapshot.attachBitmap(myBitmapData, this.getNextHighestDepth());
```

In AS3 you'd do the same except that you'd attach it to a Bitmap and add that to the display list:

```
import flash.display.Bitmap;
import flash.display.BitmapData;
var myBitmapData:BitmapData = new BitmapData(100, 80, false, 0xFF0000);
var mySnapshot:Bitmap = new Bitmap(myBitmapData);
addChild(mySnapshot);
```

There are lots of nifty things you can do to, and with, the BitmapData object through its methods, as shown in Table 10.1.

▶ **Table 10.1** Available *BitmapData* methods

Method	Description
applyFilter	Generates a filtered image from a source bitmap image and a filter object.
clone	Creates a new BitmapData object that is an exact copy of the source bitmap.
colorTransform	Adjusts the color values in a specified rectangular area of a bitmap, as specified by the supplied colorTransform object values.
compare (AS3 only)	Compares two BitmapData objects. If the two BitmapData objects have the same width and height, compare returns a new BitmapData object, in which each pixel is the "difference" between the pixels in the two source objects.
copyChannel	Transfers values from one channel of a BitmapData object into the current BitmapData object.
copyPixels	A fast method to manipulate pixels between two bitmaps (no stretching, rotation, or color effects). Copies a rectangular area of a source image to a rectangular area at the specified destination point of a BitmapData object.
dispose	Empties the memory used to store the BitmapData object.
draw	Draws a source movieclip or image into a destination image.
fillRect	Fills a rectangular area of pixels with the specified color.
floodFill	Fills an image with a specified color starting at an x,y coordinate.

Method	Description
generateFilterRect	Determines the destination rectangle that is affected by the applyFilter() method call, given a BitmapData object, a source rectangle, and a filter object.
getColorBoundsRect	Returns a rectangular area that fully encloses all pixels of a specified color in the bitmap.
getPixel	Returns an integer that represents the color value of a specific *x,y* point in a BitmapData object.
getPixel32	Returns a color value that contains alpha channel and RGB data for a specified pixel.
getPixels (AS3 only)	Generates a byte array from a rectangular region of pixel data.
hitTest	Pixel-level hit detection between a bitmap image and a point, rectangle, or other bitmap image. No stretching, rotation, or other transformation of either object is considered when the hit test is performed.
loadBitmap (AS2 only)	Returns a new BitmapData object that contains a bitmap image of the symbol identified by a specified linkage ID in the Library.
lock (AS3 only)	Locks an image so that any objects that reference the BitmapData object (Bitmap objects) are not updated when this specific BitmapData object changes.
merge	Performs per-channel blend from a source image to a destination image.
noise	Fills an image with random noise.
paletteMap	Remaps the color channel values with up to four arrays of color palette data, one for each channel. This method can be used for a variety of effects from general palette mapping (taking one channel and converting it to a color image) to gamma, curve, and level manipulation.
perlinNoise	Fills an image with Perlin noise (a random texture that's especially effective for smoke, fog and cloud effects).
pixelDissolve	Performs a pixel dissolve either from a source image to a destination image or by using the same image.
scroll	Scrolls an image over by a specified *x,y* pixel value. Edge pixels outside the scrolling area are left unchanged.
setPixel	Sets the color of a single pixel in a BitmapData object.
setPixel32	Sets the color and alpha transparency of a single pixel in a BitmapData object.
setPixels (AS3 only)	Converts a byte array into a rectangular region of pixel data.
threshold	Tests pixel values in an image against a specified threshold and sets pixels that pass the test to a new specified color value. Allows you to isolate and replace color ranges in an image.
unlock (AS3 only)	Unlocks an image so that any objects that reference the BitmapData object (such as Bitmap objects) are updated when this BitmapData object changes.

We'll only be using a couple of these with video in this chapter, such as pixel-Dissolve and of course the draw method, which captures a bitmap image. Having pixel-level control is a seriously powerful addition to Flash. You may want to look at these methods more in depth in the Flash documentation to see what other innovative applications you may be inspired to create.

Let's get started with an especially useful application of BitmapData for video applications—dynamic thumbnails.

Dynamic Thumbnails: Video Snapshots

As you probably already know, many video applications need to be updated with fresh content often, and can therefore be time-consuming to maintain. One especially tedious step is having to open the video file in your video-editing software just to export a frame for a preview. This is where BitmapData can come to the rescue. You can use BitmapData to take a snapshot of the video to use as a thumbnail. This section presents an example that shows you how to do just that.

First, we'll need to set up the FLA. Steps to create this file will be slightly different for AS2 and AS3, so skip down to the appropriate subsection for instructions.

ActionScript 2: *FLVBitmapThumb*

Create a new AS2 Flash document in Flash 8 or CS3, then follow these steps:

1. Set the Stage size to 450 × 300.

2. From the Library menu, choose New Video (ActionScript controlled) and drag the video object onto the Stage. Give it the instance name myVid. Make the size 240 × 180. Add a title if you like. Refer to Figure 10.1 for a recommended layout of the application.

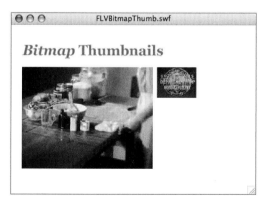

Figure 10.1 Automatically generated bitmap thumbnails

3. With this video object selected, choose Modify > Convert to Symbol (movieclip). Name the instance video_mc.

4. Next, add a new layer and name it **Actions**. Click on the first frame of the new layer and enter the following ActionScript in the Actions panel:

```
import FLVBitmapThumb;
var myFilters:FLVBitmapThumb = new FLVBitmapThumb(video_mc);
```

5. Create the class FLVBitmapThumb.as, entering the code shown in the next subsection. Save it in the same folder as your FLA.

6. Compile your SWF. When the FLV is loaded, a bitmap image will be captured, resized, and placed to the right of the video. The video will pause, and it can be triggered to play/pause by clicking on the newly generated thumbnail. (See Figure 10.1.)

FLVBitmapThumb.as

First, we import the classes we'll need, and then we'll declare our variables. We declare a public static variable for scale, to be sure our thumbnails are always created at the size specified.

```
import flash.display.BitmapData;
import mx.utils.Delegate;
import flash.geom.Matrix;

class FLVBitmapThumb
{
    public static var SCALE:Number = 0.3;
    // for a thumbnail 30% of the size of the video

    private var nc:NetConnection;
    private var ns:NetStream;
    private var targetClip:MovieClip;
    private var thumb_mc:MovieClip;
    private var bitmapData:BitmapData;
    private var wasThumbTaken:Boolean;
```

Then on to our main function, where we accept the target movieclip as a parameter. We then set the global wasThumbTaken variable to an initial value of false. This will be changed to true once we've grabbed our thumbnail snapshot. Then we add all of the usual NetStream and NetConnection code, and play the video. (We've also included an onMetaData handler here if you want to use that data in your application.)

```
public function FLVBitmapThumb(target:MovieClip)    {
        targetClip = target;
        wasThumbTaken = false;

// Create and open a new net connection
        nc = new NetConnection();
        nc.connect(null);
// Create a new stream object using the net connection
        ns = new NetStream(nc);
// Callback handler for when the Flash Player receives descriptive
// information embedded in the FLV file being played
        ns.onMetaData = function (info:Object):Void {
            trace("metadata: ");
            for (var prop:String in info) {
                trace("\t" + prop + ": " + info[prop]);
            }
        };
// Attach the stream object to the ActionScript-controlled
// video component you've placed on the stage with an
// instance name of my_video
    var video:Video = targetClip.myVid;
    video.attachVideo(ns);
// Begin playing the stream
    ns.play("http://www.flashconnections.com/flash-video-
➡ pro/ch10/StepSavi1949_edit2.flv");
```

Next we assign the onStatus handler and call makeThumbBitmap:

```
// Callback handler invoked every time a status change or error is
// posted for the NetStream object
    ns.onStatus = Delegate.create(this, handleOnStatus);

// Initiate creation of thumb bitmap holder
    makeThumbBitmap();
  }
```

The makeThumbBitmap method creates the BitmapData object and its container movieclip, and then places it on the Stage, 10 pixels to the right of the video object.

We then add an onRelease event handler, which triggers the chooseVideo method when the thumbnail is clicked:

```
private function makeThumbBitmap():Void {
var video:Video = targetClip.myVid;
// Set the width and height of the thumbnail
var bmwidth:Number = Math.round(video._width*SCALE);
var bmheight:Number = Math.round(video._height*SCALE);
// Create a new BitmapData object and fill with grey for now
bitmapData = new BitmapData(bmwidth, bmheight, false, 0x00CCCCCC);
// Create a new movieclip to hold our bitmap, attach the bitmap
thumb_mc = targetClip.createEmptyMovieClip
➥ ("thumb", targetClip.getNextHighestDepth());
thumb_mc.attachBitmap(bitmapData, 100);
// Specify its coordinates relative to the video object,
// then make it clickable
thumb_mc._x = video._x+video._width+10;
thumb_mc._y = video._y;
thumb_mc.onRelease = Delegate.create(this, chooseVideo);
}
```

The chooseVideo method toggles between video play and pause states:

```
public function chooseVideo():Void {
// Start the video if it is paused
    ns.pause();
}
```

This next method is triggered when an onStatus event is received on our NetStream. It first traces the status message, and if it was a NetStream.Buffer.Full message, it checks to see if the thumbnail bitmap was already taken. If not, we draw the contents of targetClip (the video object) into the BitmapData object, and apply the scale transformation as set out in our global variable SCALE. Finally, we pause the video and change our global wasThumbTaken variable to true.

```
public function handleOnStatus(info:Object):Void {
        trace("stream status: ");
        for (var prop:String in info) {
            trace("\t" + prop + ": " + info[prop]);
        }
// Cycle through the properties to check that the buffer is full
// then take a bitmap snapshot, scale it using a matrix.scale
// method, then pause the video and change the global variable
```

```
// thumbTaken to true
        for (var prop in info) {
            if(info.code == "NetStream.Buffer.Full") {
                if(!wasThumbTaken) {
                    var scalematrix = new Matrix();
                    scalematrix.scale(SCALE,SCALE);
                    bitmapData.draw(targetClip, scalematrix);
                    targetClip.allowSmoothing = true;
                    ns.pause();
                    wasThumbTaken = true;
                }
            }
        }
    }
```

This last method is here to remind you to always dispose of your unused bitmaps. We don't use it in this example because we always want our thumbnail on the Stage, but we kept it here to show you the code, and to remind you to use it when appropriate.

```
public function destroy():Void {
// Always good practice to have a destroy method to have
// an easy way to dispose of bitmaps when you're done with them
    bitmapData.dispose();
    thumb_mc.removeMovieClip();
    }
}
```

ActionScript 3: *FLVBitmapThumb*

Next, let's take a look at the code in AS3. You'll notice that the basic approach is the same, with just a few minor differences, as we'll point out.

Create a new AS3 Flash document in Flash CS3, and then follow these steps:

1. Set the Stage size to 450 × 300.

2. In the Properties panel, enter **Main** as the document class.

3. Create the classes Main.as and FLVBitmapThumb.as, entering the code shown in the next subsections. Save these class files in the same folder as your FLA.

4. Compile your SWF. When the FLV is loaded, a bitmap image will be captured, resized, and placed to the right of the video. The video will pause, and it can be triggered to play/pause by clicking on the newly generated thumbnail. (See Figure 10.1.)

Main.as

This is the main class for this application, which sets up our assets on the Stage and instantiates a new FLVBitmapThumb instance.

```
package
{
    import flash.display.MovieClip;
    import flash.display.StageAlign;
    import flash.display.StageScaleMode;
    import flash.events.Event;
    import flash.media.Video;
    import FLVBitmapThumb;

    public class Main extends MovieClip {
        public var myVid:Video;
        public var thumb:FLVBitmapThumb;

        public function Main() {
            stage.scaleMode = StageScaleMode.NO_SCALE;
            stage.align = StageAlign.TOP_LEFT;

            this.addEventListener(Event.UNLOAD, onUnload);

            myVid = new Video(320,240);
            addChild(myVid);
            myVid.x = 50;
            myVid.y = 50;

            thumb = new FLVBitmapThumb(this);
        }

        public function onUnload():void {
            thumb.destroy();
        }
    }
}
```

FLVBitmapThumb.as

Here we've imported the classes we'll need. You can see that, as in most AS3 applications, there are more classes that need to be specifically imported.

```
package
{
    import flash.display.BitmapData;
    import flash.display.MovieClip;
    import flash.events.NetStatusEvent;
    import flash.geom.Matrix;
    import flash.net.NetConnection;
    import flash.net.NetStream;
    import flash.media.Video;
    import flash.display.Bitmap;
    import flash.events.MouseEvent;
    import flash.events.TimerEvent;
    import flash.utils.Timer;
```

Next we move on to declaring our variables. Again, we declare a public static variable for scale. Feel free to play with the scale if you think the size we've chosen for the thumbnail is too small.

```
public class FLVBitmapThumb {

    public static var SCALE:Number = 0.3;
    // for a thumbnail 30% of the size of the video

    private var nc:NetConnection;
    private var ns:NetStream;
    private var target_mc:MovieClip;
    private var thumb_mc:MovieClip;
    private var bitmap:Bitmap;
    private var bitmapData:BitmapData;
    private var wasThumbTaken:Boolean;
```

Then we move on to our main function, which accepts the target MovieClip instance as a parameter. As in the AS2 version, we set the global wasThumbTaken variable to an initial value of false, add all of the standard NetStream and NetConnection code, then play the video.

```
    public function FLVBitmapThumb (target:MovieClip) {

        target_mc = target;
        wasThumbTaken = false;
```

```
// Create and open a new net connection
nc = new NetConnection();
nc.connect(null);
// Create a new stream object using the net connection
ns = new NetStream(nc);
ns.client = this;
// Attach the stream object to the ActionScript-controlled
// video component you've placed on the stage with an
// instance name of myVid
target_mc.myVid.attachNetStream(ns);
// Begin playing the stream
ns.play("sl_lg.flv");
```

Next we assign the onStatus handler to the NetStream and call makeThumbBitmap. Notice that we can access the NetStatus event directly in AS3; there's no need to use Delegate to maintain scope. You gotta love AS3.

```
          // wait 1 second, then initiate creation of thumb bitmap holder
          var delayTimer:Timer = new Timer(1000, 1);
          delayTimer.addEventListener(TimerEvent.TIMER_COMPLETE,
➡ makeThumbBitmap);
          delayTimer.start();

          // Callback handler invoked every time a status change or error
          // is posted for the NetStream object
          ns.addEventListener(NetStatusEvent.NET_STATUS, handleOnStatus);

     }
```

Now that the scope issue's out of our way, we can create an onMetaData method to handle our metadata events, rather than including it in our main method as we did in AS2. Again, metadata handling is not crucial to the function of this example; it's just good to have available if you want to incorporate stream data into your own application.

```
     public function onMetaData (info:Object):void {

          trace("stream metadata: ");
          for (var prop:String in info) {
               trace("\t" + prop + ": " + info[prop]);
          }

     }
```

The makeThumbBitmap method creates the BitmapData object and its container movieclip, and then places it on the Stage, 10 pixels to the right of the video object. We then add an onRelease event handler, which triggers the chooseVideo method when the thumbnail is clicked. Note that you'll need to set the useHandCursor property of the thumb movieclip to true and its buttonMode property to true to make it clickable, even if you've assigned a click handler to it.

```
private function makeThumbBitmap(evt:TimerEvent):void {
    // Set the width and height of the thumbnail
    var bmwidth:int = Math.round(target_mc.myVid.width*SCALE);
    var bmheight:int = Math.round(target_mc.myVid.height*SCALE);
    // Create a new BitmapData object and fill with grey for now
    bitmapData = new BitmapData(bmwidth, bmheight, false,
    0x00CCCCCC);
    bitmap = new Bitmap(bitmapData);
    // Create a new movieclip to hold our bitmap, attach the bitmap
    thumb_mc = new MovieClip();
    thumb_mc.addEventListener (MouseEvent.CLICK, chooseVideo);
    thumb_mc.addChild(bitmap);
    // Add the thumbnail to the target
    target_mc.addChild(thumb_mc);
    // Specify its coordinates relative to the video object,
    // then make it clickable
    thumb_mc.x = target_mc.myVid.x + target_mc.myVid.width + 10;
    thumb_mc.y = target_mc.myVid.y;
    thumb_mc.buttonMode = true;
    thumb_mc.useHandCursor = true;

}
```

The chooseVideo method toggles between video play and pause states:

```
public function chooseVideo(event:MouseEvent):void {
    // Start the video if it is paused
    ns.togglePause();
}
```

The handleOnStatus method is triggered when an onStatus event is received on our NetStream. First the status message is traced, and if it was a NetStream.Buffer.Full message, will check to see if we've already taken a thumbnail bitmap. If not, we'll create a scale matrix using the value of our global variable SCALE, draw the contents of _target_mc.video into the BitmapData object, then apply the scale matrix transformation to resample the bitmap to the specified size. And last but not least, we pause the video and change the wasThumbTaken variable to true.

```
public function handleOnStatus(event:NetStatusEvent):void {
    trace("stream status: ");
    // Cycle through the properties to check that the buffer is full
    // then take a bitmap snapshot, scale it using a matrix.scale
    // method, then pause the video and change the global variable
    // thumbTaken to true
    var info:Object = event.info;
        for (var prop:String in info) {
            trace("\t" + prop + ": " + info[prop]);
                if(info.code == "NetStream.Buffer.Full") {
                    if(!wasThumbTaken) {
                        var scalematrix:Matrix = new Matrix();
                        scalematrix.scale(SCALE,SCALE);
                        bitmapData.draw(target_mc.myVid, scalematrix);
                        ns.pause();
                        wasThumbTaken = true;


                    }
                }
            }
        }
```

This last method is here—even though we don't use it in this example—to remind you of the importance of disposing of your unused bitmaps once you've finished with them. It's just good practice, and you've got the code right here, so there's no excuse not to clean up after yourself.

```
public function destroy():void {
    // Always good practice to have a destroy method to have
    // an easy way to dispose of bitmaps when you're done with them
    bitmapData.dispose();
    thumb_mc.removeEventListener (MouseEvent.CLICK, chooseVideo);
    target_mc.removeChild(thumb_mc);
    }
}
}
```

You can apply this technique to all sorts of applications, including players with thumbnail playlists and quick on-the-fly previews. It can also be incorporated into the playlist options we outlined in Chapter 7. Now that you understand the basics of creating bitmaps from video, let's get fancy and apply this technique to video transitions.

Other Options Worth Noting

There are other ways to create thumbnails as well. You can attach a video to a small video object and then pause it. There's one issue with using this approach with progressive download, however—the video continues to load in the background even after being paused. This can be acceptable if you have just one video and one thumbnail—but if you have more than that, it can adversely affect your application's performance with all that unneeded data being downloaded in the background. So, the commonly used (yet creative) workaround is to call a nonexistent FLV to play on the same NetStream instance, which will stop the file from downloading and still give you the still video frame as a preview:

```
ns.onStatus = function (info) {
    // When buffer is full, remove your attached video,
    // pause the Netstream, then initiate play
    // of an FLV that doesn't exist.
    if(info.code == "NetStream.Buffer.Full"){
        myVideo.attachVideo(null);
        ns.pause();
        ns.play("non-existent.flv");
    }
};
```

Note: If you are using streaming video delivery, you can dynamically create thumbnails by loading the video into a small video object, jumping to a frame, and pausing the video. The file will not continue to download in the background as it does with progressive video delivery. Note, however, that you'll still have a lot of extra data loaded because the thumbnail will just be a scaled-down version of your video, containing all the pixel data of a full-sized frame. The method demonstrated in this chapter's example, FLVBitmapThumb.as, actually scales down the pixel data (or *resamples*) so you truly have a small snapshot with only the pixel data you need. You may want to combine these two approaches, taking a bitmap snapshot once the tiny video is paused, and then delete the tiny video, replacing it with the bitmap thumbnail.

Transitions and Dissolves

Flash makes it easy to create simple dissolve transitions using the BitmapData object. Using the built-in pixelDissolve method, a clean dissolve transition can be added between videos. This next example demonstrates how to set up two videos to transition between them. First, we load both videos and store bitmap snapshots of the first frame of each. Then, when switching between videos, a bitmap snapshot is taken of the current frame of the video playing. This bitmap is then dissolved into the first frame of the chosen video, which then begins to play (Figure 10.2). It all happens pretty fast, so let's walk through the scripts and see what's going on in more detail.

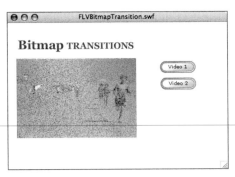

Figure 10.2 Two videos transitioning

Getting creative with the BitmapData and Bitmap objects, we can create a dissolve between two videos without having to actually capture bitmaps of the videos themselves as they play. To do this, we take advantage of the BlendMode property of the bitmap. Combining the ALPHA BlendMode and LAYER BlendMode settings, we can effectively create a dynamic mask of the video, which allows us to apply a bitmap.pixelDissolve to it and fade it out over a set length of time.

The basic structure of a pixelDissolve call in AS2 is:

```
pixelDissolve(sourceBitmap:BitmapData, sourceRect:Rectangle,
➡ destPoint:Point, [randomSeed:Number], [numberOfPixels:Number],
➡ [fillColor:Number]):Number
```

And in AS3, it's basically the same, with some changes to data types:

```
pixelDissolve(sourceBitmapData:BitmapData, sourceRect:Rectangle,
➡ destPoint:Point, randomSeed:int, numberOfPixels:int,
➡ fillColor:uint):int
```

The bracketed parameters are optional. Details for each parameter are:

- sourceBitmap is the bitmap to use as a starting point.
- sourceRect is a rectangle that defines the area of the source bitmap to use.
- destPoint is the upper-left registration point between the sourceBitmap and sourceRect.

- randomSeed is the number of pixels used to start the dissolve. numberofPixels specifies just what it says—the number of pixels to dissolve. The default is ⅟₃₀th of the source image area (width × height).

- fillColor is an ARGB color value that's used to fill pixels when both the source and destination values are the same.

Note that to continue the pixel dissolve until it's finished, you need to pass the return value of the function back in, like this:

ActionScript 2

```
dissolveSeed=bitmapData.pixelDissolve(bitmapData,bitmapData.rectangle,
➥ new Point(),dissolveSeed,pixelsToDissolve,0x00000000);
```

ActionsScript 3

```
dissolveSeed=bitmapData.pixelDissolve(bitmapData,bitmapData.rect,
➥ new Point(),dissolveSeed,pixelsToDissolve,0x00000000)
```

As you can see, the only real difference between the two languages is the syntax for specifying the bitmap source rectangle. To give you an idea of how this can work in the context of an application, we've put together a little application that transitions between two videos when a video is clicked. Let's walk through the scripts to see what's going on in more detail.

ActionScript 2: *FLVBitmapTransition*

Begin by creating a new AS2 Flash file in Flash 8 or CS3; name it **FLVBitmapTransition .fla** and set the document size to the dimensions of your video (320 × 240 in this example). Then, set up a couple of assets to display the video:

1. Go to your Library panel. In the Library pop-up menu, choose New Video (ActionScript controlled).

2. Choose Insert > New Symbol. Name it **videoPlayer**, check the Export for ActionScript option in Linkage, and set the identifier to be videoPlayer. Click OK.

3. Drag the video object from your Library onto the Stage. Position its upper-left corner at x = 0, y = 0. In the Properties panel, name the instance **videoScreen**.

4. Return to the main timeline. Select the first frame and open the Actions panel. Enter the following code:

```
var app=new App(this);
```

5. Save the file. That's all we need to do to set up our assets. Next, we'll create our two classes, App.as and VideoPlayer.as. Create these files as shown next, and save them in the same folder as your FLA.

App.as

First we'll import the only external class we'll need to explicitly call on here, Delegate:

```
import mx.events.EventDispatcher;
import mx.utils.Delegate;
class App {
```

Then we'll declare a public static variable to hold our array of two videos (change the filenames here if you want to test your own):

```
//the paths for the 2 videos to be mixed
public static var VIDNAMES:Array = ["med_lg.flv","sl_lg.flv"];
```

Next we create the two VideoPlayers and the mc, which will act as our button to toggle between videos:

```
//we will have 2 video players, layered one on top of the other
private var player1:VideoPlayer;
private var player2:VideoPlayer;
private var mc:MovieClip;
```

Then we begin the setup of our application. Create the target clip, set its alignment on the Stage, and create the two players, sending in their filenames:

```
public function App(parentClip:MovieClip) {
    this.mc=parentClip.createEmptyMovieClip("mmm",0);
    Stage.align="TL";

    //create player1 and load the first video
    player1=new VideoPlayer(mc,0);
    player1.load(VIDNAMES[0]);

    //create player2 and load the remaining video
    player2=new VideoPlayer(mc,1);
    player2.load(VIDNAMES[1]);
```

Here we add event listeners to both player objects, listening for the COMPLETE event. When triggered, we fire the playerFadeFunc method.

```
    //listen for the COMPLETE event. Signals when
    // a fade has completed. See VideoPlayer.as
    var playerFadeFunc:Function=Delegate.create
➡ (this,playerFadeCompleteHandler);

    player2.addEventListener(VideoPlayer.COMPLETE,playerFadeFunc);
    player1.addEventListener(VideoPlayer.COMPLETE,playerFadeFunc);
```

Start to play the video in the player that's on top, and start listening for clicks to begin a transition:

```
//we start player2 first, because it is on top.
player2.play();

//listen for mouseclick to start a transition
listenForClicks();
}
```

In this method, we set up the mc movieclip as a button:

```
private function listenForClicks():Void {
    //set up as a listener for clicks
    mc.onPress=Delegate.create(this,mouseClickHandler);
}
```

Here we get a bit tricky in detecting player depths. This method returns the top player if top is true. If top is false, it returns the bottom player.

```
private function getTopPlayer(top:Boolean):VideoPlayer {
    if(player1.mc.getDepth()>player2.mc.getDepth()) {
        return top?player1:player2;
    }
    else {
        return top?player2:player1;
    }
}
```

This next function is fired when the mc movieclip is clicked, and handles the transition between videos.

```
private function mouseClickHandler():Void {
    // start the bottom player
    // initially, it will not be visible,
    // because the top player obscures it
    getTopPlayer(false).play();

    // fade the top player to alpha over 1500 milliseconds
    // this will reveal the bottom player which we just started
    getTopPlayer(true).fadeOut(1500);
    // do not listen for mouseclicks any more.
    // the listener will be restored once the transition is complete.
    delete mc.onPress;
}
```

When the fade is complete, swap the player depths, playing the new video:

```
private function playerFadeCompleteHandler(e:Object):Void {
    player1.swapDepthsWith(player2);

    //as the transition had finished, we can listen for clicks again
    listenForClicks();
  }
}
```

VideoPlayer.as

Now, let's move on to the class that constructs the two video players we'll be swapping between. First we import the classes we'll need—the usual Delegate and EventDispatcher classes, and a couple of new ones: BitmapData and Point. These will allow us to create a nice bitmap transition:

```
import flash.display.BitmapData;
import flash.geom.Point;
import mx.events.EventDispatcher;
import mx.utils.Delegate;
```

Next, we set up our variables and set the timer interval. (You can edit the TIMER_INTERVAL if you'd like a faster or slower transition.) We set the size of the videos here as well.

```
class VideoPlayer {
    //event definition
    //fired when fade is complete
    public static var COMPLETE="complete";

    private var ns:NetStream;
    private var nc:NetConnection;
    private var url:String;
    private var myVid:Video;
    private var bitmapData:BitmapData
    private var dissolveSeed:Number=0;

    //transitions will be updated every 50ms
    private var TIMER_INTERVAL:Number=50;

    //video is resized to dimensions below
    public static var VIDEO_WIDTH:Number=360;
    public static var VIDEO_HEIGHT:Number=240;
```

```
//containing MovieClip
public var mc:MovieClip;
```

Here in our constructor, we set up our event dispatcher and instantiate our video objects:

```
public function VideoPlayer(parentClip:MovieClip,depth:Number) {
    //enable event dispatching
    //dummy methods dispatchEvent, addEventListener,
    //rempoveEventListener will be populated
    EventDispatcher.initialize(this);

    //create a container for all other MovieClips
    this.mc=parentClip.createEmptyMovieClip("VP"+depth,depth);
    //and attach the library item with the required
    //videoScreen instance contained within
    var videoContainer:MovieClip=
    mc.attachMovie("VideoPlayer","videoPlayer",0);

    //get the video in our mc
    myVid = videoContainer.videoScreen;

    //resize the video
    myVid._width=VIDEO_WIDTH;
    myVid._height=VIDEO_HEIGHT;
```

Next we create a bitmap object with a fill of black that is the same size as the video. We attach it to an empty movieclip, which we then attach above the videoContainer.

```
    var bitmapContainer:MovieClip=mc.createEmptyMovieClip("bitmap",1);
    bitmapData=new
    BitmapData(VIDEO_WIDTH,VIDEO_HEIGHT,true,0xFF000000);
    bitmapContainer.attachBitmap(bitmapData,0);
```

Then we set the bitmapContainer's BlendMode to alpha. This means that if the bitmap is opaque (100 alpha), then the video below it will be opaque. If the bitmap is transparent (0 alpha), then the video below it will be transparent.

```
    bitmapContainer.blendMode="alpha";

    //the parent MovieClip of a child using
    //blendMode="alpha" must be set to blendMode="layer"
    mc.blendMode="layer";
```

Next is our now-familiar NetConnection and NetStream code:

```
//create the NetConnection
nc=new NetConnection();
nc.connect(null);
ns=new NetStream(nc);

//connect the Video to the NetStream
myVid.attachVideo(ns);
}
```

And here's the method that's called when we want to swap the player depths during a transition:

```
public function swapDepthsWith(otherPlayer:VideoPlayer):Void {
    this.mc.swapDepths(otherPlayer.mc);
}
```

Here we fill our bitmap with solid black to make the video below it opaque, and begin playing the new video:

```
public function play():Void {
    bitmapData.fillRect(bitmapData.rectangle,0xFF000000);

    //begin playing from the start
    ns.seek(0);
    ns.pause(false);
}
```

The fadeOut method starts a fade from fully opaque to fully transparent. When placed above another playing video, this will give the effect of a transition between the two videos.

```
public function fadeOut(duration:Number):Void {
    var timerFunc=Delegate.create(this,timerHandler);
```

Next, we create an infoObject to be passed to the function called by the interval we are setting up. It carries all the information needed to calculate when to clear the interval.

```
    var infoObject:Object=new Object();
    infoObject.count=0;
    infoObject.repeatCount=Math.floor(duration/TIMER_INTERVAL);
    infoObject.interval=
➥ setInterval(timerFunc,TIMER_INTERVAL,infoObject);
}
```

```
private function timerHandler( infoObject:Object):Void {
    infoObject.count++;
    //pixel dissolve the bitmap to alpha 0
    //(from alpha 100% or 1.0 in AS3)
```

Here we do a bit of math—we calculate the number of pixels that will be made transparent every time this function is called. This is calculated by taking the total number of pixels in the bitmap and dividing by the number of times this function is called. Then we store the return value, which acts as a seed for the next call. In this way, only undissolved pixels will be dissolved on subsequent calls.

```
        var pixelsToDissolve:Number=
➡ VIDEO_WIDTH*VIDEO_HEIGHT/infoObject.repeatCount;
    dissolveSeed=bitmapData.pixelDissolve(bitmapData,bitmapData.rectangle,
➡ new Point(),dissolveSeed,pixelsToDissolve,0x00000000);

        if(infoObject.count>=infoObject.repeatCount) {
            clearInterval(infoObject.interval);
            //make sure the bitmap is completely transparent
            //as the integer calculations may leave
            //a few pixels that are opaque
            bitmapData.fillRect(bitmapData.rectangle,0x00000000);

            //pause and rewind the video
            ns.pause(true);
            ns.seek(0);

            //notify our listeners (in App.as) that the fade is complete
            var ev:Object={type:COMPLETE,target:this};
            this.dispatchEvent(ev);
        }
    }
```

Initially, we call this load function to begin loading the video so it will be ready to play when triggered, and then pause it for now:

```
    public function load(url:String):Void {
        //start loading the video but place it in a paused state
        this.url=url;
        ns.play(url);
        ns.pause();
    }
```

Finally, these functions will be populated the by the EventDispatcher.initialize (this) call:

```
private function dispatchEvent(ev:Object) {

}
public function addEventListener(event:String,listener:Object) {

}
public function removeEventListener(event:String,listener:Object) {

}
}
```

After you've saved these two classes, go back to your Flash document and compile your SWF. The first video will play automatically. Click on it, and you'll initiate the transition to the second video. Click again and transition back. Feel free to play with the timing and seed values (initial number of pixel changes) to alter the transition.

 Note: When using this transition approach in a real application, you may want to consider matching the audio volume level to be in sync with the video fade.

Or, for Something Completely Different: Built-in Dissolves Using the *mx.transitions* Class

Another option, if you don't want to use the `BitmapData` class to create your dissolve, is to use Flash 8's built-in transitions class. In some cases, this may be just the ticket for a nice smooth transition without having to grab bitmaps of each video.

ActionScript 2: *FLVDissolveTransition.as*

Create a new class file and enter the following code. Save this file as FLVDissolveTransition.as.

```
import mx.utils.Delegate;
import mx.managers.DepthManager;

import mx.transitions.*;

class com.flashconnections.FLVDissolveTransition {
    var target:MovieClip;
    var nc:NetConnection;
    var netStreams:Array;
    var videoClips:Array;
    var currentStream:Number;
    var vidNames:Array;
```

amazon.com

Returns Are Easy!

Most items can be returned, exchanged, or replaced when returned in original and unopened condition. Visit http://www.amazon.com/returns to start your return, or http://www.amazon.com/help for more information on return policies.

Your order of December 29, 2012 (Order ID 110-4494952-7686654)

Qty.	Item	Item Price	Total
1	**Flash Video for Professionals: Expert Techniques for Integrating Video on the Web** Larson, Lisa --- Paperback (** **P-1-H141G240** **) **X000DUPIKF** 28L5E80012BG **(Sold by Jenson Online Inc.)**	$4.00	$4.00

Subtotal	$4.00
Shipping & Handling	$3.99
Order Total	$7.99
Paid via credit/debit	$7.99
Balance due	$0.00

This shipment completes your order.

Have feedback on how we packaged your order? Tell us at www.amazon.com/packaging.

BA8

```
public function FLVDissolveTransition(target_mc:MovieClip) {
    trace("FLVDissolveTransition");

    target = target_mc;

    // Construct NetConnection
    nc = new NetConnection();
    nc.connect(null);

    // Construct NetStreams and connect to flow through NetConnection
    netStreams = new Array();
    netStreams.push(new NetStream(nc));
    netStreams.push(new NetStream(nc));

    videoClips = new Array(target.videoOne_mc, target.videoTwo_mc);

    // Specify video filenames
    vidNames = new Array("wiper_fast_lg.flv", "train_med_lg.flv");
    currentStream = 0;

    initButtons(target);

    // Play first video
    vidShow(0);

}

private function vidShow(vidNum:Number) {

    trace("vidShow");
    // extract the video name from the vidNames array
    var vidname:String = vidNames[vidNum]

    //pause the currently playing video
    netStreams[currentStream].pause();

    // and switch streams
    currentStream=(currentStream+1)%2;

    // work out the next stream and video clip to use
    var ns:NetStream = netStreams[currentStream];
    var videoclip:MovieClip = videoClips[currentStream];
```

Continues

```
                    // Move the new video on top of the last one,
                    videoclip.setDepthTo(DepthManager.kTop);

                    // initiate the transition,
                    TransitionManager.start(videoclip,{type:PixelDissolve,
                        direction:Transition.IN,
                        duration:3,
                        easing:mx.transitions.easing.None.easeNone,
                        xSections:50,
                        ySections:40});

                    // and start the video playing
                    vidPlay(videoclip, vidname, ns);


            }


            private function vidPlay(targetVid:MovieClip, vidName:String,
      ➠ ns:NetStream) {
                    trace("vidPlay");

                    // Remove the old video from the video object
                    targetVid.myVid.attachVideo(null);

                    // Attach NetStream to movieclip
                    // containing video object on the stage
                    targetVid.myVid.attachVideo(ns);

                    // Tell the NetStream which FLV to play
                    ns.play(vidName);
            }

            private function clickHandler(evtObj:Object) {
                    trace("clickHandler "+evtObj.target.selection.data);
                    vidShow(evtObj.target.selection.data);
            }

            private function initButtons() {
                    trace("initButtons");
                    target.radioGroup.addEventListener("click",
      ➠ Delegate.create(this, clickHandler));
                    target.videoOne_btn.label = "Video One";
                    target.videoTwo_btn.label = "Video Two";
            }
        }
```

Or, for Something Completely Different: Built-in Dissolves Using the *mx.transitions* Class *(Continued)*

Before you can test the code, you'll need to set up a few assets in Flash:

1. Open Flash 8 or Flash CS3 and create a new ActionScript 2 document and save it in the same folder as the FLVDissolveTransition.as class you just created.

2. Set the Stage size to 450 × 300.

3. From the Library menu, choose New Video (ActionScript controlled) and drag the video object onto the Stage. Give it the instance name **myVid**. Make the size 240 × 180.

4. With this video object selected, choose Modify > Convert to Symbol (movie clip). Name the instance **videoOne_mc**.

5. Select the movieclip you just created, then choose Edit > Copy. Create a new layer on the timeline above the current one, and call it **Video 2**. Click on the first frame of that layer, and choose Edit > Paste in Place. Name that new instance **videoTwo_mc**.

6. If the Components panel isn't already open, choose Window > Components. From the Components panel, grab a RadioButton from the User Interface list and drop it on the Stage. Name the instance **videoOne_btn**.

7. Drag another and name it **videoTwo_btn**.

8. Finally, on your main timeline, create a new layer and call it **Actions**. Open the Actions panel and enter the following ActionScript:

```
import FLVDissolveTransition;
var myTransition:FLVDissolveTransition = new
FLVDissolveTransition(this);
```

Test your movie. The first video should play automatically. Choose the second one and you'll see a nice mosaic dissolve transition from the old video to the new (see graphic below, which uses the built-in *mx.transitions* classes). This effect can be used instead of the bitmap transition presented in this chapter if it provides you with the effect you're looking for. *(Shout out to Seb Lee-Delisle for this example!)*

ActionScript 3: *FLVBitmapTransition*

In this AS3 version, the initial setup is simpler:

1. Create a new AS3 Flash document in Flash CS3.

2. In the Properties panel, set the size to the dimensions of your video (320 × 240 in this example) and enter App as your Document class.

3. Then create the App.as and VideoPlayer.as classes as shown next and save them in the same folder as your FLA.

The basic functionality of this version is the same as the AS2 version, so we'll just jump in the code below when there's a significant syntax or structure difference. Let's take a look.

App.as

This is our main class, so here we're specifying our video names, setting up the display, and instantiating our video objects:

```
package
{
    import flash.display.*;
    import flash.net.*;
    import flash.events.*;

    public class App extends Sprite {
        //the paths for the 2 videos to be mixed
        public static var VIDNAMES:Array = ["med_lg.flv","sl_lg.flv"];

        //we will have 2 video players, layered one on top of the other
        private var player1:VideoPlayer;
        private var player2:VideoPlayer;

        public function App() {
            init();
        }
```

Here we initialize the display, aligning everything to the top-left corner of the Stage (note the different syntax here for Stage alignment):

```
        private function init():void {
            stage.align=StageAlign.TOP_LEFT;

            //create player1 and load the first video
            player1=new VideoPlayer();
```

```
player1.load(VIDNAMES[0]);

//add it to the display list
this.addChild(player1);

//create player2 and load the remaining video
player2=new VideoPlayer();
player2.load(VIDNAMES[1]);

//add it to the display list.
//as it was added last, it will be on top, obscuring player1
this.addChild(player2);
```

Next, we set up listeners to watch for the COMPLETE event, signaling that a fade has completed. (See VideoPlayer.as.)

```
        player2.addEventListener
➡ (Event.COMPLETE,playerFadeCompleteHandler,false,0,true);
        player1.addEventListener
➡ (Event.COMPLETE,playerFadeCompleteHandler,false,0,true);

        //we start player2 first, because it is on top.
        player2.play();

        //listen for mouseclick to start a transition
        listenForClicks();
    }
```

Then we set up a listener to register clicks and trigger a transition:

```
    private function listenForClicks():void {
        this.stage.addEventListener
➡ (MouseEvent.CLICK,mouseClickHandler,false,0,true);
    }
```

In this method, we determine which player is on the top and which is on the bottom. Since there is nothing else in our playlist in this example, these are at depths 0 and 1, respectively. ActionScript 3 allows us to simplify the fade here a bit, giving us the top and bottom players without having to call out to an additional method to determine which is which:

```
    private function mouseClickHandler(e:MouseEvent):void {
        var bottomPlayer:VideoPlayer=VideoPlayer(this.getChildAt(0));
        var topPlayer:VideoPlayer=VideoPlayer(this.getChildAt(1));
```

```
                        //start the bottom player
                        //initially, it will not be visible,
                        //because the top player obscures it
                        bottomPlayer.play();

                        //fade the top player to alpha over 1500 milliseconds
                        //this will reveal the bottom player which we just started
                        topPlayer.fadeOut(1500);

                        //prevent user from starting another fade
                        //before this one is complete.
                        //do not listen for mouseclicks any more.
                        //the listener will be restored once the transition is complete.
                        this.stage.removeEventListener
➡     (MouseEvent.CLICK,mouseClickHandler,false);
                }

                private function playerFadeCompleteHandler(e:Event):void {
                        //once the top player has completely faded to
                        //alpha 0, bring the bottom one to the front
                        this.swapChildren(player1,player2);

                        //the transition has finished, so we can listen for clicks again
                        listenForClicks();
                }
            }
        }
```

VideoPlayer.as

Next, we move on to the VideoPlayer class, which creates our video objects and their behaviors.

```
        package
        {
            import flash.display.*;
            import flash.media.Video;
            import flash.net.*;
            import flash.geom.*;
            import flash.utils.*;
            import flash.events.*;
```

Here we extend Sprite and initialize our variables, setting dissolveSeed to 0 to start and TIMER_INTERVAL to 50 ms. We also set our video dimensions here, so if you're using videos of a different size, change the values:

```
public class VideoPlayer extends Sprite {
    private var ns:NetStream;
    private var nc:NetConnection;
    private var url:String;
    private var myVid:Video;
    private var bitmap:Bitmap;
    private var bitmapData:BitmapData
    private var timer:Timer;
    private var dissolveSeed:int=0;

    //transitions will be updated every 50ms
    private const TIMER_INTERVAL:int=50;

    //video is resized to dimensions below
    private const VIDEO_WIDTH:int=360;
    private const VIDEO_HEIGHT:int=240;

    public function VideoPlayer() {
        init();
    }
```

Next, we initialize our VideoPlayer object, setting up the NetConnection and NetStream, and then instantiate a Video object:

```
    private function init():void {
        //create the NetConnection
        nc=new NetConnection();

        //standard procedure for non-streaming content
        nc.connect(null);

        //create the NetStream
        ns=new NetStream(nc);
        ns.bufferTime=5;

        //create the Video at the specified size
        myVid = new Video(VIDEO_WIDTH, VIDEO_HEIGHT);
```

Here we create our bitmapData object, the same size as the video and filled with solid black:

```
bitmapData=new BitmapData
➧ (VIDEO_WIDTH,VIDEO_HEIGHT,true,0xFF000000);
bitmap=new Bitmap(bitmapData);

ns.client=this;

//connect the Video to the NetStream
myVid.attachNetStream(ns);
```

We of course need to add our objects to the display list. We do so in the order we want them stacked, so here bitmap will be on top of myVid.

```
//layer the bitmap over the video
this.addChild(myVid);
this.addChild(bitmap);
```

As in the AS2 example, we need to set the bitmap's blendMode to ALPHA, meaning that if the bitmap is opaque (1.0 alpha), then the video below it will be opaque. If the bitmap is transparent (0 alpha), then the video below it will be transparent.

```
bitmap.blendMode=BlendMode.ALPHA;

//the parent DisplayObject of a child using
//BlendMode.ALPHA must be set to BlendMode.LAYER
this.blendMode=BlendMode.LAYER;
```

Next we add listeners and create a Timer, but we don't start it yet. The parameters 100 and 0 are just placeholder values for now; they will be changed before the timer is started in the fadeOut method.

```
timer=new Timer(100,0);
timer.addEventListener
➧ (TimerEvent.TIMER,timerHandler,false,0,true);
timer.addEventListener
➧ (TimerEvent.TIMER_COMPLETE,timerCompleteHandler,false,0,true);
}

public function play():void {
//fill the bitmap with solid black
//to make the video below opaque
bitmapData.fillRect(bitmapData.rect,0xFF000000);

//begin playing from the start
```

```
    ns.seek(0);
    ns.resume();
}


//starts a fade from fully opaque to fully transparent
//when placed above another playing video, this will
//give the effect of a transition between the 2 videos
```

The fadeOut method resets the Timer, sets its interval, and starts it running. Remember, each time the Timer fires, it triggers the timerHandler method, and when it's complete, it triggers the timerCompleteHandler method.

```
public function fadeOut(duration:int):void {
    //reset the timer
    timer.reset();
    timer.delay=TIMER_INTERVAL;

    //timer will fire this many times over the specified duration
    timer.repeatCount=Math.floor(duration/TIMER_INTERVAL);

    //start the timer
    timer.start();
}


private function timerCompleteHandler(e:TimerEvent):void {
    //make sure the bitmap is completely transparent
    //as the integer calculations may leave a few
    //pixels that are opaque
    bitmapData.fillRect(bitmapData.rect,0x00000000);

    //pause and rewind the video
    ns.pause();
    ns.seek(0);

    //notify our listeners (in App.as) that the fade is complete
    var ev:Event=new Event(Event.COMPLETE);
    this.dispatchEvent(ev);
}


private function timerHandler( e:TimerEvent):void {
```

```
            var pixelsToDissolve:int=
➧ VIDEO_WIDTH*VIDEO_HEIGHT/timer.repeatCount;

            //store the return value, as this acts as a seed
            //for the next call
            //in this way only undissolved pixels
            //will be dissolved on subsequent calls

            dissolveSeed=bitmapData.pixelDissolve
➧ (bitmapData,bitmapData.rect,new Point(),
➧ dissolveSeed,pixelsToDissolve,0x00000000);
        }

        public function load(url:String):void {
            //start loading the video but place it in a paused state
            this.url=url;
            ns.play(url);
            ns.pause();
        }
```

This class is a NetStream client, so the following two methods are required to avoid throwing errors:

```
        public function onMetaData(info:Object):void {


        }


        public function onCuePoint(info:Object):void {


        }
```

And finally, to be good Flash citizens, we include a destroy() method. Just in case this instance may not be needed, we can delete it from memory.

```
        public function destroy():void {
            this.removeChild(bitmap);
            bitmapData.dispose();
        }
    }
}
```

Now, just go back to your Flash file and compile your SWF. Click on the video to trigger the transition back and forth.

Having access to the pixels in an image opens up a ton of possibilities; this example is just the tip of the iceberg. Next, let's create an application that uses the BitmapData object in a fun way: taking snapshots from a video.

The FotoBooth Application

OK, so you've learned some rather practical uses for the BitmapData object. Now let's have some fun with the bitmap object and video—with a little application that mimics an old-style photo booth. It snaps stills from your video (or a webcam) at set intervals and saves them as bitmaps on the Stage. Nifty!

Figures 10.3 and 10.4 show our final FotoBooth application in action.

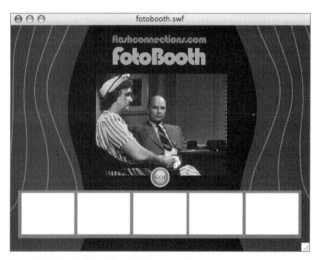

Figure 10.3 Application before initiating snapshots

Figure 10.4 Application after snapshots are taken

Basically, this application loads a video, and when initiated by the user, takes five consecutive snapshots at set intervals. These snapshots will be resized and saved as smaller bitmaps inside five movieclips positioned below the video. We're sure you can think of lots of interesting ideas for web applications using this technique, especially when you bring in the unpredictable element of a webcam. Let's see how it's done.

Before we start coding, we'll need to set up some assets in Flash. The AS3 approach is slightly different, so if you're working in Flash CS3, skip ahead to the specific AS3 instructions.

ActionScript 2: FotoBooth Application

Begin by creating a new AS2 Flash document in Flash 8 or CS3. Then follow these steps to set up the FotoBooth application:

1. Set the stage size to 550 × 400 and the background color to black.

2. From the Library menu, choose New Video (ActionScript controlled) and drag the video object onto the Stage. Give it the instance name **myVid**. Make the size 240 × 180.

3. With this video object selected, choose Modify > Convert to Symbol (movieclip). Name the instance **video_mc**.

4. Double-click video_mc to edit it. Add two layers. Name one **snapshots** and the other **button**.

5. Click on the button layer. From the Window menu, choose Common Libraries > Buttons. The Buttons Library will open. From that list, choose buttons circle bubble > circle bubble grey, as shown in Figure 10.5, and drag it onto the Stage. Give it an instance name of **start_btn**. In the Transform panel, reduce the size of the button to 60%. If you'd like to change the button text (as we did in our example application), double-click the button, choose the text layer, and unlock it if it's locked. Then double-click on the text on the Stage and change the text to **GO!**. Then set its point size to 15 and recenter the text on the button.

6. Return to editing video_mc and select the snapshot layer. Draw a box and size it to 96 pixels wide by 72 pixels high with a stroke of 2 pixels, a stroke color of #CCCCCC, and a fill of None. With just this stroke selected, choose Modify > Convert to Symbol (movieclip). Name the instance **snap1_mc**. Duplicate this movieclip four times and space the copies across the lower portion of the Stage, as shown in Figure 10.3. Give each one an instance name, in order: **snap2_mc**, **snap3_mc**, **snap4_mc**, and **snap5_mc**. You can draw a gray box behind them as shown in the figure to make it look like a photo strip if you wish.

Figure 10.5 The Buttons Library

7. Add a title and any other graphics you'd like. Have a little fun with it.

8. Then, return to the main timeline. Create a new layer and call it **Actions**. Select the first frame and enter the following code into the Actions panel:

```
import FotoBooth;
var myFilters:FotoBooth = new FotoBooth(video_mc);
```

9. Save the file as **FotoBooth.fla**.

10. Now, move on to the ActionScript. Create a new ActionScript file in your favorite editor and place it in the same folder as FotoBooth.fla. Name it **FotoBooth.as,** and enter the code in the following section.

11. After entering the code, save the file. Go back to your FLA and compile. The video will load, then when you press the GO! button, a series of snapshots will appear below your video, just like an old-time photo booth!

FotoBooth.as

As usual we start by importing the classes we need:

```
import flash.display.BitmapData;
import flash.geom.Matrix;
import mx.utils.Delegate;
```

Then we start out by declaring our global variables, including some that we'll want to remain constant—THUMB_COUNT, THUMB_SCALE, and SNAP_SHOT_DELAY—declaring them as public static variables:

```
class FotoBooth {
    // Number of thumbnail images
    public static var THUMB_COUNT:Number = 5;

    // Thumbnail scale size
    public static var THUMB_SCALE:Number = 0.6;

    // delay 1.5 seconds between snapshots
    public static var SNAP_SHOT_DELAY:Number = 1500;

    private var nc:NetConnection;
    private var ns:NetStream;
    private var targetClip:MovieClip;
    private var bitmapDataArray:Array;
    private var shotCounter:Number;
    private var myInterval:Number;
```

Then, we move on to our main method, where we begin by establishing our scope as targetClip, instantiating a BitmapData array, and initializing the shotCounter at 0. Then we have the usual NetConnection and NetStream code.

```
    public function FotoBooth(target:MovieClip) {
        targetClip = target;
        bitmapDataArray = new Array();
        shotCounter = 0;

        // Construct NetConnection
        nc = new NetConnection();
        nc.connect(null);

        // Construct NetStream and connect to flow through NetConnection
        ns = new NetStream(nc);
```

Next we show two different options: playing an FLV or attaching a webcam. For now, we're using the FLV as the source, with the webcam code commented out (more on that after we step through the rest of the code).

```
        // BEGIN FLV SOURCE
        // Attach NetStream to movieclip containing video object
        // on the stage, and play file
        targetClip.myVid.attachVideo(ns);
```

```
            ns.setBufferTime(3);
            ns.play("http://www.flashconnections.com/flash-video-
➥ pro/ch10/StepSavi1949_edit2.flv");
            // END FLV SOURCE

            /*
            // BEGIN WEBCAM SOURCE
            //Instantiate Camera and Microphone
            var local_cam:Camera = Camera.get();
            var local_mic:Microphone = Microphone.get();
            //Connect Camera instance to local video
            myVid.attachVideo(local_cam);
            // END WEBCAM SOURCE
            */
```

Next we trigger the method that sets up our bitmap holder movieclips and assign a method to our button click:

```
            // Initialize bitmap holders
            makeThumbBitmap();
            targetClip.start_btn.onRelease = Delegate.create(this,
➥ startInterval);
        }
```

Here we cycle through the bitmap holders and create a new BitmapData object in each:

```
        private function makeThumbBitmap():Void {
            // Create a new BitmapData object for each snapshot
            // and set pixel dimensions of the bitmap
            for (var i:Number = 1; i<=THUMB_COUNT; i++) {
                bitmapDataArray[i] = new BitmapData(96, 72, true);
                targetClip["snap"+i+"_mc"].attachBitmap(bitmapDataArray[i],
➥ 100+i, "auto", true);
            }
        }
```

Next, we set up the interval that starts when the user clicks the GO! button, and then hide the button:

```
        public function startInterval():Void {
            // Trigger the snapshots and hide the start button
            myInterval = setInterval(this, "takeSnapshots", SNAP_SHOT_DELAY);
            targetClip.start_btn._visible = false;
        }
```

Next is the method that actually takes the snapshots, which is triggered by myInterval. We cycle through each of the five snapshots, scaling each of them down using a matrix.scale() method to preserve memory. Then, when the maximum thumb count is reached, we trace a message saying we're done, and then clear the interval:

```
private function takeSnapshots():Void {
    // Take snapshots until the max THUMB_COUNT is reached,
    // then clear interval
    if (++shotCounter<=THUMB_COUNT) {
        var scalematrix:Matrix = new Matrix();
        scalematrix.scale(THUMB_SCALE, THUMB_SCALE);
        bitmapDataArray[shotCounter].draw(targetClip.myVid,
➡ scalematrix);
        if (shotCounter == THUMB_COUNT) {
            trace("Finished taking " + THUMB_COUNT + " snapshots.");
            clearInterval(myInterval);
        }
    }
}
```

Finally, we add a utility function to dispose of the BitmapData arrays after we're done with them. This function is not used here; we just included it so you'd have it handy if you want to use this script for other custom applications. You'll thank us later.

```
public function destroy():Void {
    // Always good form to have a destroy method to have
    // an easy way to dispose of bitmaps when you're done with them
    for (var i:Number = 1; i<=THUMB_COUNT; i++) {
        if (bitmapDataArray[i].dispose != undefined) {
            bitmapDataArray[i].dispose();
        }
    }
}
```

ActionScript 3: FotoBooth Application

If you want to cut right to the chase, you can download our example FLA from www.sybex.com/go/flashvideo. If you'd like to create your own FLA, here's how.

Begin by creating a new AS3 Flash document in Flash CS3. Then perform the following steps to create the FotoBooth application:

1. Set the Stage size to 550×400 and the background color to black.

2. Next, create a simple button. (In this example, we are creating our own buttons instead of using components. You could use the components if you'd rather; you'll just need to customize the sample code if you choose to do so.) Choose Insert > New Symbol. Draw a circle about 40 pixels in diameter on the Stage. On top of this circle, type **GO!** using the text tool. Give your symbol the name **GoButtonUpState**. In the Library, right-click the symbol and choose Linkage, then click Export for ActionScript and Export in First Frame in the dialog box, leaving the class and base class settings at the default values, and click OK. Then, right-click on the symbol in the Library again and choose Duplicate. Name this first copy **GoButtonOverState**. Set its Linkage to Export for Action-Script as well. Go through this process one more time, creating a third button state called **GoButtonDownState** and changing its Linkage settings. Edit each symbol to have a different color circle background.

3. Using the Type tool, add a title. (Refer to Figure 10.4 to see how we've set up our Stage.) Select the text box and choose Modify > Convert to Symbol and give it the name **FotoBoothTitle**. Export the movieclip for ActionScript as you did with the buttons, leaving the default values for class and base class. In our example, we also added some curtains. You can add any curtain-like artwork you can come up with, giving the movieclip the name **Curtains**. Be sure the top-left corner of this artwork is set to 0, 0. (If you decide not to include curtains, you'll need to edit that code out of our example.)

4. Then, return to the main timeline. At this point, all of your assets are in the Library and nothing is on your Stage. In the Properties panel, enter **Main** as your document class.

5. Save the file as **FotoBooth.fla**.

6. Now, on to the ActionScript. Create two new ActionScript files in your favorite editor, as shown next (Main.as and Fotobooth.as). Save Main.as and Fotobooth.as in the same folder as FotoBooth.fla.

Main.as

Let's start out with our Main class, which basically sets up the Stage and imports our FotoBooth class, which we'll be creating next.

```
package
{
    import FotoBooth;
```

```
import flash.display.StageAlign;
import flash.display.StageScaleMode;
import flash.display.Shape;
import flash.display.MovieClip;
import flash.display.SimpleButton;
import flash.media.Video;

public class Main extends MovieClip
{
    public var video_mc:MovieClip;
    public var video:Video;
    public var start_btn:SimpleButton;

    public var snap1_mc:MovieClip;
    public var snap2_mc:MovieClip;
    public var snap3_mc:MovieClip;
    public var snap4_mc:MovieClip;
    public var snap5_mc:MovieClip;

    public function Main()
    {
```

Here we're setting up our assets on the Stage. Feel free to change the coordinates here to better align the elements you create in your version.

```
        stage.scaleMode = StageScaleMode.NO_SCALE;
        stage.align = StageAlign.TOP_LEFT;
        // Create the FotoBooth Title
        var fbTitle:MovieClip = new FotoBoothTitle();
        addChild(fbTitle)
        fbTitle.x = (stage.stageWidth-fbTitle.width)/2;
        fbTitle.y = 20;
        // Create the Curtains
        var curtains:MovieClip = new Curtains();
        addChild(curtains)
        curtains.x = (stage.stageWidth-curtains.width)/2;
        curtains.y = (stage.stageHeight-curtains.height)/2;
        // Create the Video Player container
        video_mc = new MovieClip();
        addChild(video_mc);
        video_mc.x = 22;
        video_mc.y = 86;
```

```
// Create the Video component
video = new Video(240,180);
video_mc.addChild(video);
video.x = (stage.stageWidth-video.width)/2 - video_mc.x;
// Create the Start Button
var up:MovieClip = new GoButtonUpState();
var ov:MovieClip = new GoButtonOverState();
var dn:MovieClip = new GoButtonDownState();
start_btn = new SimpleButton(up,ov,dn,up);
video_mc.addChild(start_btn);
start_btn.width = start_btn.height = 35;
start_btn.x = (video.width-start_btn.width)/2 + video.x;
start_btn.y = (video.height-(start_btn.height/2)) + video.y;
// Add Snap Shot Holders
var snapbg:Shape = new Shape();
snapbg.graphics.beginFill(0xCCCCCC);
snapbg.graphics.drawRect(0,0,516,92);
snapbg.graphics.endFill();
video_mc.addChild(snapbg);
snapbg.x = -8;
snapbg.y = start_btn.y + 50;
snap1_mc = new MovieClip();
video_mc.addChild(snap1_mc);
snap1_mc.x = snapbg.x + 10;
snap1_mc.y = snapbg.y + 10;
snap2_mc = new MovieClip();
video_mc.addChild(snap2_mc);
snap2_mc.x = snapbg.x + 110;
snap2_mc.y = snap1_mc.y;
snap3_mc = new MovieClip();
video_mc.addChild(snap3_mc);
snap3_mc.x = snapbg.x + 210;
snap3_mc.y = snap1_mc.y;
snap4_mc = new MovieClip();
video_mc.addChild(snap4_mc);
snap4_mc.x = snapbg.x + 310;
snap4_mc.y = snap1_mc.y;
snap5_mc = new MovieClip();
video_mc.addChild(snap5_mc);
snap5_mc.x = snapbg.x + 410;
snap5_mc.y = snap1_mc.y;
```

Whew! OK, our assets are all set up; now let's instantiate a FotoBooth object, and off we go. Let's take a look at that class next.

```
                    // New FotoBooth
                    var fotoBooth:FotoBooth = new FotoBooth(this);
            }
        }
    }
```

FotoBooth.as

Here's where the action begins. This class actually grabs the video and saves the bitmaps. Let's step through and see what's going on. First, we import all the classes we'll need. Note that we are importing the Camera and Microphone classes here; these are needed only if you want to use a webcam as a source, instead of an FLV. We'll talk more about that in the next section.

```
package com.flashconnections
{
    import flash.display.MovieClip;
    import flash.display.BitmapData;
    import flash.geom.Matrix;
    import flash.net.NetConnection;
    import flash.net.NetStream;
    import flash.utils.Timer;
    import flash.events.MouseEvent;
    import flash.events.TimerEvent;
    import flash.display.Bitmap;
    import flash.media.Video;
    import flash.media.Camera;
    import flash.media.Microphone;
```

Next we set up some static variables that control the size of the snapshots, the number of snapshots, and the length of delay between them:

```
    public class FotoBooth {
        // Number of thumbnail images
        public static var THUMB_COUNT:Number = 5;
        // for a thumbnail a quarter the size of the video
        public static var THUMB_SCALE:Number = 0.4;
        // delay 1.5 seconds between snapshots
        public static var SNAP_SHOT_DELAY:Number = 1500;
```

```
private var _conn_nc:NetConnection;
private var _stream_ns:NetStream;
private var _target_mc:MovieClip;
private var _bitmapDataArray:Array;
private var _shotCounter:Number;
private var _timer:Timer;
```

Next we set up our video source. We include both FLV and webcam code here. We also initialize the number of snapshots taken, setting the shotCounter variable to 0.

```
public function FotoBooth(target:MovieClip) {
    _target_mc = target;
    _bitmapDataArray = new Array();
    _shotCounter = 0;
    // Construct NetConnection
    _conn_nc = new NetConnection();
    _conn_nc.connect(null);
    // Construct NetStream and connect to flow through
    // NetConnection
    _stream_ns = new NetStream(_conn_nc);
    _stream_ns.client = this;

    // BEGIN FLV SOURCE
    // Attach NetStream to movieclip containing video object
    //on the stage, and play file
    _target_mc.video.attachNetStream(_stream_ns);
    _stream_ns.bufferTime = 3;
    _stream_ns.play("http://www.flashconnections.com/flash-
➡ video-pro/ch10/StepSavi1949_edit2.flv");
    // END FLV SOURCE

    /*
    // BEGIN WEBCAM SOURCE
    //Instantiate Camera and Microphone
    var local_cam:Camera = Camera.get();
    var local_mic:Microphone = Microphone.get();
    //Connect Camera instance to local video
    _targetmc.video.attachVideo(local_cam);
    // END WEBCAM SOURCE
    */
```

Next, we create the `BitmapData` objects that will hold our snapshots, set up the event listener on our button, and create a timer that will handle the delay between snapshots:

```
// Initialize bitmap holders
makeThumbBitmap();
_target_mc.start_btn.addEventListener (MouseEvent.CLICK,
➡ startInterval);
    _timer = new Timer(SNAP_SHOT_DELAY, THUMB_COUNT);
    _timer.addEventListener(TimerEvent.TIMER, takeSnapshots,
➡ false, 0.0, true);
    }
```

Next is our function to set up the `BitmapData` objects. We draw an empty rectangle to act as placeholders for the bitmaps we'll be taking.

```
private function makeThumbBitmap():void {
    var bm:Bitmap;
    var bmd:BitmapData;
    // Create a new BitmapData object for each snapshot
    for (var i:Number = 1; i<=THUMB_COUNT; i++) {
        bmd = new BitmapData(96, 72, true, 0xCCCCCC);
        bm = new Bitmap(bmd);
        _target_mc["snap"+i+"_mc"].addChild(bm);
        _target_mc["snap"+i+"_mc"].graphics.lineStyle(0,0xFFFFFF);
        _target_mc["snap"+i+"_mc"].graphics.drawRect(0,0,96,72);
        _bitmapDataArray[i] = bmd;
    }
}
```

When the GO! button is clicked, the startInterval method will be triggered, starting the timer and hiding the button:

```
public function startInterval(event:MouseEvent):void {
    _timer.reset();
    _timer.start();
    _target_mc.start_btn.visible = false;
}
```

Here's where the action is—for each `BitmapData` object, a bitmap will be captured and resampled down to snapshot size, then attached to the object on the Stage. If all five shots have been taken, the shotCounter will reset to 0, the button will be visible again, and we'll stop our timer.

```
public function takeSnapshots(event:TimerEvent):void {
    if (++_shotCounter<=THUMB_COUNT) {
```

```
                var scalematrix:Matrix = new Matrix();
                scalematrix.scale(THUMB_SCALE, THUMB_SCALE);
                _bitmapDataArray[_shotCounter].draw(_target_mc.video, ➡
                scalematrix);
            }
            if (_shotCounter==THUMB_COUNT) {
                _target_mc.start_btn.visible = true;
                _shotCounter = 0;
                _timer.stop();
            }
        }
    }
```

And last but not least is our fiscally responsible destroy method, which allows you to clear the memory of any bitmap objects you no longer need:

```
    public function destroy():void {
        // Always good form to have a destroy method to have
        // an easy way to dispose of bitmaps when you're done with them
        for (var i:Number = 1; i<=THUMB_COUNT; i++) {
            if (_bitmapDataArray[i].dispose != undefined) {
                _bitmapDataArray[i].dispose();
            }
        }
    }

    public function onMetaData (info:Object):void {
        trace("stream metadata: ");
        for (var prop:String in info) {
            trace("\t" + prop + ": " + info[prop]);
        }
    }
  }
}
```

Finally, compile your SWF. The video will play automatically. When you're ready to snap some shots, click the GO! button. A series of five bitmaps will be taken as your video plays. Fun! Now, let's kick it up a notch, using a webcam instead of a video. Did you remember to comb your hair this morning?

Snapshots from a Webcam

For even more kitschy fun, you can hook up a webcam to this app and take some snapshots of yourself (Figure 10.6). We've included the code in our previous examples. Just plug a webcam into your computer, then comment out this FLV source block in the FotoBooth.as file, like this (in ActionScript 2):

```
/*
// BEGIN FLV SOURCE
// Attach NetStream to movieclip containing video object
// on the stage, and play file
targetClip.myVid.attachVideo(ns);
ns.setBufferTime(3);
ns.play("http://www.flashconnections.com/flash-video-
➡ pro/ch10/StepSavi1949_edit2.flv");
// END FLV SOURCE
*/
```

and uncomment the webcam source block:

```
// BEGIN WEBCAM SOURCE
//Instantiate Camera and Microphone
var local_cam:Camera = Camera.get();
var local_mic:Microphone = Microphone.get();
//Connect Camera instance to local video
targetClip.myVid.attachVideo(local_cam);
// END WEBCAM SOURCE
```

Or in ActionScript 3:

```
/*
// BEGIN FLV SOURCE
_target_mc.video.attachNetStream(_stream_ns);
_stream_ns.bufferTime = 3;
_stream_ns.play("http://www.flashconnections.com/flash-video-
➡ pro/ch10/StepSavi1949_edit2.flv");
// END FLV SOURCE
*/
```

and uncomment the webcam source block:

```
// BEGIN WEBCAM SOURCE
//Instantiate Camera and Microphone
var local_cam:Camera = Camera.getCamera();
```

```
var local_mic:Microphone = Microphone.getMicrophone();
//Connect Camera instance to local video
_target_mc.video.attachCamera(local_cam);
// END WEBCAM SOURCE
```

Figure 10.6 Snapshots from a webcam video source

So, instead of attaching a NetStream, setting a buffer (no buffer needed with a local webcam), and playing an FLV file, you'll get your local webcam and microphone, then attach them to the myVid instance. Piece of cake!

Now, plug in a webcam and test the application. You should see yourself instead of an FLV. Strike a pose and take some snapshots. Don't worry—no one else will see the photos; saving them to disk is beyond the scope of this book (although it *is* possible with the Flash Media Server server-side File class or with Apollo, Adobe's platform for developing desktop applications). There are also ways, just using Flash 8 or higher, to save out the BitmapData to an array and then send that array to a PHP or Remoting script, which in turn saves a JPEG to the server. You'd then have to retrieve the URL to that file so the user could download their photo. Like we said, it's a bit beyond the scope of this book, but it's good to know it's possible!

You could get even more creative with this example, adding a button toggle to choose between FLV or webcam source, or even automatically detect a webcam and if there's no webcam, play an FLV. Have some fun with it!

Well, that last webcam example was just a teaser of what's to come. The next chapter will deal with webcams and live video using Flash Media Server 2. If you've never messed with FMS2, or have been intimidated by it in the past, never fear. We'll give you a clear overview of what it can do and the know-how to do it.

Summary

In this chapter you learned about the power of the BitmapData object and how it can be used creatively in Flash video applications. You should now understand:

- What the BitmapData object is, and what you can do with it
- How to create bitmap thumbnails from an FLV file for dynamic playlists and previews
- How to create transitions and dissolves between videos
- How to take video snapshots from FLVs or a webcam

Next, we'll explore the exciting and fascinating world of Flash Media Server 2. We'll give you a whirlwind tour of live video, streaming video delivery, remote shared objects, server-side code, and more.

Live Video and Webcams: FMS

11

I (Lisa) discovered Flash Communication Server (FCS, or FlashCom) back in 2002. A friend of mine had an idea for a surveillance product that was simple to use, even for those with the most basic computer skills. He had noticed that most of the surveillance systems out there at the time had a huge learning curve—tons of special equipment, custom wiring, and a large monetary investment. (This was overkill for the average person who just may want to bop in to see if their dog's sleeping on the furniture.) Since I had just graduated from a postgrad new-media program (and was looking for something constructive to do that summer), he asked me to figure out how to build it.

Chapter Contents

The Video Revolution Will Be…Webcast
FMS2 Live! What You Need to Know
From Your Webcam to the World
What Else Can This FMS2 Thing Do?
Smart Bandwidth Streaming
FMS Hit List: Lisa's Tips and Tricks

FCS was the clear and obvious answer. It gave us an entirely web-based interface, with no special hardware, software, or wiring required. The user could broadcast using anything from a cheap $20 webcam to a high-definition security camera with night vision. Because it was wrapped in a Flash shell, we (that would be the royal "we") could build an interactive framework around it, with multiple camera angles, account login, guest account access—even motion detection with e-mail notification.

My summer with FCS was full of trial and triumph. Much time was spent on the now-defunct (but still searchable) ChattyFig FlashCom list, learning from the sages there how to write server-side scripts, throttle bandwidth, keep spotty connections alive...and before I knew it, I had an application—a real, robust, fully functional video application—that even your grandmother could use. And, with support here and there from an amazing developer community, I created it all myself! I was hooked.

After reading this chapter, we hope you'll catch the FMS bug as well. You'll get a glimpse of the powerful tools offered by the latest version, Flash Media Server 2 (FMS2), to work with video, audio, and data. We'll walk you through setting up a development environment and give you an overview of how FMS2 works. Of course, you can always just use it for simply streaming video or audio, but we bet your head will be filled with ideas for much richer applications by the end of this chapter.

Let the romance begin!

The Video Revolution Will Be...Webcast

The revolution in online video we're seeing today gained momentum slowly and steadily. In crept faster Internet connections, faster processors, more savvy surfers, and more efficient video codecs, all dovetailing at once, giving us today's burgeoning online video market. Luckily for us Flash developers, Flash was at the forefront of this technology, delivering video without any extra plug-ins or player downloads. They just kinda snuck video in there...and we ran with it.

Enter Flash Communication Server, now dubbed Flash Media Server (FMS). Offering tools to integrate data, streaming video and audio, live video, and user inter-action, FMS has opened up a world of possibilities. Not only can developers of varying skills deliver streaming video, but we can also create amazing, ingenious, robust, col-laborative multimedia applications.

All that's fine and good—now what exactly *is* FMS, you ask?

What FMS Is and How It Works

The Flash Media Server opens up a persistent connection to a viewer, or "client" (through a SWF) using Real-Time Message Protocol (RTMP). This provides an uninter-rupted two-way data stream between the client and the server that can contain video, audio, or data.

Why It's So Cool

RTMP differs from your standard HTTP connection in that it's an open line of communication, flowing both ways. For example, HTTP receives a request from a client, and then answers that request. In other words, the client *pulls* data from the server. RTMP, however, is much more powerful because it can automatically *push* data to connected clients. This opens up a ton of possibilities for interactive applications. Add video and audio to the mix—and *fugeddaboutit*!

Where/How You Can Use It

FMS is a great solution for applications such as:

- Video blogging
- Video on demand
- Streaming with intelligent bandwidth and version detection
- Videoconferencing
- Collaborative environments, whiteboard, chat, and sharing data
- Multiplayer games
- Live web event broadcasts, either with your own custom application or Adobe's Flash Media Encoder

So, now that you're all jazzed to start your own revolution via RTMP, let's go over the information you need to get started.

> **Note:** This chapter is a brief overview of FMS; you'll walk away with the tools and understanding you need to get started, but there's a lot more to FMS than we could ever cover in one chapter. (The learning curve can be worth it, though!) To help you further your knowledge, we've included some helpful links and resources at the end of the chapter to point you in the right direction.

FMS2 Live! What You Need to Know

You're probably feeling ready to dive in and start building your first application. Don't worry, we'll get to that in a bit—but you'll need to do a little planning first. (Do we ever let up with all the *planning*!) Do you have an account with an FMS host? Or do you want to run your own server? Regardless, you'll need to set up your work environment before you can start your first FMS app. Luckily, on the development end, Flash is all you need. To test the apps, though, you'll need a server running FMS. Let's take a look at your hosting options; then we'll go over the basic elements of FMS. Finally, we'll give you some code examples and bring it all together by building our very own two-person videoconference application from scratch!

Hosting: Choices, Choices, Choices

Since you're reading this book, you've likely already decided that Flash video is a better solution than, say, Windows Media or QuickTime for your specific application. And if you need streaming video delivery, FMS is your de facto choice. (Caveat: See the sidebar "Revolutionary FMS Alternatives" for a discussion of possible FMS alternatives.)

Great, that's settled! Hold on—you actually have yet another choice to make: will you use a Flash Video Streaming Service (FVSS), go with an FMS service provider, or host the video on your own server with an FMS license? Let's take a look at the differences and see which option is a good fit.

Flash Video Streaming Service (FVSS) Plug and play is for you. You just want to serve some FLVs, and you want them to play back quickly and smoothly. You like having an automated system to log into and upload new videos whenever you (or your clients) need to. You need the reliability and scalability offered by a larger content delivery network. All you need is the RTMP address of their server to plug into your connection string in Flash and you're good to go. As covered back in Chapter 3, the larger players, and Adobe's authorized partners in this space, are Akamai and Limelight Networks.

FMS Service Provider You need a little more flexibility. You've developed an application that doesn't just leverage FLV streaming but also has some other interactive elements such as a live chat, videoconferencing, or server-side authentication. An FMS service provider may be for you. Also offering fast, optimized video delivery, these companies are basically FMS-centric FVSSs (see Chapter 3 for more discussion). However, they offer more than just FLV streaming: they give you access to your own FMS "vhost" account. A vhost, or virtual host, account gives you access to upload both FLVs and full FMS applications. Unlike most straightforward FVSS accounts, you can run your own custom server-side scripts, record video, save files, and more. You can do just about everything that FMS offers, but—and this can be a big "but"—you don't have access to the overall FMS server settings that you may need to tweak for some custom FMS applications. Often, you won't ever need to change those settings, but sometimes you want the option to do so.

If you just want to dive in and get started developing FMS applications, we recommend opening one of these accounts. Providers such as Influxis.com have very low-cost monthly accounts to get you started.

Hosting It Yourself You like having control. You don't want anyone to tell you that you can't make changes to your own server's configuration, darn it! You want to dig into the inner workings of FMS and bend it to your will. Maybe you're working on a small, custom application that you're going to host yourself, or you work for a large company with an IT department that will be deploying an FMS-based load-balanced server farm and you want to get the settings just right. Regardless of any specific project, you'll likely want to test your FMS applications locally to streamline your production workflow. Luckily for us, Adobe has a developer license available—and better yet, it's free! (Even better news—the user license states that you can use it on commercial projects as well. You're limited to 10 consecutive connections but that's usually enough for development or proof-of-concept deployment. *Thank you, Adobe!*)

FMS runs on either Windows or Linux. The specific system requirements are:

- Windows Server 2000 or 2003 (We run our local development FMS license on Windows XP, but it's not officially supported.)
- Linux: RedHat Enterprise v3.0 or v4.0

Your computer should be pretty beefy as well, at least a Pentium 4, 3.2GHz or better (Dual Xeon or higher recommended), 1GB of available RAM, and a 1GB Ethernet card. In our experience, you can get away with a slightly slower machine for development if need be. But once your app is ready for real testing, you'll want to run it on a well-equipped server.

Revolutionary FMS Alternatives

Although we specifically refer to Flash Media Server as the streaming solution throughout this chapter, you should know that there are alternatives available. FMS is not the end-all and be-all for streaming video, audio, and data in Flash. Depending on your application's needs, you may be able to utilize one of these other options.

Red5

An open source project (Lesser General Public License), Red5 is a server written in Java that supports:

- Streaming video (FLV)
- Streaming audio (MP3)
- Live stream publishing
- Shared objects
- Remoting
- AMF3 (since version 0.6rc2)

The Red5 project is community-driven, but there are several companies emerging that are focused on Red5 support and commercial application development. With several CDNs looking to get it implemented as a service at this writing, Red5 is well on its way to becoming a robust RTMP server

Continues

Revolutionary FMS Alternatives *(Continued)*

solution. The potential downside? Well, it depends on how you feel about open source. Support is only as reliable as the open source community (which, in this case, though, is pretty darn good, with stellar developers John Grden and Chris Allen guiding the project and plenty of sharp developers dedicated to building it). It also takes some server admin knowledge to get configured (and some Java development experience if you want to go beyond just streaming media). But if you are up for it, it's a robust alternative, offering much more extensibility than FMS. Red5 works with all standard video classes, so your FMS applications should port over smoothly to Red5 from FMS. Another benefit, because Red5 is open source and based on widely adopted technologies, such as Spring Framework and Mina protocol layer, it's a great cross platform solution that works on Windows, Mac OSX and Linux. Being Java-based and open source, you can extend it like crazy, dig in as deep as you like and compile and deploy your apps within whatever platform you're on, even OSX. The best part? It's free.

http://osflash.org/red5/

Red5-minimal

Also, as of this review, there's a small embedded version of Red5 named Red5-minimal, which is based on Red5 0.6rc2, and provides just streaming media capabilities. It can be configured as a library for any Java project.

http://oss.viewdle.com/red5-minimal/

Wowza Media Server Pro

Another server written in Java, this one was developed by a team of Adobe ex-pats who built it from the ground up. It also streams video and audio and supports shared objects, as well as the following:

- Server-side scripting (Java, not Server-Side ActionScript)

- Logging and administration

- Multiplatform (Windows, Linux, Mac OS X, Solaris, and more)

- 64-bit architecture

Wowza is feature-rich and well supported. The biggest downside to this alternative (for some of us) is its use of Java on the server side instead of Server-Side ActionScript (SSAS). And this one, though not as expensive as FMS, is still not free ($750–$5,000 depending on the number of simultaneous connections you need).

http://www.wowzamedia.com

Revolutionary FMS Alternatives *(Continued)*

haXeVideo

Another open source solution, haXeVideo is a multithread FLV streaming server written using the haXe programming language. Because it's written to do just one thing, the source code is optimized and the server is lightweight. Note, however, that haXeVideo is still in beta at this time.

http://code.google.com/p/haxevideo/

Unity 2

Written by Colin Moock, Unity 2 is a server-side Java application that acts as a socket server allowing a free flow of data from server to client for applications such as chat, games, business applications, and more. Note, though, that it's for data only; it doesn't support video or audio. It ships with lots of ready-to-use multiuser Flash applications and a Development Kit. It's actually been out for a few years now, but we decided it was worthy of a mention here as it can be useful in some specific applications. It can be used in conjunction with FMS if need be.

http://www.moock.org/unity/

Setting Up a Development Environment

The good news is, you can program for FMS with nothing more than the tools you now use to develop other Flash applications.

However, if you plan to spend a lot of time developing applications for FMS, we recommend that you set up your own Developer Edition FMS locally. The simplest workflow we can suggest is to run FMS and develop on the same machine, preferably running Windows. (The Mac user in us is cringing!) It's just the most straightforward way to set things up; you don't have to worry about access over the local network (as you would if you were running two machines locally, one for development and the other for FMS), and you have full access to all of the FMS core settings (which you wouldn't have if you just used an FMS service provider account).

That being said, if you are just experimenting with FMS, you don't need to mess with server settings, or you're on a Mac, you'll probably want to sign up for an entry-level account with an FMS service provider.

It's a bit outside of our focus here to walk you through the installation of FMS, but it's pretty simple, especially on Windows. You can find detailed installation instructions and recommendations in the FMS docs.

Note: You can use AS1 or JavaScript 1.5 to develop server-side scripts, and AS1, 2, or 3 to develop your client-side scripts.

File Structure

It's important to understand where files are stored, as well as the overall directory structure of an application. No matter what your setup—hosted with an FMS service provider, your own server, or your local machine for testing—the basic folder structure within FMS is going to be the same. It's quite simple; let's have a look.

The first thing you need to understand is that each FMS application has its own directory inside the applications directory. For example, the path to an application called MyApp would look like this:

```
/applications/MyApp/
```

Each application should have a main server-side file associated with it. This file can have the name of the application followed by the .asc extension, or just be called main.asc. It would be inside the applications directory:

```
/applications/MyApp/main.asc
```

This is where SSAS files will reside. In addition to your application's main.asc file, you can create as many .asc files as you need; you'd then import them into your main.asc file at runtime. This approach can be convenient if you have a complex application and you want to keep your code compartmentalized.

When FMS records FLV streams, it saves them in an instance-specific directory inside of a directory called streams, which is inside its main application directory. If either directory doesn't exist yet, FMS creates it. So, if you recorded a stream from the application MyApp and you called that instance of the application myInstance, the path would be as follows:

```
/applications/MyApp/streams/myInstance/myVideo.flv
```

This directory would also contain any FLVs you'd like to access and stream via that application instance.

Remote shared objects get the same treatment. They are stored in an instance-specific directory inside a directory called sharedobjects, like so:

```
/applications/MyApp/sharedobjects/myInstance/...
```

(The shared objects are not actually files that you can upload/download or edit; they are only referenced via FMS and can only be edited using the sharedObject class methods.)

Note: If you don't specify an application instance when you connect to the application, an instance name of _definst_ will be used.

Note: It is recommended that you use all lowercase for application and stream names with FMS2. That way, you shouldn't run into problems if you move your applications to servers with different configurations or platforms.

The Basics

There are two core technologies inside Flash Media Server that make it so powerful: *streams* and *remote shared objects*.

Streams

Streams are a basic element of FMS. A stream can contain an FLV or an MP3.

Each viewer receives their own stream when they view a video (live or recorded) or listen to an audio file. If you are broadcasting a live video, that is an outgoing stream. As the number of connections increases, the number of streams needed increases exponentially. For example, in a two-way videoconferencing application, there would be four active streams. Each participant has one incoming stream and one outgoing stream. The number of streams can multiply fast as you add participants, however—a 4-person videoconference would require a whopping 12 streams (see Figure 11.1)! That's a lot of bandwidth. Keep that in mind when building your apps, and set your maximum bandwidth per stream accordingly.

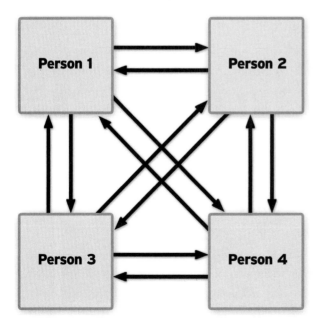

Figure 11.1 Mapping the streams

Remote Shared Objects

Ah... shared objects. Aside from the actual video streaming, shared objects are arguably the most powerful tool in your FMS toolbox.

You may be familiar with the local shared object available in Flash. It acts as a "cookie," saving data locally that you can retrieve from the client at a later time, such as the next time they visit your site. Remote shared objects are like local shared objects on steroids.

Remote shared objects (RSOs) allow real-time data sharing between multiple SWF clients, and can be stored on the FMS server itself for later retrieval. You can use them to synchronize data between all clients in an application. They can store high scores; the state the last person left the application in when they signed out; or the location of a draggable object on the Stage, animated in real time as another person drags it around. Or they can store information on who was in the chatroom before you arrived and what time they left. The uses are virtually infinite!

You can break down the uses for remote shared objects into two general categories:

Storage and retrieval of data The remote shared object can store data on the Flash Media Server that other clients can access when they connect to that instance of the application. By using the built-in onSync event, any changes to the data in the RSO by the client will automatically be updated on the server. For example, say you created a Flash-based wiki. Every time someone updated the text on the page, anyone also connected to that application instance would see the text update in real time, and anyone who visited the page after that would see the updated text as well because it's stored *persistently* on the server.

Real-time sharing of data For example, you could have a shared video playlist. One client could choose a video to watch, and it would play for all clients connected to the application. Of course, this could lead to some playground-caliber sharing issues, as often demonstrated in the now-infamous Fridge Magnet application by Stefan of Flash-ComGuru (http://www.flashcomguru.com/apps/letters/index.cfm). I have yet to be able to spell out more than a word or two before someone starts stealing my letters!

Remote shared objects can be either persistent or nonpersistent. Persistent means that they are actually stored on the server (in the sharedobjects directory of the application instance) and their values can be accessed by clients when they connect to that instance. Nonpersistent means that they are shared among all connected clients, but they are purged from memory after the last client closes the connection.

Then, to make it even more confusing, you can have server-side shared objects or client-side remote shared objects. Client-side remote shared objects are shared between connected clients. Server-side remote shared objects can be shared between servers. You'd use server-side RSOs if you needed to share data between two different FMS applications—if you had a shared "lobby" area that had an updated list of chatrooms that may be hosted on different Flash Media Servers, for example.

Next, let's take a look at the ActionScript media classes that are available for use in FMS applications.

The Media Classes

On the *client side*, you have six classes that relate to FMS functionality:

Camera This class allows you to capture, display, and record video from an attached webcam (or other video source, such as supported video cards). You can attach the camera to a video object to display it in Flash by calling the Video.attachVideo method in AS2 or the Video.attachCamera method in AS3.

Microphone This class allows you to capture, play, and record audio from your computer's built-in microphone, or from another source plugged into the sound card. You can use MovieClip.attachAudio to play back the audio from either the microphone or the NetStream. By doing this, you can then control the properties of the sound, such as volume, in AS2. In AS3, you can use the soundTransform property of the NetStream to control the volume.

NetConnection This class has the same use as in progressive video delivery, but instead of passing null, you pass the RTMP path to your application instance on your Flash Media Server.

NetStream This class has the same use as in progressive video delivery; it carries a one-way stream of video or audio data, either live or prerecorded.

SharedObject This class offers real-time data sharing between connected SWFs, and can be persistent locally or remotely.

Video This class allows you to display video on the Stage in Flash without embedding it into your SWF file. The video can be live or recorded.

You've likely encountered most of those client-side classes. Here are a few you may not be familiar with yet—the *server-side* media classes, used, of course, in SSAS:

Application Each FMS application has a single application object, which lasts until the application instance is unloaded from the server. The application object can be used to accept or reject connection attempts, register and unregister proxies, or even create functions that are triggered when an application starts or stops.

Client This class gives you a way to handle each connection, or client, to a specific FMS application. When the client connects to the application, FMS automatically creates a client object, and destroys it when they leave. Properties of the Client class can give you information about the version, operating system, and IP address of a connected client, and can allow you to set bandwidth limits and even call methods on the client SWF.

File This class allows access to the server's file system. You can create, edit, and delete files using this class's methods.

LoadVars This class lets you send variables to and from a specified URL.

NetConnection The server-side NetConnection class operates much like the client-side version, but here you're creating a two-way connection between an FMS application and an application server, another Flash Media Server, or another instance of an application on the same FMS server. This allows for server load balancing, real-time data updates, and more.

SharedObject This class operates basically the same way as the client-side version, but here you can share data between application instances, or even between applications on other Flash Media Servers.

Stream Server-side streams give you even more flexibility than client-side streams. You can play or record streams strictly on the server side, either remotely on another FMS or between application instances on the same server.

WebService This class is used to create and access WSDL/SOAP web services. The WebService, SOAPFault, SOAPCall, and Log classes make up the WebService package. It's important to note that the WebService class cannot retrieve complex data or arrays returned by a web service, and it has no security features.

XML This class lets you load, parse, send, build, and manipulate XML document trees, just like the client-side class.

XMLSocket This class creates an open connection to a server identified by an IP address or a domain name. This lets the server immediately send messages without a request from the client, providing low latency for applications such as chat and multiplayer games. Related to the XMLSocket class is the XMLStreams class, which transmits data in a slightly different way, and is optimized for Jabber or IM communication.

This is, of course, a simple overview of the classes used in FMS applications. Next, let's take a look at how a basic connection to FMS would be set up.

Note: Some people *hate* code with suffixes. Personally, we prefer it, because it tells you at a glance what type of object you're dealing with (in addition to helpful code hints). Some FMS-specific objects and their associated suffixes are provided in Table 11.1, for your reference.

▶ **Table 11.1** Object Types and Associated Suffixes

Object Type	Suffix String
Camera	_cam
Microphone	_mic
NetConnection	_nc
NetStream	_ns
SharedObject	_so
Video	_video

Connecting to FMS2

The following code will tell Flash to connect to the instance called myInstance, of an application called myApplication, which is hosted on the same server as the SWF file:

```
nc.connect("rtmp:/myApplication/myInstance");
```

(Note the use of a single slash in the URL. Keep an eye on that in these examples, it can trip you up.) Another connection string option, used for local testing, would be:

```
nc.connect("rtmp://localhost/myApplication/myInstance");
```

or:

```
nc.connect("rtmp://127.0.0.1/myApplication/myInstance");
```

This next code will connect to the instance called myInstance, of an application called myApplication, on a server that is different from that of the SWF file:

```
nc.connect("rtmp://www.myFMSDomain.com/myApplication/myInstance");
```

OK, now that you've got the basics down, you're ready to dive into a real application so you can get a better understanding of how an FMS application works!

From Your Webcam to the World

One of the coolest features of FMS (in our opinion) is being able to send and receive live video. Using just a simple webcam and a few lines of ActionScript, you can create a completely custom live broadcast application. Talk about "power to the people!"

To complete this exercise, you'll of course need a webcam and microphone (built-in or external), and an FMS server. If you don't have your own developer's edition FMS set up locally, you can get a trial account with an FMS service provider to experiment. (Visit our blog at http://www.flashconnections.com for recommendations and discount links.) Once you've got that all set up, we can dive in and see how it's done.

videoConf.fla

In this example, we'll try to roll as many of the basic FMS functions in as possible so you can see them in action, without making it too overwhelming. We'll create a tidy little two-person videoconferencing application that prompts each participant for their name, and then broadcasts their webcam and microphone (see Figure 11.2). If more than two people try to log in at once, they'll get a message that the room is full. This application uses the following basic features of FMS:

- Live streaming video and audio (broadcasting and receiving)
- Nonpersistent remote shared objects to sync login names
- Simple server-side scripting to give feedback in the FMS Admin Console

Figure 11.2 Completed *videoConf.swf* application

The asset setup is the same in both AS2 and AS3, but the code is a bit different. In addition to some syntax differences, AS3 is much stricter about the sequence of connections and events in FMS applications. AS2 can be particular as well (where the status handler methods are placed within the code can be crucial to whether the handler will fire), but AS3 is even more so. You'll see that we need to add some additional checks and handlers to be sure that the streams do not try to connect before the Net-Connection has fully connected, for example. Then there are the defaultObjectEncoding commands that need to be set up (and were not well documented!). Let's walk through setting up the application on the server first, then the assets, and finally we'll walk through both the AS2 and AS3 code.

Server-Side Application Setup

First, let's set up our application file on the FMS server, so we have something to connect to. If you're running your own FMS locally, you'll just want to create a new folder inside the Applications folder and call it fvpvideoconf. You'll place your main.asc file in here.

Also, locate your FMS Administration Console SWF that came with FMS. Open it in a browser so you can monitor your server-side stats and traces as you develop your application. You can also use this interface to restart your application if need be. This Admin console is your friend; use it often!

To create the main.asc file, just open up your favorite text editor and enter the following code:

```
application.onAppStart = function() {
    trace("Chatroom created!");
};
```

```
application.onConnect = function(client, myName) {
    client.name = myName;
    trace(client.name+" has connected");
    application.acceptConnection(client);
    trace(client.name+" has been accepted");
};
application.onDisconnect = function(client) {
    trace(client.name+" has left.");
};
```

This is a basic server-side script that gives some feedback in the FMS Console when clients connect and disconnect.

Now, if you happen to be using Influxis, here's how to set up the new application in that interface:

1. Log into your account, and click the File Admin tab.

2. Choose Add New Application, and enter **fvpvideoconf** as the application name. Choose the option to create your own main.asc file (Figure 11.3). Click OK. Either paste in the previous code or upload the main.asc file if you've created it already.

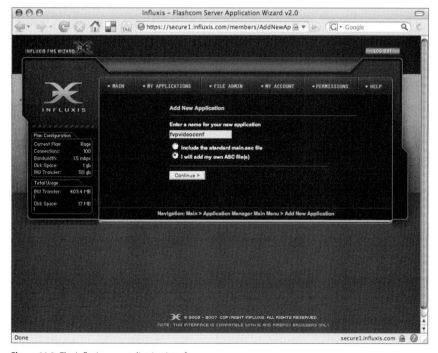

Figure 11.3 The Influxis new application interface

3. You'll then be shown a screen with the connection string to this application. Copy this string and save it for later. You'll need to paste it into your NetConnection code, like so:

```
nc.connect(
➡ "rtmp://yourInfluxisAccountNumber.rtmphost.com/fvpvideoconf",
"myName");
```

4. Your application is all set up. While you're logged in, you should now open the FMS Admin Console so you can see what's happening on the server as you test your application. Select the My Applications tab, and then click the FCS Application Inspector link. At the bottom of this page, you'll see a link to open the Flash Media Server 2 Administration Panel. Click this link and a new window will open, prompting you to log in with the admin login provided to you by Influxis. Once you log in here (Figure 11.4), you'll be able to see everything going on behind the scenes, including stream and connection data, shared object instantiation, server-side traces, and more.

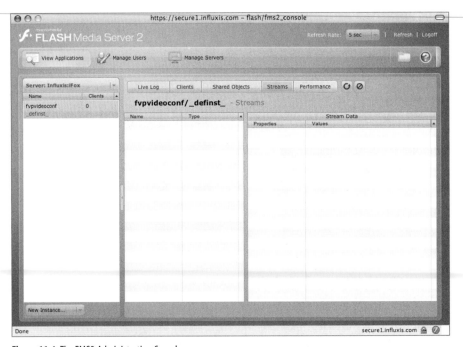

Figure 11.4 The FMS2 Administration Console

Setting Up Your Assets in Flash

As we said, the asset setup is the same for both versions (Figure 11.2):

1. Create a new FLA in either Flash 8 or Flash CS3.

2. From the drop-down menu in the Library, choose New Video. Drag this video object to the Stage and name it **myVid**.

3. Create a text box beneath the video object. In the Parameters panel, make it dynamic text, 240 pixels wide by 30 pixels high, and Verdana Bold at a point size of 22. Give it an instance name of **myName**.

4. Select both items and choose Modify > Convert to Symbol. Give the resulting symbol an instance name of **videoOne_mc**. Place it at x = 24, y = 120.

5. Duplicate the symbol, place it to the right of the original, and call the new symbol **videoTwo_mc**.

6. Next, we'll create the movie clip for our login. From the Components menu, drag a TextInput box onto the Stage above the videos. Give it an instance name of **name_txt**.

7. Draw a box to the right of the TextInput box that's 76 pixels wide by 22 pixels tall. On top of it, using the Text tool, type the word **SUBMIT**. Select both items and choose Modify > Convert to Symbol. Give the symbol an instance name of **submit_btn**.

8. Select the new submit_btn symbol and the name_txt box, then choose Modify > Convert to Symbol. Give this new symbol an instance name of **loginWindow**. Now you have a single login movie clip that we can hide when we no longer need it.

9. Almost there…now we just need a way to get some feedback about our connection. To do this, we drag another TextInput box onto the Stage, this time near the bottom, beneath the videos. (A dynamic text field would also work here, if you don't want to use a text field component.) Make it 150 pixels wide, and give it an instance name of **status_ti**. Our connection status code will appear there to let us know what's going on behind the scenes.

10. Now, on to the code. Create a new layer called **Actions**, and add the Action-Script from the following sections to the first frame (in either AS2 or AS3, as appropriate). Follow the comments for explanations about what's going on—paying close attention to the sometimes subtle differences between the AS2 and AS3 code.

Note: As you'll notice, we are just putting all this code on the first frame on the timeline in the Flash IDE rather than creating a class-based application. Obviously, OOP class-based setup is preferred in professional deployment, but we want you to focus on the basic workings of FMS here, and admittedly, OOP structure can sometimes get in the way.

ActionScript 2:

```
// Construct NetConnection
var nc:NetConnection = new NetConnection();
nc.connect(
➠ "rtmp://yourInfluxisAccountNumber.rtmphost.com/fvpvideoconf",
➠ "myConf");

// Construct NetStreams and connect to flow through NetConnection
var out_ns:NetStream = new NetStream(nc);
var in_ns:NetStream = new NetStream(nc);

// Show NetConnection status feedback, and connect
// shared objects when nc is successful
nc.onStatus = function(infoObj:Object) {
    if (infoObj.code == "NetConnection.Connect.Success") {
        status_ti.text = "Connected";
        personOne_so.connect(nc);
        personTwo_so.connect(nc);
    } else {
        status_ti.setStyle("color", 0xff0000);
        status_ti.text = "Connection Failed!";
    }
}

function hideLogin():Void {
    // Hide login window and assign login name to variable
    loginWindow._visible = false;
    myName = loginWindow.name_txt.text;
    // Check to see if the first person has logged in yet,
    // if not, assign this client to personOne
    if(personOne_so.data.nameString == undefined){
        setupVideo(myName, 1);
        personOne_so.data.nameString = myName;
// If personOne is logged in, check to see if a
// second client is logged in already. If not,
// assign this client to personTwo
    } else if (personTwo_so.data.nameString == undefined) {
        //var nameTwo:String = myName;
        setupVideo(myName, 2);
```

```
        personTwo_so.data.nameString = myName;
// If both slots are assigned, give feedback
// that room is full
    } else {
        loginWindow._visible = false;
        status_ti.setStyle("color", 0xff0000);
        status_ti.text = "Room Full";
    }
}

function setupVideo(myName, person:Number):Void {
    //Instantiate Camera and Microphone
    var local_cam:Camera = Camera.get();
    var live_mic:Microphone = Microphone.get();
    live_mic.setRate(5);
    live_mic.setSilenceLevel(20, 2000);
    //Connect Camera and Mic instances to outgoing NetStream
    out_ns.attachAudio(live_mic);
    out_ns.attachVideo(local_cam);
    // Assign correct outgoing and incoming streams,
    // depending on designation as personOne or personTwo
    if(person == 1) {
        // Populate display of videos and names
        videoOne_mc.myVid.attachVideo(local_cam);
        videoOne_mc.myName._visible = true;
        videoTwo_mc.myName._visible = true;
        videoOne_mc.myName.text = personOne_so.data.nameString;
        videoTwo_mc.myName.text = personTwo_so.data.nameString;
        // Publish this client's video, and play back other video
        out_ns.publish("vOne", "live");
        in_ns.play("vTwo");
        videoTwo_mc.myVid.attachVideo(in_ns);
    } else {
        // Populate display of videos and names
        videoTwo_mc.myVid.attachVideo(local_cam);
        videoOne_mc.myName._visible = true;
        videoTwo_mc.myName._visible = true;
        videoOne_mc.myName.text = personOne_so.data.nameString;
        videoTwo_mc.myName.text = personTwo_so.data.nameString;
```

```actionscript
        // Publish this client's video, and play back other video
        out_ns.publish("vTwo", "live");
        in_ns.play("vOne");
        videoOne_mc.myVid.attachVideo(in_ns);
    }
}


// Initial setup of Stage, show login, hide name textfields
loginWindow.submit_btn.onRelease = function() { hideLogin() };
videoOne_mc.myName._visible = false;
videoTwo_mc.myName._visible = false;
// Instantiate shared objects which will hold client names
var personOne_so:SharedObject = SharedObject.getRemote("pOne", nc.uri);
var personTwo_so:SharedObject = SharedObject.getRemote("pTwo", nc.uri);


// Set up handlers to update the client names when they change
personOne_so.onSync = function(list) {
    videoOne_mc.myName.text = personOne_so.data.nameString;
}
personTwo_so.onSync = function(list) {
    videoTwo_mc.myName.text = personTwo_so.data.nameString;
}
```

ActionScript 3:

```actionscript
// Required for AS3 and FMS2 to
// communicate in the proper format
NetConnection.defaultObjectEncoding = flash.net.ObjectEncoding.AMF0;
SharedObject.defaultObjectEncoding = flash.net.ObjectEncoding.AMF0;


// Initial setup of Stage, show login, hide name textfields
// Instantiate shared objects which will hold client names
loginWindow.submit_btn.addEventListener(MouseEvent.CLICK, hideLogin);
loginWindow.visible = false;


// Instantiate shared objects which will hold client names
var personOne_so:SharedObject;
var personTwo_so:SharedObject;


// Construct NetStreams and connect to flow through NetConnection
```

```
var out_ns:NetStream;
var in_ns:NetStream;

// Construct NetConnection
var nc:NetConnection = new NetConnection ();
nc.objectEncoding = ObjectEncoding.AMF0;
nc.addEventListener(NetStatusEvent.NET_STATUS, onNetStatus);
nc.connect("rtmp://3yrgt1807fg.rtmphost.com/fvpvideoconf/", "myConf");

// required function
function onMetaData(info:Object):void {
    trace("onMetaData: ");
    for (var prop:String in info) {
        trace("\t" + prop + ": " + info[prop]);
    }
}

// Show NetConnection status feedback, and connect
// shared objects when nc is successful
function onNetStatus(event:NetStatusEvent):void {
    trace ("onStatus: " + event);
    for (var prop:String in event.info) {
        trace("\t" + prop + ": " + event.info[prop]);
    }
    if (event.info.code == "NetConnection.Connect.Success") {
        // Don't show login until connection has been made
        setupLogin();
        // Person One
        personOne_so = SharedObject.getRemote("pOne", nc.uri);
        personOne_so.addEventListener(SyncEvent.SYNC, onSync);
        personOne_so.addEventListener(NetStatusEvent.NET_STATUS, onSync);
        personOne_so.connect(nc);
        // Person Two
        personTwo_so = SharedObject.getRemote("pTwo", nc.uri);;
        personTwo_so.addEventListener(SyncEvent.SYNC, onSync);
        personTwo_so.addEventListener(NetStatusEvent.NET_STATUS, onSync);
        personTwo_so.connect(nc);
        // In Stream
        in_ns = new NetStream(nc);
```

```
        in_ns.addEventListener(NetStatusEvent.NET_STATUS, onMetaData);
        // Out Stream
        out_ns = new NetStream(nc);
        out_ns.addEventListener(NetStatusEvent.NET_STATUS, onMetaData);
    }
    if (event.info.Description != undefined) {
        status_ti.text = event.info.Description;
    }
}


function setupLogin():void {
    loginWindow.name_txt.text = "";
    loginWindow.visible = true;
    videoOne_mc.myName.visible = false;
    videoTwo_mc.myName.visible = false;
}


function hideLogin(event:MouseEvent):void {
    // Hide login window and assign login name to variable
    loginWindow.visible = false;
    var myname:String = loginWindow.name_txt.text;

    // Check to see if the first person has logged in yet,
    // if not, assign this client to personOne
    if (personOne_so.data.nameString == undefined) {
        setupVideo (myname, 1);
// If personOne is logged in, check to see if a
// second client is logged in already. If not,
// assign this client to personTwo
    }
    else if (personTwo_so.data.nameString == undefined) {
        setupVideo (myname, 2);
// If both slots are assigned, give feedback
// that room is full
    } else {
        loginWindow.visible = false;
        status_ti.text = "Room Full";
    }
}
```

```
function setupVideo(myname:String, person:Number):void {
    //Instantiate Camera
    trace("setupVideo "+person+" "+myname);
    // Show names
    videoOne_mc.myName.visible = true;
    videoTwo_mc.myName.visible = true;
    var local_cam:Camera = Camera.getCamera ();
    // If client has no camera, give feedback and disallow login
    if (local_cam == null) {
        status_ti.text = "You need a camera";
        setupLogin ();
    } else {
        // Connect Camera instances to outgoing NetStream
        out_ns.attachCamera(local_cam);
        // Instantiate Microphone
        var live_mic:Microphone = Microphone.getMicrophone();
        if (live_mic != null) {
            live_mic.rate = 5;
            live_mic.setSilenceLevel(20, 2000);
            //Connect Mic instances to outgoing NetStream
            out_ns.attachAudio(live_mic);
        }
        // Assign correct outgoing and incoming streams,
        // depending on designation as personOne or personTwo
        if (person == 1) {
            // Note different syntax in AS3 for setting
            // the value of a shared object data slot
            personOne_so.setProperty("nameString", myname);
            // Populate display of videos and names
            videoOne_mc.myVid.attachCamera(local_cam);
            videoOne_mc.myName.text = personOne_so.data.nameString;
            // Publish this client's video, and play back other video
            out_ns.publish("vOne", "live");
            in_ns.play("vTwo");
            videoTwo_mc.myVid.attachNetStream(in_ns);
        } else {
            personTwo_so.setProperty("nameString", myname);
            trace("set myname = "+personTwo_so.data.nameString);
```

```
// Populate display of videos and names
videoTwo_mc.myVid.attachCamera(local_cam);
videoOne_mc.myName.text = personOne_so.data.nameString;
videoTwo_mc.myName.text = personTwo_so.data.nameString;
// Publish this client's video, and play back other video
out_ns.publish("vTwo", "live");
in_ns.play("vOne");
videoOne_mc.myVid.attachNetStream(in_ns);
      }
    }
  }

function onSync(syncEvent:SyncEvent):void {
  trace ("onSync fired");
  if(personOne_so.data.nameString) {
    videoOne_mc.myName.text = personOne_so.data.nameString;
  }
  if(personTwo_so.data.nameString) {
    videoTwo_mc.myName.text = personTwo_so.data.nameString;
  }
}
```

11. Save your FLA as **videoConf.fla**. Compile your SWF. Enter your name in the login box and click the Submit button. Your webcam and name should appear on the left side.

12. Of course, to test this application, you'll either need a friend with a webcam or a second webcam attached to your computer. If you have a second webcam, just open up a second instance of videoConf.swf. Then right-click anywhere on the SWF to access your Flash Settings, where you can select the second camera as your source. If you have the Admin Console open as we suggested, you should see a trace in the Output panel whenever anyone enters or leaves the conference.

Note: Although you can stream video using the On2 VP6 codec through FMS2, when you record video using your webcam to FMS2, it is still using the Spark video codec and the Nellymoser audio codec. There are third-party server utilities you can plug in to a Flash Media Server to record VP6 content, but these utilities take a bit of configuration, and they aren't cheap. And you're stuck with Nellymoser (there's no option for MP3 at this time). In our opinion, Spark is just fine, though, for typical videoconferencing applications; VP6 may actually introduce some latency since it's processor intensive to compress and decompress. (You may wish you had MP3 available for audio, however, especially if you're trying to broadcast something like a live concert.)

Pretty cool, eh? And you thought FMS was rocket science. This app is just the tip of the proverbial iceberg, though, and it should spark some ideas for other cool applications using FMS. Here are a couple, just to get you thinking:

- Use the drawing API and remote shared objects to create a "whiteboard" on top of the video that you can draw on. You could give your friend a mustache, and she can see it on her video display in real time!

- Using the pixel-level access that Flash now provides, create an application that detects motion on a webcam—you could use this input for games, to trigger recording, or to add filter effects.

We're sure you can come up with some even more ingenious uses. When you do, be sure to let us know via our blog (http://www.flashconnections.com) and we'll add your application to our FMS Showcase.

Note: Make sure your Stage size is at least 215 by 138 pixels; Flash needs at least this much Stage real estate to display the Player Settings panel. Your users will need that to set up their camera and microphone.

Video Did Not Kill the Radio Star

In addition to video, FMS also allows you to stream MP3s. This only requires a small change to the code used to stream FLVs. For reference, here's how you'd stream an FLV:

```
// plays myVideo.flv on the stream ns, using a Video Object
var nc:NetConnection = new NetConnection();
nc.connect("rtmp:/myApp/");
var ns:NetStream = new NetStream(nc);
myVid.attachVideo(ns);
ns.play("myVideo.flv");
```

Here's an example where we attach the audio to a video object:

```
// plays myAudio.mp3 on the stream ns, using a Video Object
var nc:NetConnection = new NetConnection();
nc.connect("rtmp:/myApp/");
var ns:NetStream = new NetStream(nc);
myVid.attachVideo(ns);
ns.play("mp3:myAudio");
```

Continues

> ### Video Did Not Kill the Radio Star *(Continued)*
>
> And here we attach the audio to a movieclip instead:
>
> ```
> // plays myAudio.mp3 through the stream ns, using a MovieClip object
> var nc:NetConnection = new NetConnection();
> nc.connect("rtmp:/myApp/");
> var ns:NetStream = new NetStream(nc);
> myMovieClip_mc.attachAudio(ns);
> ns.play("mp3:myAudio");
> ```
>
> Did you catch it? The only change is to add mp3 to the URL in the ns.play command. Niiiice.

What Else Can This FMS2 Thing Do?

FMS offers much more than just a way to serve streaming video. It's full of tools you can put to work in sophisticated rich media applications. Let's take a look at some of its capabilities.

File Class

The new latest version of FMS added the powerful File class to our arsenal. The File class lets an application write to the server's file system. That's right—without Flash Remoting or any other server-side technologies, we can now create, append, and delete text files directly in SSAS. Without using a database server, we can store valuable information, such as log files and other data, that can then be read back into Flash or any other application that reads and processes text files (such as log-parsing software). You can also use the directory listing functionality of the File class to read contents of a directory to build a playlist of streams on the fly, for example.

 Note: Always mindful of security, Flash Media Server only allows access to files within the sandbox (limited directories) specified for your application's virtual host.

Server-Side Data Manipulation

In addition to the File class for storing and retrieving data, FMS also features two other server-side data classes: LoadVars and XML. The LoadVars class is similar to the client-side class that you may already be familiar with; it lets you send/load all the variables in an object to and from a specified URL. The only real difference in this implementation is that the send/load operation is done on the server side of the application, rather than the client side.

The SSAS XML class operates the same way as the LoadVars class; the only difference is that XML data is transmitted as an XML Document Object Model tree, and the LoadVars data is transferred as ActionScript name and value pairs. LoadVars also allows you to send/load just the variables you want (instead of all variables), which can be helpful in streamlining your application's performance.

By performing these operations on the server side, you have more flexibility in your data handling and can more efficiently synchronize data between clients. Instead of several clients polling a database for updated data, for example, now the server can poll once, and then send the updated information to all subscribed clients.

Note: The XMLSocket and XMLStreams classes are also available in SSAS. XMLSocket can be used for low-latency applications such as basic chatrooms; for IM or Jabber-compatible applications, the XMLStreams class offers a compatible transfer format. For more in-depth information about the differences, consult the SSAS documentation.

Server-to-Server Communication

FMS allows you to open connections between FMS server(s) via SSAS. You can use the NetConnection.connect method to make these connections to share data, video, and audio via RTMP or SSL, or to connect to an application server to make standard HTTP calls. This gives you a great deal of flexibility as a developer to create robust and flexible applications.

Bandwidth Management

There are several ways you can control the amount of bandwidth used by each connected client in FMS, using either server-side or client-side scripting.

One way is by monitoring the connection on the client side, using client-side NetStream information objects. One status message, NetStream.Play.InsufficientBW, indicates that data being received through the NetStream is slower than it should be. You can listen for this message and respond either by giving feedback to the client in the form of a "warning" message, or by switching the content on the NetStream to a lower-quality version automatically.

Another method of bandwidth control is to use the server-side Client.setBand-widthLimit method for incoming data or the client-side Camera.setQuality method for outgoing data.

A more heavy-handed approach, but equally effective, is to change the bandwidth limits globally in the Flash Media Server configuration file (config.xml).

Controlling bandwidth consumption is an important consideration in FMS applications. You should research these options more thoroughly when beginning development of real-world projects, and choose the most appropriate option for your specific application. More detail can be found in the documentation, *Developing Flash Media Server Applications*.

Server-Side Streaming

By now you're quite familiar with creating streams on the client side. But did you know you can create them on the server side as well? This can be handy for creating applications where there is a continuous stream that clients drop in to watch, much like conventional television and radio. You just create the "channel" stream(s) on the server side and viewers can tune in.

Creating a server-side stream is as simple as creating one on the client side; you just call the Stream.get method in your application's main.asc file. You can also use this method to play streams from other Flash Media Servers.

Load Balancing

With FMS, you can implement Edge servers (at extra cost, of course), which allow you to publish live streaming video to a large audience by distributing the bandwidth load among multiple servers. These proxy servers, as they are also referred to, intelligently distribute the bandwidth demands of very large events. However, if you're not anticipating a large number of consecutive stream requests, you likely wouldn't need to invest in Edge servers. But now you know load-balancing functionality is available with FMS if you ever should require it.

Control Access to Streams and Recording

By default, all streams and shared objects associated with an FMS application instance are available to any connected client. SSAS in FMS2 gives you the ability to apply a dynamic access control list (ACL). ACLs allow you to restrict access (creating, reading, or updating) to all or some of your streams and shared objects.

Using the server-side Client object, you can use readAccess and writeAccess methods to define *string tokens*, or strings that are allowed in the names of streams and shared objects, to be accepted for that particular client. For example, to restrict all connected clients to subscribe only to shared objects with names that begin with myAppSO, you'd add this line in your application's main.asc file, in the Application.onConnect handler:

```
client.readAccess = "myAppSO/";
```

If you want to restrict your connected clients access to write to only shared objects whose names begin with myAppSo/public, you'd add this line:

```
client.writeAccess = "myAppSO/public/";
```

You can allow access to more than one string token in the same command:

```
client.readAccess = "myAppStreams/public/;myAppSO/public/";
```

Also, because you can pass additional variables into your connection script in Flash, you can include a variable indicating the SWF client's level of access, which can then be used to assign access privileges. For example, if you used this command to connect:

```
nc.connect("rtmp:/myApp/myInstance", "admin");
```

you could set admin accounts to have open readAccess and writeAccess, then restrict it to public directories if "guest" was passed instead. In this way, you can easily implement a basic access control system in your FMS application.

Secure Applications

Two encryption methods are available to ensure the security of your applications and data in FMS.

One approach is to use Secure Sockets Layer (SSL), which is supported for both incoming and outgoing connections. You'll need to obtain an SSL certificate from a provider such as VeriSign, and configure both your server settings and your FMS applications accordingly. FMS uses an open source SSL implementation, called OpenSSL. Consult the FMS documentation for more details if you wish to set up an application on SSL.

Another approach specific to FMS is Real-Time Messaging Protocol over SSL (RTMPS). This is basically a standard RTMP connection, but on a secure port, through a TCP socket. Like standard SSL, RTMPS transfers encrypted data to avoid interception by hackers and other miscreants. This does add some server load, unfortunately, and may affect the performance of your application. Therefore, it's recommended that you only use RTMPS for applications that transmit highly sensitive data. To implement RTMPS, you simply replace rtmp with rtmps in the URL of your NetConnection.connect call.

Smart Bandwidth Streaming

FMS offers you the functionality to deliver video to a client based on their bandwidth speed. To do this, you'll need access to your FMS vhost.xml configuration file. If you have this access, or your host can make the edits for you, keep reading to find out how it's done.

Start by encoding your video content at different bit rates and store them in appropriate directories, such as:

```
c:\myApp\streams\35k\myVideo.flv
c:\myApp\streams\140k\myVideo.flv
c:\myApp\streams\300k\myVideo.flv
```

You can even include different codecs to accommodate clients running Flash Player 7 or older:

```
c:\myApp\streams\spark35k\myVideo.flv
c:\myApp\streams\spark140k\myVideo.flv
c:\myApp\streams\spark300k\myVideo.flv
```

Next, you'll need to edit the vhost.xml file to tell FMS what version of the Flash Player the connected client is using, and assign them a corresponding virtual key. Inside the VirtualKeys tag, set the virtual key for Flash Player 7 and below to spk and set the virtual key for Flash Player 8 and later to vp6, as shown:

```
<VirtualKeys>
<Key from="WIN 8,0,0,0" to="WIN 9,0,0,0">vp6</Key>
<Key from="MAC 8,0,0,0" to="MAC 9,0,0,0">vp6</Key>
<Key from="WIN 6,0,0,0" to="WIN 7,0,55,0">spk</Key>
<Key from="MAC 6,0,0,0" to="MAC 7,0,55,0">spk</Key>
</VirtualKeys>
```

Next, edit the <VirtualDirectories> tag, which tells the server to look for client keys as shown below and assign the appropriate path to the video files (we'll be appending slow, medium, or fast to the virtual keys in a moment):

```
<VirtualDirectory>
<Streams key="spkslow">foo;c:\myApp\streams\spark35k</Streams>
<Streams key="spkmedium">foo;c:\myApp\streams\spark140k</Streams>
<Streams key="skpfast">foo;c:\myApp\streams\spark300k</Streams>
<Streams key="vp6slow">foo;c:\myApp\streams\35k</Streams>
<Streams key="vp6medium">foo;c:\myApp\streams\140k</Streams>
<Streams key="vp6fast">foo;c:\myApp\streams\300k</Streams>
<Streams key="">foo;c:\myApp\streams</Streams>
</VirtualDirectory>
```

Finally, you'll need to edit your application's server-side main.asc file. In the application.onConnect handler, create a bandwidth detection script (discussed more in depth in the FMS documentation), and depending on the speed detected, append the appropriate string to the value of each client's virtual key (their player version), like so:

```
client.virtualKey += "slow"
client.virtualKey += "medium"
client.virtualKey += "fast"
```

Now FMS will detect the player version, assign either spk or vp6 to the virtualKey, and then append fast, medium, or slow to that key. The FLV will then be served from the appropriate directory as specified in the <VirtualDirectory> tag. More details about this approach, and other options available, can be found in the FMS documentation.

FMS Hit List: Lisa's Tips and Tricks

Video is sexy, audio is cool, but IMHO, the most powerful feature of FMS is the Remote Shared Object. When thinking of FMS, most people think video and audio, but the Remote Shared Object (RSO) could well be the most versatile feature, ripe for integration into your existing applications. Through RSOs, you can allow multiple clients to communicate with each other, share data and images—almost anything you can dream up. Through proxied RSOs, clients can communicate between applications, and even between servers.

Trace, trace, trace! The infoObject is your *friend*. When developing anything in FMS, before writing anything else, set up traces of your SSAS infoObjects and print your client-side infoObjects to a dynamic text field in your movie. Also trace and print your shared object and local variable values. Though this is a pretty basic programming protocol, it's *really* important in FMS. It can be temperamental and moody, so it's best to keep a close eye on it.

Go ahead, try out those components—get it out of your system. Your experience may differ, but I have found that when programming any sort of custom application, building my own communication elements and staying away from the supplied components has given me more nimble, lightweight applications (and fewer headaches). In almost every case where I tried to customize a component, it turned out to be more work and more file size overhead than simply making my own. Plus, you know exactly what's going on inside your own components, in contrast to the pre-built ones, which tend to be like "black boxes."

Don't fear SSAS. Being essentially JavaScript 1.5 with some added objects (and a few missing ones), Server-Side ActionScript is not as intimidating as it may seem. Utilizing trace commands and the FMS Admin Console, you can monitor and control connections, assign user IDs, send function calls to active instances of your applications (and vice versa), and a whole lot more. Some of the syntax is different from client-side ActionScript, however, so be sure to keep the docs handy.

Your applications should be built for speed. Multiuser communication is naturally bandwidth and processor intensive. Add video, audio, and constantly synching data objects and things can get bogged down pretty quickly. Keep this in mind from the very beginning of development. For example, if you have live video with gaps, be sure to set the silence levels to stop broadcasting when there's no sound. If you have 10 items in a shared object array and only one slot changes often, keep that one in its own shared object so you don't have to transfer all 10 with each update. All these things will help your bottom-line performance.

Lock it down. When developing a new application, it's usually best to go ahead and operate wide open, and then tighten up your security once you have everything working correctly. You can restrict access to your FMS applications to specific domains in the Server.xml file, or by requiring the client.referrer in your application to be from your domain, among various other security methods. See the sidebar "Our FMS Bookmarks" for more information.

Learn and relearn. It seems to me that every time I start a new project in FMS, I think, "Yeah, that can be done, no problem!"—and it can be done. But unless you are programming FMS full time, expect lots of debugging, and keep your references handy. It's usually a bumpy (but rewarding) ride.

Obviously, this chapter has provided a quick overview of what's involved in FMS application development. We wanted to give you an understanding of what FMS is and what it can do. You should now be able to bravely jump into the FMS pool, knowing how deep it is—confident that you can swim!

Our FMS Bookmarks

This is our current list of helpful URLs and resources as of press time, but we'll keep it up to date on our companion website, http://www.flashconnections.com/flash-video-pro/.

The #1 Ultimate Resource

FlashMedia List:

> http://www.flashcomguru.com/flashmedialist/

And the archives of the previous #1 Ultimate Resource (now defunct, but with searchable archives), FlashComm List:

> http://chattyfig.figleaf.com/mailman/listinfo/flashcomm/

Our FMS Bookmarks *(Continued)*

Other Resources

The FMS Resource Center, which features tools to get you started with FMS. The files are hosted in an Acrobat Connect meeting room. To download them, go to

http://fms.adobe.acrobat.com/resources/

and enter **guest** in the login form.

Peldi's FMSWiki:

http://www.peldi.com/fmswiki/index.php?title=Main_Page

Adobe's Chris Hock presents the FMS FAQ:

http://www.flashcommunicationserver.net/index.htm

Some FMS components to get you started:

http://www.adobe.com/devnet/flashmediaserver/articles/components.html

Handy-dandy port tester, helpful if you need to work through firewall issues:

http://www.adobe.com/cfusion/knowledgebase/index.cfm?id=tn_16466

And, of course, the ever-enlightening Adobe DevCenter:

http://www.adobe.com/devnet/flashmediaserver/index.html

Blogs

Stefan's forums, tutorials, articles:

http://www.flashcomguru.com

Fabio Sonnati:

http://flashvideo.progettosinergia.com

Summary

So, now you understand that FMS is for more than just streaming FLVs. In this chapter you learned:

- What FMS is, and how it works

- What applications are possible with FMS

- Hosting choices

- FMS alternatives for streaming

- How to set up your development environment

- FMS file structure

- The basic classes and methods available to FMS applications, on both the server side and client side

- How to create a two-person video chatroom

- How to stream MP3s

- Smart bandwidth streaming methods using FMS

- Helpful tips and resources for continuing your (hopefully) budding romance with FMS

We hope this chapter, along with the rest of this book, gave you the insight and tools you need to develop some innovative, rock-solid Flash video applications. It was our goal to give you a good well-rounded resource that you can keep by your side and return to often.

Be sure to read the Appendix, where a developer talks about using, and extending, the MVC-based video player framework in a real-world application.

Real-World Deployment of an MVC Media Player

Jim Kremens, http://www.listenerinteractive.com/book

In Chapter 5, we developed a general-purpose MVC framework that we extended into an MVC media player. MVC code tends to be rather elaborate— there's a lot of setup involved. The rationale for enduring that setup is that it can make it simpler to deploy new versions of an application by merely writing a new View; you don't need to reinvent the wheel each time you're hired to write a media player—you only need to consider your View *class.*

Appendix Contents

Our Client's Requirements
Refactoring Higher-Level Framework Code
Refactoring MVC Media Player Code
Adding Multiple Components to the View
Media Player Conclusion
Taking It to the Next Level

That said, the framework in Chapter 5 is, well, a framework. It's not a complete media player, and if you tried to deliver it to your client as such, they might frown upon your efforts. To make the code as easy as possible to understand, many essential aspects of a media player were left unimplemented. This appendix will attempt to flesh out lots of the little widgets and things that make a Flash media player unique. Let's imagine that someone has hired us to do just that!

 Note: You can download the complete AS2 source code for this appendix at www.sybex.com/go/flashvideo.

Our Client's Requirements

Our client has delivered to us a detailed, clearly written and illustrated functional spec (on the back of a napkin!). From this document, we deduce that our player will need the following widgets:

- Volume slider
- Seek bar
- Download progress bar
- Mute button
- Play/Pause button
- Fast-Forward button
- Rewind button
- Elapsed/Total Time display

The first thing we need to do as developers is group these things into like categories. This will help us to establish relationships that we can use to build class hierarchies when we actually write the code. In other words, understanding how objects are similar will help us write code that those objects can share.

Now the list looks like this:

- Sliders: Volume, seek bar, download progress
- Buttons: Mute, Play/Pause, Fast-Forward, Rewind
- Displays: Elapsed/Total Time

That feels more manageable, doesn't it? To complicate things, however, the functional spec includes details about animation states—this is Flash, after all. Here are some of those requirements:

- When a video starts playing, the title of the current video animates in.
- The player will also play advertisements. When ads play, the controls need to be "grayed out" and disabled.

Refactoring Higher-Level Framework Code

These requirements got us thinking…in addition to all the components we're going to need to write, we'll also require some core services that the MVC framework we've written does not provide. Once we get these preliminaries out of the way, we'll be able to focus on actually building our player.

Implementing *EventBroadcaster*

To disable various controls when ads play, it will make sense to implement some variant of the Observer pattern. In this case, we'll use an EventBroadcaster. EventBroadcasters are useful when there is a one-to-many relationship to handle. In this case, there will be one event—for now we'll call it onAdPlay—and many potential widgets that will need to respond to that event by disabling themselves.

For the AS2 version of this player, we'll use a custom EventBroadcaster that I wrote for the FHTML library (http://www.runtimeflash.com—more on that later). This class has a few unique features. First, the method signature is a little friendlier than the Macromedia/Adobe AS2 variant. Here are a few example calls to get the hang of it:

```
//basic method signature
object.addEventListener(eventName:String,
                        scope:Object,
                        functionToCall:String
);


//example call
model.addEventListener("onPlayMedia", this, "disable");
```

In this example, when model broadcasts its onAdPlay event, the disable method of the object specified by this will be called. Notice that the function to be called is referenced by its name (a string), not a function reference. This offers more flexibility when coding, as strings can be constructed dynamically—read in from XML, for example.

Also, you can pass in additional arguments:

```
//example call
model.addEventListener("onAdplay", this, "disable", 1, 2, 3);
```

In this case, the disable method will receive the parameters 1, 2, and 3 after the other parameters it normally receives.

If the syntax seems vaguely familiar, it might be because it's *vaguely* similar to setInterval in that you specify a scope, a method (as a string), and potentially the additional arguments you want to pass to that method:

```
setInterval(this, "myFunc", 30, 1, 2, 3);
```

Using a Code-Based Animation Library

To handle the various animation states, we'll employ a tween sequencing package. There are a few open source packages of this type, but the most well-loved (for AS2) is Fuse (written by Moses Gunesch; http://www.mosessupposes.com). Rather than tweening one property at a time (like the built-in Tween classes), Fuse makes it easy to string together complex visual behaviors and create engaging user experiences. Here's a sample:

```
var f:Fuse = new Fuse(

[
{target:mc, alpha:100, seconds:1.2, ease:"easeInHard"},
{target:otherMc, alpha:100, y:-165, seconds:2,
➡ ease:"easeInHard"}
]

);
f.start(true);
```

Because they are in an array, this code will cause two tweens to run at once. (If not, they would run one at a time.) In short, Fuse lets you specify multiple targets, properties, and values and determine whether tweens run concurrently or sequentially.

Refactoring MVC Media Player Code

It makes sense for core-level services like event broadcasting and tween sequencing to exist in packages outside our MVC Media Player package. Now it's time to take a look inside the MVC framework itself and determine what basic functionality will need to be added or changed.

Changing How MVC Connections Are Made

One of the stated goals of the framework is to make it easy to create different views of our media player. Practically, this means that the only class you should ever really have to touch is your View class. But in actuality, the code as written made that slightly difficult. So, before proceeding, we should correct that problem by changing the way certain MVC relationships are established. The change is fairly esoteric, so skip ahead if the nuances of MVC don't interest you.

Looking at our original implementation of MVCMediaPlayer, we see that the init method looks like this:

```
public function init(val:MovieClip):Void {
    setView(new MediaPlayerView(
```

```
                new MediaPlayerModel(),
                new MediaPlayerController(),
                val
        )
    );
    getModel().init();
    getView().init();
    getController().init();
    __mpModel = MediaPlayerModel(getModel());
}
```

Let's refactor init by renaming it configure and making it look like this:

```
public function configure(val:MovieClip, view:MediaPlayerView,
⇒ x:Number, y:Number, w:Number, h:Number, playList:Array):Void {
    setView(view);
    getModel().init();
    getView().init();
    getController().init();
    __mpModel = MediaPlayerModel(getModel());
    initCoordinates(x, y, w, h);
    populatePlaylist(playList);
    getView().layout();
```

configure accepts a lot of arguments, but as we'll see in a minute, it allows us to configure our media player in one line of code. But a little more housekeeping first...

In MediaPlayerView, let's change the constructor from this:

```
public function MediaPlayerView(
model:Model,
    controller:Controller, container:MovieClip)
{

    super(model, controller, container);
}
```

to this:

```
public function MediaPlayerView(container:MovieClip) {
    super(new MediaPlayerModel(),
        new MediaPlayerController(),
        container);
}
```

This allows us to choose the Controller and Model we're going to use from within our View. Because the View is typically the only class we'll be changing, this is handy. And now, to make it easier to use different views with our MediaPlayer application, let's use the configure method we created earlier. In MediaPlayer, our initMediaPlayer method now looks like this:

```
private function initMediaPlayer(bool:Boolean, mc:MovieClip):Void {
    player = new MVCMediaPlayer();
    player.configure(mc, new MediaPlayerView(mc), COORDS.x,
➡ COORDS.y, COORDS.w, COORDS.h, xObject.item);
    player.playMedia(String(player.getPlaylist().getItemAt(0).
➡ path.getValue()));
```

With these details out of the way, we can start to make some changes that will provide for new functionality. To do that, we'll add methods to our Model, View, and Controller. Hint: Methods are your friends!

Adding Necessary Methods to the Interfaces

The framework exploits a one-to-one ratio between interfaces and classes. For some, this might seem extreme, but it makes it easy to change implementations of classes. Want new methods in all of your Views that implement a given interface? Just add the methods to the interface. Want to change a method signature everywhere it appears? Change the declaration in the interface. The compiler (and ideally, your editor) will alert you to all of the changes you need to make in your actual classes. When writing complex systems, interfaces are an excellent way to keep a handle on things. Whereas classes themselves are basically a description of the instances they will create, interfaces serve as a description of those classes; they help you manage your classes.

This coding style is often called "programming to the interface." Using an editor designed for these purposes can make all the difference. An excellent choice for Action-Script is FDT: http://fdt.powerflasher.com/flashsite/flash.htm. For example, using FDT, if you write an interface, and then a class that implements that interface, FDT will automatically stub out all of the methods for you.

So, let's start to add some methods. In an MVC system, the Controller determines which methods of the Model are actually exposed to the View. So, if we're going to change things in this system, the Controller is the place to start.

Controller

If we look at out widget list from the beginning of the appendix, it seems that the following widgets are seeds that can find no purchase in IMediaPlayerController as it currently stands:

- Fast-Forward Button
- Rewind Button

- Mute Button

- Play/Pause Toggle Button

So, to provide the services that these widgets will need, it makes sense to add the following highlighted methods, so now our Controller looks like this:

```
public function getMPModel():MediaPlayerModel;
public function getMPView():MediaPlayerView;
public function play():Void;
public function playMedia(path:String):Void;
public function pause():Void;
public function stop():Void;
public function setMediaPosition(val:Number):Void;
public function getMediaPosition():Number;
public function setVolume(val:Number):Void;
public function getVolume():Number;
public function playNext():Void;
public function playPrevious():Void;

public function fastForward(val:Number):Void;
public function rewind(val:Number):Void;
public function mute():Void;
public function unMute():Void;
public function toggle():Void;
```

Model

Of course, in order to actually do anything, these methods will have to have corollary methods in the Model. And if this media player is going to play in the big leagues, we're also going to have to further expand the functionality of the Model to include still more services. See the comments in the code for the rationale behind these additions to our IMediaPlayerModel interface:

```
/*
These methods provide access to the sound object, which was
   unimplemented in the previous version of the Model. To set volume,
   mute and unmute, we need a sound object, right?
*/
public function setSound(val:Sound):Void;
public function getSound():Sound;

/*
```

One of the display panels the client requested is a time elapsed/total
time panel. This method allows us easy access to media duration,
which we need to calculate that number.
*/
public function getMediaDuration():Number;

/*
Not surprisingly, the client requested a download progress bar.
Internally, this method will calculate the percentage of the media
file that has loaded and then send that number to the View where it
can easily be displayed.
*/
public function handleLoadProgress():Void;

/*
The functional spec also stipulates a seek bar. To implement this, we
need to be aware of media position, and we also need to send
position updates to the View where they can be displayed. This method
will do just that…
*/
public function handlePosition():Void;

/*
When each video loads, an onMetaData event is automatically fired. It
provides various pieces of information about the video—height, width,
framerate, duration, and so on. We keep track of some of those
properties; this method simply provides a way to clear them as needed.
*/

public function resetMetaData():Void;

/*
This is just a convenience method, an alternative to saying
getConnection().connect(val);
*/
public function connect(val:String):Void;

/*

This method is closely related to playMedia. It loads the media
    specified, but doesn't automatically play it. You might use it to prepare
the media, load a JPEG snapshot of the video, or whatever…
*/
public function initMedia(path:String):Void;

/*
As the player will play ads, it needs to automatically play into and
    out of those ads. setContinuousPlay and getContinuousPlay provide
    access to a Boolean value that determines whether this functionality
    is available.
*/
public function setContinuousPlay(val:Boolean):Void;
public function getContinuousPlay():Boolean;

View

If you've been following along (praise you, Gentle Reader!), it will be apparent to you
that we'll need to add methods to our View interface that correspond with the ones
we've added to the Controller and Model. And here they are—again, see comments for
explanation:

    // in IMediaPlayerView…
    /*
    Here's the best way to understand the next four methods: let's say that
        the user clicks a button in the View. That button calls a
        corresponding method in the Controller, which calls a method in the
        Model, which actually does the thing requested – fast-forward,
        rewind, mute or unmute. Then the Model calls one of the following
        methods in the View. And, if we choose, we can then display the fact
        that, for example, the video is muted!
    */
    public function onFastForward(val:Number):Void;
    public function onRewind(val:Number):Void;
    public function onMute():Void;
    public function onUnMute(val:Number):Void;

    /*
    The Model is friendly and hands us current media position, total media
        duration and percentage played so that we can display those values.
    */

```
public function onPositionChange(position:Number, duration:Number,
➡ percentage:Number):Void;


/*
Here the Model provides the View with a number that reflects the
   percentage of the media file that has been downloaded so far.
*/
public function onLoadProgress(percentage:Number):Void;


/*
This method is fired if you call initMedia().
*/
public function onInitMedia(path:String):Void;


/*
Very handy-fires when the media file ends.
*/
public function onMediaEnd():Void;


/*
Fires when a successful connection to the media stream has been made.
*/
public function onConnect(val:String):Void;


/*
As the spec requires the player to play ads, we keep track of an
   adIsPlaying variable in the View. This code could go in the Model.
   For purists, it clearly should. But I decided to keep it in the View,
   as doing so prevented us from needing to make a whole new
   implementation of our Model. The following method provides public
   access to the private adIsPlaying variable.
*/
public function setAdPlaying(val:Boolean):Void;
```

Implementing New Methods in the Classes

Now we've got a handle on what methods we need to add, but so far we've only discussed interfaces; let's talk about how these methods are implemented in the actual Model, View, and Controller classes. First, we'll deal with the Model.

Note: Although some coders keep their private variables at the bottom of the class (thinking perhaps that because they aren't meant to be accessed directly, they should be kept out of sight and out of mind), I prefer to list them at the top. I think they offer an excellent snapshot of what a class is actually doing. When you think about it, the class exists, at least in part, to manipulate these variables.

Also, it's a convention of mine to use double underscore prefixes for variables that are accessible via public getter/setter methods and no prefix at all for variables that are purely internal to the class.

Model

Here are the private variables in MediaPlayerModel:

```
private var __mpView:MediaPlayerView;
private var __connection:NetConnection;
private var __stream:NetStreamExt;
private var __playlist:IPlaylist;
private var __sound:Sound;
private var __duration:Number;
private var __volume:Number = 100;
private var __continuousPlay:Boolean = true;

private var posInterval:Number;
private var prgInterval:Number;

private var playing:Boolean = false;
private var initialized:Boolean = false;
private var currentPath:String;
```

Just reading those variable names gives you a pretty good idea of the kinds of information we'll be working with in MediaPlayerModel. Mainly, there's a reference to the View (this prevents constant recasting), a NetConnection, a NetStream, a Playlist, and a Sound object. Most of the code in the class exists in service of these objects. Typically, each method in the Model will work with one of these objects, and then notify the View that it has done so.

In our initial version of this MVC Media Player, almost all of the methods in the Model were merely "stubbed out"—in other words, barely implemented, if at all. Let's take a look at how they have been fleshed out. The methods mainly fall into three categories:

- Transport methods (play, pause, stop, etc.)
- Time-based methods (methods called on an interval)
- Event-based methods (responses to NetStream, etc.)

Model: Transport Methods

Everything starts with the transport methods, so let's begin there. We'll cover just the interesting ones.

 Note: There's a lot of detail in here—it's the guts of the Media Player. One of the core precepts of this project is that you shouldn't necessarily have to think about what's going on behind the scenes; the goal is to quickly make new Views that respond to events from the Model. But then again, in the real world, it's always a good idea to know how things really work!

The toggle method allows a playButton to toggle between play and pause. If it's clicked for the first time, it calls playMedia; otherwise, it simply toggles between play and pause.

```
public function toggle():Void {
    //if clicked for the first time
    if (initialized == false) {
        playMedia(currentPath);
        getMPView().onPlay();
        initialized = true;
    }
    else if (playing == true) pause();
    else this.play();
}
```

The playMedia method, as its name suggests, is a big one!

```
public function playMedia(path:String):Void {

    //set the current path
    currentPath = path;

    //set playing status
    playing = true;

    //clear any metadata that was stored last time…
    resetMetaData();

    //start tracking download progress on an interval
    startProgressInterval();

    //start tracking media position on an interval
```

```
startPositionInterval();

//do what you need to do with the NetStream object
    getStream().close();
    getStream().play(path);

//Check if the Media is an ad.
    if (MediaPlayerUtils.isAd(getPlaylist()))getMPView().
➡ setAdPlaying(true);
    else getMPView().setAdPlaying(false);

//Let the View know we just started playing media
    getMPView().onPlayMedia(path);


}
```

The play and pause methods are interesting for two reasons:

- They show how to deal with the position interval in each case. (It's important to stop the intervals!)
- They show the correct ways to deal with the NetStream object to make it play, pause, stop, and so forth.

```
public function play():Void {
    playing = true;
    startPositionInterval();
    getStream().pause(false);
    getMPView().onPlay();
 }
public function pause():Void {
    playing = false;
    stopPositionInterval();
    getStream().pause(true);
    getMPView().onPause();
 }
public function stop():Void {
    playing = false;
    stopPositionInterval();
    getStream().seek(0);
    getStream().pause(true);
    getMPView().onStop();
}
```

We need setMediaPosition and getMediaPosition for our seek bar, which allows us to seek to any point in a stream:

```
public function setMediaPosition(val:Number):Void {

    //calculate the position
    var pos:Number = getMediaDuration() * (val/100);
    getStream().seek(pos);

    //notify the View
    getMPView().onSetMediaPosition(val)


public function getMediaPosition():Number {
  return getStream().time;
}
```

fastForward and rewind are a little different, as they don't allow for random access to the stream, but, um, fast forward or rewind through it:

```
public function fastForward(val:Number):Void {
    var pos:Number = getStream().time + val;
    getStream().seek(pos);
    getMPView().onSetMediaPosition(pos)
    getMPView().onFastForward(pos);
}
public function rewind(val:Number):Void {
    var pos:Number = getStream().time - val;
    getStream().seek(pos);
    getMPView().onSetMediaPosition(pos)
    getMPView().onRewind(pos);
}
```

The duration of the media file is stored in the __duration variable when the onMetaData event of the FLV stream is fired. We retrieve it here:

```
public function getMediaDuration():Number {
    return __duration;
}
```

Here's how we work with sound. Like the other methods, we manipulate an object and then let the View know that we've done so.

```
public function setVolume(val:Number):Void {
    __volume = val;
```

```
    getSound().setVolume(val);
    getMPView().onSetVolume(val);
  }
  public function getVolume():Number {
    return __sound.getVolume();
  }
  public function mute():Void {
    getSound().setVolume(0);
    getMPView().onMute();
  }
  public function unMute():Void {
    getSound().setVolume(__volume);
    getMPView().onUnMute(__volume);
  }
```

Model: Time-Based Methods

Here are our methods for starting and stopping the intervals that monitor position and load progress. It's often useful to wrap whatever interval-based operations you're going to be handling (even onEnterFrames) into startXInterval and stopXInterval methods that can be easily called.

```
private function startPositionInterval():Void {
  posInterval = IntervalUtils.setInterval(this, "handlePosition", 100);
}
private function stopPositionInterval():Void {
  IntervalUtils.clearInterval(posInterval);
}
private function startProgressInterval():Void {
prgInterval = IntervalUtils.setInterval(this, "handleLoadProgress", 100);
}
private function stopProgressInterval():Void {
  IntervalUtils.clearInterval(prgInterval);
}
```

IntervalUtils is a handy way of managing intervals (in AS2) written by Kenny Bunch (http://www.kennybunch.com/index.php?p=16). If you've ever wrestled with starting and stopping intervals, this class will ease your pain.

Model: Event-Based Methods

Finally, here are our event-based methods. In our private initConnection method, we mapped events from the NetStream object to methods in our class like so:

```
getStream().onMetaData = Proxy.create(this, handleOnMetaData);
getStream().onStatus = Proxy.create(this, handleOnStatus);
```

Now we can catch those events and forward them to the View:

```
public function handleOnMetaData(val:Object):Void {
    if (__duration != undefined) __duration = val.duration;
    getMPView().onMetaData(val);
}
```

This one is particularly helpful in that it allows us to both catch all status events and determine that a video has ended:

```
public function handleOnStatus(val:Object):Void {
    if (val.code == "NetStream.Play.Stop") {
        stopPositionInterval();
        stopProgressInterval();
        getMPView().onMediaEnd();
    }
    getMPView().onStatus(val);
}
```

Again, handlePosition is called on an interval while the video is playing. The View is provided with all of the numbers it will need to display position, media duration, and percentage of media played.

```
public function handlePosition():Void {
    var pos:Number = getMediaPosition();
    var dur:Number = getMediaDuration();
    getMPView().onPositionChange(pos, dur,(pos / dur) * 100);
}
```

handleLoadProgress is also called on an interval and sends the View the data it needs to display the percentage of media loaded.

```
public function handleLoadProgress():Void {
    var perc:Number = (getStream().bytesLoaded/
➡ getStream().bytesTotal)
*100;
    getMPView().onLoadProgress(perc);
}
```

View

Like the Model, the View required a great deal of fleshing out. The easiest way to get a high-level understanding of the changes is to look at the widget list again:

- Volume slider
- Seek bar
- Download progress bar
- Mute button
- Play/Pause button
- Fast-Forward button
- Rewind button
- Elapsed/Total Time display

Each of these is now a class member of the View:

```
private var volumeBar:HSlider;
private var seekBar:SeekBar;
private var progressBar:MovieClip;
private var muteBtn:MovieClip;
private var unmuteBtn:MovieClip;
private var playButton:PlayButton;
private var ffBtn:FFButton;
private var rwBtn:RWButton;
private var mediaInfo:MediaInfo;
```

Although some of these are simple enough to remain basic MovieClips, most are now instances of their own class. The View serves as a vehicle to bring them together, feed them events, and modify their behavior.

Adding Multiple Components to the View

Now that we're at the point where we're starting to flesh out the UI of our Media Player, it's important then to note that our Media Player framework is not, for example, a GUI toolkit. It doesn't provide the zillions of nice little hooks that a programmer might like for adding widgets to the stage. It merely provides us with a View where we can instantiate those widgets and feed them with the information they need to operate in the context of our player.

That means, of course, that the way in which you add widgets is up to you. You are free to use any GUI framework that you like. There are lots of open source options out there. (In fact, I'll refer to a framework of my own toward the end of this chapter that has a different slant than most.) But, for our purposes here, we'll proceed as simply as possible; that way we can focus on the code needed to do the particular task of each widget. In the end, what we end up with will not be a GUI framework, but rather a collection of gizmos. Even so, they will have things in common, and it makes sense to provide the minimal scaffolding needed to place them in a class hierarchy.

Core Component Class

To that end, notice that we've added a core component class (com.flashconnections .ui.component.Component). Here it is; see the comments for clarification:

```
class com.flashconnections.ui.component.Component

extends MovieClip

implements IComponent

{

/*
Components often will contain data that changes. It can be handy to
    broadcast the fact that the data has changed using this name:
*/
public static var ON_CHANGE:String = "onChange";

/*
These are the basic methods that any class must implement to use our
    AS2 EventBroadcaster (see above). They are mixed into this class
    using internal methods of EventBroadcaster.
*/
public function addEventListener(event:String, scope:Object,
➡ handler:String):Void{}
public function removeEventListener(event:String, scope:Object,
➡ handler:String):Void{}
public function broadcastMessage():Void{}
public function destroyListeners():Void{}

/*
Here's a little untyped variable to keep track of some piece of
    information—a number, a string, a piece of XML. Components often do
    that…
```

```
*/
private var __val;

/*
Our constructor initializes this class with EventBroadcaster, allowing
  it to broadcast messages, add event listeners of its own, etc.
*/
public function Component() {
    EventBroadcaster.initialize(this);
}

/*
We'll need to be able to set and get our value (__val)
*/
public function setValue(val):Void {
    __val = val;
}
public function getValue() {
    return __val;
}

/*
init methods are always useful…
*/
public function init(val:Object):Void {
}

/*
Show and hide are the bare minimum for a UI component. Actually, these
    are handled by Movieclip._visible, but if you prefer regular methods
    to intrinsic methods…
*/
public function show():Void {
}
public function hide():Void {
}


}
```

Unless they are very simple, most of our components will inherit directly from this class, which itself extends MovieClip.

It would have been possible to produce code-only components that used the drawing API or externally loaded assets to produce their visual aspect. Programmers tend to prefer this kind of methodology (myself included!). In fact, it's a *very* good idea to work this way if at all possible. But it's usually not possible. Alas… Still, although drawing items on the Stage and then writing classes that make use of them might make it easier to work with designers, it is essentially akin to hard-coding, and can go a long way toward preventing reuse of code if you're not careful.

Note: This chapter tracks our real-world progress expanding on a code framework. In the course of our efforts, it became clear that our client did not want us to produce a "code-only" media player. They preferred to have their designers create mockups that we then coded against.

Let's have a look at each component in turn. Remember that we grouped them conceptually earlier in this chapter:

- Sliders: Volume, seek bar, download progress
- Buttons: Mute, Play/Pause, Fast-Forward, Rewind
- Display: Elapsed/Total Time

And notice that our component package now includes the following subpackages:

- slider
- button
- display

I love it when a plan comes together!

Note also that our View now contains the following private references:

```
private var playButton:PlayButton;
private var ffBtn:FFButton;
private var rwBtn:RWButton;
private var volumeBar:HSlider;
private var seekBar:SeekBar;
private var mediaInfo:MediaInfo; //displays time and title

private var muteBtn:MovieClip;
private var unmuteBtn:MovieClip;
private var nextButton:MovieClip;
private var prevButton:MovieClip;
private var progressBar:MovieClip;
```

We'll use these references in the various methods we've exposed in the View. Let's start with the Elapsed/Total Time display, as it's pretty simple.

Elapsed/Total Time Display

Although we haven't mentioned it yet, in addition to displaying the elapsed and total times, this component is also meant to display the name of the currently playing clip. Note the variables.

```
private var timeField:TextField;
private var titleField:TextField;
```

These correspond to two actual text fields inside our mediaInfo movieclip—one to display time, one to display the title.

Inside our View, whenever a piece of media is played, the onPlayMedia method is triggered, which itself calls initControls and initDisplays:

```
public function onPlayMedia(path:String):Void {
    initControls();

//call initDisplays, passing current playlist
//item and 'true'
    initDisplays(MediaPlayerModel(getModel()).getPlaylist().
➟ getCurrentItem(), true);
}
```

The method signature for initDisplays looks like this:

```
private function initDisplays(playlistItem:Object,
➟ initMediaInfo:Boolean):Void {
```

So it's expecting both a reference to the current playlist item and a flag to indicate whether we should initialize the mediaInfo component. If so, we call the init method of the mediaInfo component, passing it the current playlist item.

```
if (initMediaInfo) mediaInfo.init(playlistItem);
```

Here's what that init method looks like. Other than triggering a simple Fuse animation to "roll" the text field in from the top, it really couldn't be simpler. We just assign the value of the title text field to the title property of the playlistItem that we passed in.

```
public function init(playlistItem:Object):Void {
    var f:Fuse = new Fuse({target:display, start_y:-20, y:2.5});
    f.start(true);
    titleField.text = playlistItem.title.getValue();
}
```

Note: We are using the Model to extract information from an XML playlist and pass it to the View, where it ends up being used in components like this one. If this confuses you, you might want to review Chapter 7, where we discuss the various mechanisms that make our playlist work.

So, to review, each time a new piece of media starts playing, the View's onPlayMedia method supplies the mediaInfo component with the current playlist item. It then extracts the title from this playlist item.

But what about elapsed time? Here's how it works.

Remember from our discussion of the Model that MediaPlayerModel calls MediaPlayerView.onPositionChange on an interval (only while media is playing!). If we look inside MediaPlayerView.onPositionChange, we can see that it in turn calls mediaInfo.onPositionChange, forwarding values for position, duration, and percentage:

```
public function onPositionChange(position:Number, duration:Number,
➥ percentage:Number):Void {
   //we'll get to the seek bar later!
   seekBar.slideBar._xscale = percentage;

   //hand mediaInfo the goodness it needs…
   mediaInfo.onPositionChange(position, duration, percentage);
}
```

Now look inside mediaInfo.onPositionChange:

```
public function onPositionChange(position:Number,
➥ duration:Number, percentage:Number):Void {
   timeField.text = DateUtils.format12(position) + " / " +
➥ DateUtils.format12(duration);
}
```

We use a utility method (in DateUtils) to properly format the date for display in our component. We won't go into the details of this method, as, like everything, it's involved. In truth, it's just one of those utility methods you'll want to keep around, because the next time you need to format a date in this manner, you probably won't remember how!

Mute/Unmute Buttons

The mute/unmute buttons are simple enough not to need classes of their own—they're just movieclips. We just tell them to call the mute and unmute methods of the Controller when they are clicked and everything else takes care of itself. Hooray! In MediaPlayerView.layout:

```
//store a local reference to the Controller for ease of //use
var cntrl:MediaPlayerController =
➡ MediaPlayerController(getController());

//assign click behaviors to mute and unmute buttons
   muteBtn.onRelease = Proxy.create(cntrl, cntrl.mute);
   unmuteBtn.onRelease = Proxy.create(cntrl, cntrl.unMute);
```

Note: Remember that our FLA, to our chagrin, includes assets drawn on the Stage. That means that nowhere in our classes will you see code that instantiates our components. This can be confusing to developers coming to Flash from other languages.

Fast-Forward and Rewind Buttons

The remaining buttons are all slightly more complex. Let's think about this for a second—not including displays, we need to create the following types of components: buttons and sliders. Both are varieties of controls. So, let's make a Control class and a Button class to allow these components to share code. Here's the relevant code of the Control class. Note that it extends Component:

```
class com.flashconnections.ui.component.Control

extends Component

{public function Control() {
   onPress = Proxy.create(this, doOnPress);
   onRelease = onReleaseOutside = Proxy.create(this, doOnRelease);
}

private function doOnPress():Void {}
private function doOnRelease():Void {}
```

So, each button or control will trigger its doOnPress and doOnRelease methods when they are pressed or released. Simple enough.

Let's now take a look at our implementation of a fast-forward button. See the comments for explanations of the code:

```
class com.flashconnections.ui.component.button.FFButton

extends MPButton
{

/*
this is just a variable, perhaps poorly named, that we will increment
*/
private var size:Number = 0;

public function FFButton() {
    //enable the button
    enable();

    //deal with the 'hit' clip, which exists inside
    //our mc on the stage

    hit._visible = false;
    hitArea = hit;
}

//////

/*
All controls fire their doOnPress method when pressed, so this one will
    as well. Note that doOnEnterFrame is set to execute on each frame.
*/
private function doOnPress():Void {
    if (isEnabled()) {
    gotoAndStop("down");
        pressed = true;
        onEnterFrame = doOnEnterFrame;
        }
}

/*
```

```
    Here we really just kill the onEnterFrame handler and reset the size
        variable.
    */
    private function doOnRelease():Void {
        if (isEnabled()) {
        gotoAndStop("up");
        pressed = false;
        size = 0;
        delete onEnterFrame;
        }
    }


    /*
    What happens on each frame when the button is pressed? A message is
        broadcast indicating that the status of this component is changed.
        And, with it, we send along our incremented size variable.
    */
    private function doOnEnterFrame():Void {
        broadcastMessage(ON_CHANGE, Math.min(size+=.001, 100));
    }
```

So on each frame (while the button is pressed) we broadcast a message with the new "value" of the fast-forward button. That value needs to be picked up somewhere, and it is. If you look in MediaPlayerView.layout, you'll see the following code:

```
    ffBtn.addEventListener(Component.ON_CHANGE, cntrl, "fastForward");
```

That code translates to: "Listen for an onChange event from the fast-forward button. When you hear it, call the fastForward method on the Controller." And of course, calling the fastForward method on the Controller calls fastForward in the Model, which actually fast-forwards the NetStream object! It works!

The Rewind button code is almost identical to our fastForward code, so we won't discuss it here.

Play/Pause Button

The play/pause button is basically a toggle button. All of the code in this section exists to manage the visual aspect of the button. The real action happens in the onRelease handler, which broadcasts an ON_CHANGE event. That event is picked up by the View, which passes it onto the Controller, which calls toggle in the Model.

In short, onRollover and onRollout cause the movieclip playhead to go to different frame labels, depending on the current playstate. There are certainly other ways to make a toggle button, but this one allows your favorite designer to draw elements directly into a movieclip, which is something that designers like to do.

Here's the complete code for our play/pause button. As always, follow along in the comments:

```
class com.flashconnections.ui.component.button.PlayButton

extends MPButton

implements IPlayButton

{

/*
Allocate two variables to track playstate.
*/
public static var PLAY:String = "play";
public static var PAUSE:String = "pause";

//default playstate is 'play'
public var playState:String = PLAY;


public function PlayButton() {

    //enable button and hit area.
      enable();

/*
    A movieclip named 'hit' exists inside our playButton
    (and all of our buttons for that matter). We make it invisible, but
    then assign it to our playButton's 'hitArea' property. That means
    that whenever we roll over 'hit', the playButton's rollover behavior
    will be triggered.
*/
hit._visible = false;
hitArea = hit;

//map functions to mouse interactions
    onRollOver = function() {
        if (isEnabled()) gotoAndStop(playState + "Over");
    };
```

```
        onRollOut = function() {
            if (isEnabled()) gotoAndStop(playState + "Up");
        };
        onRelease = onReleaseOutside = function() {
            if (isEnabled()) {
              togglePlayState();
              gotoAndStop(playState + "Down");

              //broadcast change... View is listening!
              broadcastMessage(ON_CHANGE);
            }
        };
    }
    public function togglePlayState():Void {
        if (playState == PAUSE) playState = PLAY;
        else if (playState == PLAY) playState = PAUSE;
    }


    /*
        To link this class conceptually with the movieclips on the stage,
        playstates and mousestates correspond to actual named frames in a
        timeline. So, this movieclip needs to have six frames: playUp,
        playOver, playDown, pauseUp, pauseOver and pauseDown. This allows us
        to have different visual cues for the up, over, and down mouse
        events whether the video is playing or paused.
    */

    public function setPlayState(val:String):Void {
        playState = val;
        gotoAndStop(playState + "Up");
    }
    public function getPlayState():String {
        return playState;
    }
```

And, as with our fast-forward button (and all of our controls, for that matter), we tell the View to listen for an ON_CHANGE event from our playButton. When it hears that message, it will call toggle in the Controller, which starts our happy MVC dance.

See the following code in MediaPlayerView.layout:

```
playButton.addEventListener(Component.ON_CHANGE, cntrl, "toggle");
```

Volume Slider

The volume slider is, I'm afraid to say, a slider. As such, it participates in all manner of slider silliness, which is encapsulated in our Slider class, which extends Control. This time, for brevity, let's look at our ISlider interface:

```
public function setPosition(val:Number):Void;
public function getPosition():Number;
public function setMax(val:Number):Void;
public function getMax():Number;
public function setMin(val:Number):Void;
public function getMin():Number;
```

As Slider extends Control, it will inherit Control's default press and release handlers, namely doOnPress and doOnRelease. Here we override the default implementations:

```
private function doOnPress():Void {
    pressed = true;
    onEnterFrame = setPosition;
}
private function doOnRelease():Void {
    pressed = false;
    delete onEnterFrame;
}
```

And so, any time the slider is pressed, we begin calling setPosition on every frame. What happens in setPosition? The Volume slider is an HSlider (horizontal), so if we look in HSlider, we see the following:

```
public function setPosition(val:Number):Void {
/*
    if a value is passed in, use it to set the value
    of __pos. If not, set _pos to the //value of _xmouse
*/
__pos = val ? val : _xmouse;


/*
    Set the slideBar width to whichever is less: getPosition() or getMax()
*/
slideBar._width = Math.min(getMax(), getPosition());


/*
    Pass getPosition()/getMax() to setValue(), where it will be broadcast
    out to the View.
```

```
*/
setValue(getPosition()/getMax());
}
```

Up a level, in Control, the result of getPosition()/getMax() is sent out to whomever might be listening:

```
public function setValue(val):Void {
    __val = val;
    broadcastMessage(ON_CHANGE, val * 100);
}
```

And in the View, not surprisingly, we see:

```
volumeBar.addEventListener(Component.ON_CHANGE, cntrl, "setVolume");
```

Are you starting to see a pattern? The volume bar broadcasts an ON_CHANGE event every time its value changes. That value is picked up in the View, which calls the Controller, which calls the appropriate method in the Model. The Model then lets the View know that the value has changed so that the View might respond if needed.

Seek Bar

The seek bar and download progress bar are similar to the volume slider. Like the volume slider, the seek bar overrides the default implementation of setPosition:

```
public function setPosition(val:Number):Void {
    __pos = val ? val : _xmouse;
    slideBar._width = Math.min(getMax(), getPosition());
    setValue(getPosition()/getMax());
}
```

Download Progress Bar

The progress bar barely merits mention, except for the fact that it is an excellent example of our MVC framework doing all of the work for us. In our View, see:

```
public function onLoadProgress(percentage:Number):Void {
    progressBar._xscale = percentage;
}
```

The Model automatically handles download progress and sends the View everything we need to display it. We get the percentage for free! Just set the _xscale of a movieclip to match it and there you go.

Media Player Wrapup – MVC pays off!

After all of the work setting up an MVC framework, an MVCMediaPlayer framework, and a simple Component framework, it might be difficult to see the simple payoff of this project through all of the behind-the-scenes complexity. The best way to bring that back into focus is to imagine, once again, that you've been hired to create a media player for a client. How will you start?

We posit that the best place to look is at ImediaPlayerView, the interface for our View. The following are all of the methods that you will need to implement. You can almost think of the process as filling out a form:

```
public function getMPController():MediaPlayerController;
public function getMPModel():MediaPlayerModel;
public function setVideoInstance(val:Video):Void;
public function getVideoInstance():Video;
public function setAdPlaying(val:Boolean):Void;

public function onConnect(val:String):Void;
public function onMetaData(val:Object):Void;
public function onStatus(val:Object):Void;
public function onLoadProgress(percentage:Number):Void;

public function onPlay():Void;
public function onInitMedia(path:String):Void;
public function onPlayMedia(path:String):Void;
public function onPause():Void;
public function onStop():Void;
public function onFastForward(val:Number):Void;
public function onRewind(val:Number):Void;
public function onSetMediaPosition(val:Number):Void;
public function onPositionChange(position:Number,
➡ duration:Number, percentage:Number):Void;
public function onMediaEnd():Void;
public function onSetVolume(val:Number):Void;
public function onMute():Void;
public function onUnMute(val:Number):Void;

//from super…
public function init():Void;
public function layout():Void;
```

So, what visual cues will you create when onPlay, onPause, onPositionChange, and onMediaEnd are fired? How about onConnect, onStatus, and onLoadProgress? These visual elements can really distinguish your work! The framework provided makes it easy to get the information that each of these elements would need.

In short, the way you actually implement your View is up to you!

Taking It to the Next Level

We've just written some pretty intense OOP code. It was a lot of work! Why bother? Because you can reuse it. The goal of MVC—and of object-oriented programming in general—is to promote reuse of code and avoid duplication of effort. Because Flash projects tend to be so design intensive, they often have difficulty realizing this goal. In fact, most high-end Flash projects that are made using traditional Flash development practices are one-offs. As a result, they tend to be incredibly difficult (and expensive) to work on or extend. In effect, they are like handmade airplanes. Nothing in them gets reused the next time around because they contain very few reusable parts.

Our premise was that, if you're going to be hired to write a Flash media player, it's probable that much of what you'll be doing will deal with the visual aspects of that player; if you use MVC, you might only need to change your View code. Even if you do need to work with the Model, having it separated from the View can only be a good thing. Keeping code in discrete modules makes for a happy programmer.

But MVC is not the only way to skin this cat. Many efforts have been made to make Flash development less difficult. There are a number of wonderful open source (and not open source) frameworks out there that can increase your productivity. Remember, though, frameworks have a learning curve; you'll need to learn how to do things within the context of a given framework before you can get anything done at all. Then, presumably, if the framework is a good one, you will benefit from this preliminary effort; your project will be more manageable and less of a nightmare to change; you'll be able to reuse code and avoid duplicate effort—and maybe you'll even make more money!

The open source Flash community is growing faster than ever. You can get a glimpse into this brave new world and the projects and frameworks in development that might help you here:

http://osflash.org/open_source_flash_projects/

And, although this list is by no means exhaustive, here are some well-proven frameworks that you might want to look into implementing as part of your workflow:

http://osflash.org/projects/actionstep/

http://osflash.org/enflash/

http://osflash.org/as2lib/

Of course, in case you've been living in a cave, there's Flex:

http://www.adobe.com/products/flex/

And, for 3D in Flash, check out:

http://sandy.media-box.net/blog/

http://www.papervision3d.org

Each of these is, like Flash itself, a compile-time solution. They assume that the developer will create, hone, and compile an application. A lot of the logic that might then normally exist in the server layer is often rolled into the client—hence the "thick client" metaphor. This often provides for a better user experience; applications can maintain a persistent user interface with minimal page refreshes.

Typical web applications, on the other hand, are structured differently. They assume that most of your business logic will reside on the server and that the user interface should be a very thin client that serves to respond to that layer. If you're interested in creating Flash content that follows this metaphor, there's FHTML: http://www.fhtml.org. *(Disclaimer: I'm the author of the FHTML framework!)*

FHTML lets you generate flash UI from XHTML markup and simple style sheets at runtime (not compile time), thereby making it easier to create and deploy Flash content. The goal of the project is to provide all of the coolness of Flash while sacrificing nothing of the HTML/browser user experience—content degrades to HTML, and more importantly, is fully search-engine indexable.

Basically, most of what you can create in the Flash IDE you can also create dynamically using FHTML. And because FHTML features a liquid layout engine, many other things that are nearly impossible to create with the Flash IDE are suddenly very easy. For example, to put a video on the page, in FHTML you just say:

```
<video src="myVideo.flv" />
```

To set some properties for that video, do this:

```
<!--Put a video on the page and set its properties -->
<video
    class="myVideoStyle"
    coord = {x:'right', y:'bottom', w:320, h:240};
    filter = "__defaultFilters"
    show = "__videoShowAnimation"
    hide = "__videoHideAnimation"
    over = "__videoOverAnimation"
    out = "__videoOutAnimation"
    playlist = "myPlaylist.xml"
    />
```

It's only possible to scratch the surface here, but this example:

- Places a video instance on the page
- Uses a style sheet to set loads of other properties that we're not even considering here (via the class attribute)
- Places the video so that it will stay aligned to the right and bottom edges of its parent as the parent resizes
- Applies a filter preset (shadow, glow, etc.) to the video (presets of all types are stored in a preset file)
- Applies animation sequences for show, hide, rollover, and rollout
- Hands the video a playlist

That's a pretty simple way to achieve a result that usually requires a lot of code.

With the rapid growth of these frameworks and the incredible speed of the Flash 9 VM, this is an exciting time to be a Flash developer. Go Flash!

Index

Note to the Reader: Throughout this index **bold-faced** page numbers indicate primary discussions of a topic. *Italicized* page numbers indicate illustrations.

A

abstract objects, 58
access control lists (ACLs), 308
access control to streams and recording, 308–309
Accordion components, 132
ACLs (access control lists), 308
Action Message Format (AMF), 187
ActionScript 2 (AS2) versions
    vs. AS3, **64–66**
    bandwidth checking, **111–114**
    cue points
        captions, **173**, *174*, *175*
        chapter links, **178–180**, *178*
        dynamic, **171**
        reading, **168–169**
    dissolves
        bitmaps for, **246–254**
        transitions class, **254–257**
    filters, **210–215**
    FotoBooth application, **266–270**, *267*
    masks, **193–198**, *198–199*
    Media Player
        structure, **94–98**
        XML playlist in, **149–151**
    metadata
        reading, **160**, *161*
        video duration, **162–163**
    progressive delivery, **46–47**, *47–48*
    streaming delivery, **50–51**
    transitions, **221–225**
    video snapshots, **235–239**, *235*
    videoconferencing application, **298–300**
ActionScript 3 (AS3) versions
    vs. AS2, **64–66**
    bandwidth checking, **114–118**
    cue points
        captions, **174–176**
        chapter links, **180–182**
        dynamic, **171–172**
        reading, **169–170**

dissolves, **258–265**
filters, **215–220**
FotoBooth application, **270–277**
masks, **199–206**, *207*
Media Player, **152–154**
metadata
    reading, **160**, *161*
    video duration, **163–164**
progressive delivery, **48–49**, *50*
streaming delivery, **51–52**
transitions, **225–230**
video snapshots, **239–245**
videoconferencing application, **300–305**
ActionScript Virtual Machine (AVM2), 65
addASCuePoint method, **166–167**
addEventListener method
    Component, 332
    VideoPlayer, 254
Administration Console, 296
Adobe DevCenter, 313
Align property, 79
alpha channels
    filters with, **207–208**, *208*
    vs. masks, 193
    transparency, **19–20**, 193
    video settings, **34–35**
alternatives in proposals, **12–13**
AMF (Action Message Format), 187
Animation Codec setting, 20
animHandler method, 195, 205
AnimMask.as file, 200
App.as file
    AS2, **248–250**
    AS3, **258–260**
Application class, 291
applyFilter method, 233
archiving, **127**
arrays
    cue points, 165
    in ListBoxes, **137–138**, *138*
    pixel data, 232
ASDT plug-in, 67
aspect ratio
    in frames, 26, *26*
    pixels, **32**
assert statements, 103
asset files, **126**

associative arrays, 165
AsyncErrorEvent handlers, 170
attachBitmap method, 232
audio
    compression, **27**, **34**
    importance, 18
    streaming, 305–306
    synching, 33
audiocodecid metadata, **158–159**
audiodatarate metadata, 158
audiodelay metadata, 158
autoexposure, 18
autofocus, 18
automatic playing, 79, **142–144**, *142*, *144*
autoPlay property, 79
AVM2 (ActionScript Virtual Machine), 65

B

back button considerations, **40–41**
background for transparent videos, **19**
bandwidth
    buffering for, **109–110**
    and data rate, 31
    detecting, **110**
        AS2, **111–114**
        AS3, **114–118**
    in encoding, **30**
    FMS, 289, **307–308**
    smart streaming, **310–311**
bark method, 91
beginBitmapFill method, 232
BevelFilter filter, 209
bit rate
    audio, **34**
    encoding, **27**
BitmapData object, **231**
    dissolve transitions, **246–247**
        AS2, **247–254**
        AS3, **258–265**
        transitions class, **254–257**
    dynamic thumbnails
        AS2, **235–239**, *235*
        AS3, **239–245**
    FotoBooth application, **265–266**, *265*
        AS2, **266–270**, *267*
        AS3, **270–277**
    overview, **232–235**
blogs, FMS, 313
BlurFilter filter, 209, **212–213**
blurHandler method, FunWithFilters
    AS2, 211
    AS3, 219

bookmarks
    cue points, **176–177**
    in interactive video, 134
BoxMask.as file, 201
broadcastMessage method, 332
browsers, testing on, **105–106**
buffering, video, **109–110**
bufferLength property, 88
bufferTime property, 88
bug handling, **107–108**
Bunch, Kenny, 329
buttons, 132, **337–338**
bytesLoaded property, 88
bytesTotal property, 88

C

caching with progressive downloads, 44, **55–56**
Camera class, 291
canSeekToEnd metadata, 158
Captionate tool, **188**, *188–189*
captions, cue point
    AS2, 173, *174*, *175*
    AS3, **174–176**
CBR (constant bit rate) compression, 28
CDNs (content-delivery networks), **53**, 119, *120*
    FVSS, **53**
    hosting, **54**
certificates, SSL, 309
changeHandler method
    FunWithFilters, **219–220**
    FunWithMasks, **205–206**
    FunWithTransitions, **229–230**
chapter links, cue points for, **177**
    AS2, **178–180**, *178*
    AS3, **180–182**
Charles utility, 30, 107
checkDataLoaded function, 143
checklists, wrap-up, **127–128**
chooseVideo method, 238, 243
classes
    deployment methods in, **324–331**
    in OOP, 58
Click.TV site, 134, *135*
clickable thumbnails, 132
clickHandler method
    FLVDissolveTransition, 256
    FunWithFilters, 214
    FunWithMasks, 196
    FunWithTransitions, 224
clients
    deployment requirements, 316
    FMS classes, **291–292**

needs, **2–5**
remote shared objects, 290
separation anxiety, 127
source videos from, **16–17**
clone method, 233
close method, 88
code-based animation libraries, 318
codecs, 21
ColorMatrixFilter filter, 209, 213–214
colorMatrixHandler method, FunWithFilters
    AS2, 211
    AS3, 219
ColorTransform filter, 209, 213, 233
colorTransformHandler method, FunWithFilters
    AS2, 211
    AS3, 219
ComboBox components, 132
comments in interactive video, 134
compare method, 233
Component class, 332–334
compression
    audio, **27**, **34**
    types, **28**
concrete state functionality, 63, *63*
configure method, 319
connect method, 322
connections
    in deployment, 318–319
    to FMS, 293
    testing speed, **106–107**
constant bit rate (CBR) compression, 28
content-delivery networks (CDNs), **53**, 119, *120*
    FVSS, **53**
    hosting, **54**
content updates, **130–131**
context functionality, 62, *63*
Control class, 337
Controller.as class, 89
controllers
    FMS interface methods, 320–321
    in MVC pattern, **60–62**, *60*, *62*
controls, customizing, **83–84**, *84*
CoordinateSpace.as class, 90
copyChannel method, 233
copyPixels method, 233
copyright issues, **55–56**
Core.as class, 89
core package, 89
Create Motion Tween option, 225
cue points, **155–156**, 165
    adding, **166–167**
    bookmarks, **176–177**
    captions, **173–176**, *174*
    chapter links, **177–182**, *178*

contents, **165**
dynamic ActionScript, **170–172**, *172*
NetStream, **168–170**
purpose, **165**
types, **167–168**
CuePoint_trace.swf file, AS2, 168–169
CuePoint_trace_AS3.swf file, 169–170
CuePoint_trace_comp.swf file
    AS2, 171
    AS3, 171–172
CuePoints_captions.swf file, 175
CuePoints_captions_AS3.swf file, 176
cuePoints metadata, 159
CuePoints_ns_captions.swf file, 173, *174*
CuePoints_ns_captions_AS3.swf file, 174–175
CuePoints_playlist.swf file, 178–180, *178*
CuePoints_playlist_AS3.swf file, 180–182
cuePoints property, 79
currentFps property, 88
custom display, 132
customizing UI controls, **83–84**, *84*

D

data rate, **27**, **30–31**
day rates in proposals, 11
debugging, **107–108**
defining client needs, **2–5**
deinterlacing, **28–29**, *29*
deliverables in wrap-up, 126
delta frames, 27
deployment, Media Player, 315–316
    class methods, **324–331**
    client requirements, **316**
    Component class, **332–334**
    connections, **318–319**
    download progress bar, **343**
    elapsed/total time display, **335–336**
    fast-forward/rewind buttons, **337–338**
    higher-level framework code, **317–318**
    interface methods, **320–324**
    mute/unmute buttons, **336–337**
    play/pause button, **339–341**
    progressive, **118**, *118–120*
    seek bar, **343**
    streaming, **121–124**, *122–124*
    view components, **331–332**
    volume slider, **342–343**
    wrapup, **343–344**
design patterns, **59–60**
    MVC, **60–62**, *60*, *62*
    state, **62–64**, *63*
destroy method
    FLVBitmapThumb, 239, 244

FotoBooth
AS2, 270
AS3, 277
VideoPlayer, 264
destroyListeners method, 332
detection, bandwidth, 110
AS2, 111–114
AS3, 114–118
development environment for FMS, 287
digital rights management (DRM), 44, 55–56
Digital Video (DV) format, 20
directories
automatic playing from, 142–144, *142, 144*
FMS, 288–289
disable method, 317
dispatchEvent method, 254
display standards, 20
dispose method, 233
dissolve transitions, 246–247
AS2
bitmaps for, 247–254
transitions class, 254–257
AS3, 258–265
documentation files, 126
Dog class, 91
doOnEnterFrame method, 339
doOnPress method
Control, 337–338
ISlider, 342
doOnRelease method
Control, 337, 339
ISlider, 342
download progress bar, 343
downloads, progressive, 44–45
AS2, 46–47, *47–48*
AS3, 48–49, *50*
scripted pseudo-streaming, 184–187, *185–186*
vs. streaming, 42–45, *43*
dragMeHandler method, 195, 205
draw method, 233
DRM (digital rights management), 44, 55–56
dropShadow method, 212
DropShadowFilter filter, 209
dropShadowHandler method, FunWithFilters
AS2, 212
AS3, 219
duration of videos, metadata for, 159,
161–164, *161*
DV (Digital Video) format, 20
DVDs
FLVs on, 54–55
source videos on, 17
dynamic ActionScript cue points, 170–172, *172*

dynamic playlists, 129–130
content updates, 130–131
ListBox arrays, 137–138, *138*
sequential playback, 144–146
shuffle playback, 146–147
steps, 131–132, *132–133*
XML, 148–154
XML data in ListBoxes, 139–141, *141*
dynamic thumbnails
AS2, 235–239, *235*
AS3, 239–245

E

Eclipse code editor, 67–69, *68*
ECMA-standard-based languages, 65
elapsed/total time display, 335–336
Emacs code editor, 67
embedding in SWF, 43, *43*
encapsulation in OOP, 58
encoding, 15, 21, 29
alpha channel video settings, 34–35
audio compression, 34
bandwidth target, 30
data rate, 30–31
frame size, 32
keyframe intervals, 33–34
optimal frame rate, 33
options, 21–24, *22–23*
reference, 26–29, *26, 29*
standards and formats, 20
tips, 24–25
video analysis for, 30
equity, working for, 12
EventBroadcaster class, 317–318
events
cue points, 167
MediaPlayerModel methods, 330
expiring caches, 56
Express Install option, 41

F

fadeOut method, 252, 263
fast-forward/rewind buttons, 337–338
fast pans and zooms, 18
fastForward method
IMediaPlayerController, 321, 339
MediaPlayerModel, 328
FCS (Flash Communication Server), 281–282
FDT plug-in, 67, 69, *70*
feedback, 40

fees in proposals, **11–12**
FFButton method, 338
ffmpeg encoder, 24, 73
ffmpeX encoder, 24
FHTML framework, 346–347
File class, 291, 306
file properties, Sorenson Squeeze, **157**
file structure, FMS, 288–289
fillColor data type, 232
fillRect method, 233
filters, **191**
    alpha channels, **207–208**, *208*
    classes for, **210–220**
    overview, **208–209**
final project walkthrough, **126**
findCuePoint method, 166
findNearestCuePoint method, 166
findNextCuePointWithName method, 166
Flash 8 Video Encoder, 21
Flash Communication Server (FCS), 281–282
Flash Debug Player tool, 108
Flash Debugger tool, 108
Flash Detection Kit, 41
Flash Live Video (FLV) format, 16
Flash Media Server (FMS), 44, **281–282**
    access control, **308–309**
    alternatives, **285–287**
    applications, **283**
    bandwidth management, **307–308**
    client side classes, **291–292**
    connections, **293**
    development environment, **287**
    file structure, **288–289**
    hosting, 53–54, **284–285**
    load balancing, **308**
    operation, **282–283**
    planning, **283**
    remote shared objects, **290**
    secure applications, **309**
    server-side data manipulation, **306–307**
    server-side streaming, **308**
    server-to-server communication, **307**
    smart bandwidth streaming, **310–311**
    streaming MP3s, **305–306**
    streams, **289**
    tips and tricks, **311–313**
    videoconferencing application, **293–294**
        AS2, **298–300**
        AS3, **300–305**
        asset setup, **296–297**
        server-side setup, **294–296**
Flash Media Streaming Service (FMSS), 121
Flash Player detection, **41**

Flash Professional 8 (FP8) encoder, 21
Flash Video Import Wizard, 21–22, *22*
Flash Video Streaming Service (FVSS), 45, **53**, 284
FlashDevelop code editor, 67
Flashloaded components, 42
FlashMedia List site, 312
FlashVideoProFilters package, 215–216
FlashVideoProMasks package, 200–201
FlashVideoProTrans package, 227
Flex Client ActionScript Debugger tool, 108
FlexBuilder2, 67
flexibility for playlists, 131
Flomag, Rick, 184
floodFill method, 233
flow, **38–42**, *39*
flow charts, **39–40**, *39*
FLV (Flash Live Video) format, 16
FLV MetaData Injector (FLVMDI) utility, 74, **187**
FLV QuickTime Export plug-in, 22, 24
FLV to Video Converter, *55*
flv2fmpeg4 utility, 73
FLVBitmapThumb.as file
    AS2, **235–239**, *235*
    AS3, **239–245**
FLVBitmapTransition file
    AS2, **247–254**
    AS3, **258–265**
FLVDissolveTransition.as file, 254–257
FLVMDI (FLV MetaData Injector) utility, 74, **187**
FLVPlayback component
    AS3, **78**
    benefits, **77**
    for cue points, **170–172**
    customizing, **82–84**, *84*
    full-screen mode, **86**
    implementing, **78–80**
    instantiating and configuring, **80–82**, *81*
    limitations, **77–78**
    methods, **166–167**
    skins, **82–86**, *84*
FLVPlayback Skins folder, 85
FLVPlayerBasic class
    AS2, **46–47**, 50–51
    AS3, **48–49**
FLVPlayerBasicBwCheck class
    AS2, **111–114**
    AS3, **115–118**
FLVs, creating, **21–24**, *22–23*
FLVTool2 utility, 73, **187**
FMS. *See* Flash Media Server (FMS)
FMS FAQ, 313
FMS Resource Center, 313
FMSS (Flash Media Streaming Service), 121

FMSWiki site, 313
formats, 16–17
FotoBooth application, **265–266**, *265*
 AS2, **266–270**, *267*
 AS3, **270–277**
FotoBooth.as file, **267–270**
frame rate
 optimal, **33**
 setting, **27**
frame size, 26, *26*, **32**
framerate metadata, 159
Fridge Magnet application, 290
full-screen mode, **86**
functionality, **38–42**, *39*
FunWithFilters.as file
 AS2, **210–215**
 AS3, **215–220**
FunWithMasks.as file
 AS2, **193–198**, *198–199*
 AS3, **199–206**, *207*
FunWithTransitions.as file
 AS2, **221–225**
 AS3, **225–230**
FVSS (Flash Video Streaming Service), 45, **53**, 284

G

gaffes, **7–8**
generateFilterRect method, 234
getBytesTotal function, 112
getColorBoundsRect method, 234
getContinuousPlay method, 323
getMax method, 342
getMediaDuration method
 IMediaPlayerModel, 322
 MediaPlayerModel, 328
getMediaPosition method
 IMediaPlayerController, 321
 MediaPlayerModel, 328
getMin method, 342
getMPController method, 344
getMPModel method
 IMediaPlayerController, 321
 ImediaPlayerView, 344
getMPView method, 321
getNext method, 151
getPixel method, 234
getPixel32 method, 234
getPixels method, 234
getPlaylist method, 151
getPlayState method, 341
getPosition method, 342

getRandomVideo function, 147
getSound method, 321
getTopPlayer method, 249
getValue method, 333
getVideoInstance method
 ImediaPlayerView, 344
 MediaPlayerView.as, 96
getVolume method
 IMediaPlayerController, 321
 MediaPlayerModel, 329
grab method
 BoxMask, 201
 FunWithMasks, 205
GradientGlowFilter filter, 209
Gunesch, Moses, 318

H

handleLoadProgress method
 IMediaPlayerModel, 322
 MediaPlayerModel, 330
handleOnMetaData method, 330
handleOnStatus method
 FLVBitmapThumb, 238, 243–244
 MediaPlayerModel, 330
handlePosition method
 IMediaPlayerModel, 322
 MediaPlayerModel, 330
hasNext method, 151
haXeVideo application, 287
HD (High-Definition Video) format, 20
height
 aspect ratio, 26, *26*
 metadata, 159
hide method, 333
hideLogin method, videoconferencing application
 AS2, **298–299**
 AS3, 302
High-Definition Video (HD) format, 20
higher-level framework code in deployment, **317–318**
highest-quality source videos, 16
hitTest method, 234
hosting
 choices, **52–55**
 FMS, 53–54, **284–285**
hotFlashVideo extension, 183
hotspots, **182–184**, *183–184*
hourly fees in proposals, **11–12**
HSlider class, 342–343
HTTP connections vs. RTMP, 283

I

ifc folder, 90
IISlider interface, 342
IMediaPlayerModel interface, 321–322
incoming FMS streams, 289
Influxis host, 54, 121–124, *122–124*
infoObject, 311
inheritance in OOP, 58
init method, 318–319
    App, 258–259
    Component, 333, 335
    ImediaPlayerView, 344
    MediaPlayer.as, 94
    MediaPlayerView.as, 96
    VideoPlayer, 261–262
initButtons method
    FLVDissolveTransition, 256
    FunWithFilters, 214
    FunWithTransitions, 224
initCoordinates method
    MediaPlayer.as, 94
    MediaPlayerView.as, 96
initDisplays method, 335
initMedia method, 323
initMediaPlayer function, 150, 153, 320
integrating XML playlist into MVC Player,
    148–154
interactive video, **133–136**, *135–136*
Interface package, 90
interfaces
    deployment methods in, **320–324**
    description, 91
interframe (temporal) compression, 28
interlaced video, **28–29**, *29*
IntervalUtils utilities, 329
interviews for client needs, **4–5**
intraframe (spatial) compression, 28
ISlider interface, 342–343

J

Java Runtime Environment (JRE), 68
jumpcuts in interactive video, 135

K

keyframe intervals, **33–34**
keyframes
    for cue points, 168
    description, **27**
Kremens, Jim, 76

L

launching, **118, 126**
    progressive deployment, **118**, *118–120*
    soft launches, **108**
    streaming deployment, **121–124**, *122–124*
layout method
    ImediaPlayerView, 344
    MediaPlayerView.as, 96
length of video metadata, **161–164**, *161*
letgo method, 206
libraries, code-based animation, 318
lighting scenes, 18
links
    chapter, **177**
        AS2, **178–180**, *178*
        AS3, **180–182**
    relative, 106
ListBoxes
    simple arrays in, **137–138**, *138*
    XML data in, **139–141**, *141*
listenForClicks method, 249, 259
live video. *See* Flash Media Server (FMS)
load balancing
    CDNs, 53
    FMS, 308
load method, 253, 264
loadBitmap method, 234
LoadVars class, 291, 306–307
lock method, 234

M

Main.as file
    FLVBitmapThumb.as, 240
    FotoBooth application, **271–274**
    Media Player, **152–153**
main.asc file, 82, 288, 294–295
makeThumbBitmap method
    FLVBitmapThumb
        AS2, 238
        AS3, 243
    FotoBooth
        AS2, 269
        AS3, 276–277
mashups, 135
masks, **191**
    classes for, **193–206**, *198–199, 207*
    overview, **192–193**
media classes for FMS clients, 291
MediaPlayer.as class, 90, **94–95**, 149–150
MediaPlayerController.as class, 89

MediaPlayerModel, 325
    event-based methods, 330
    time-based methods, 329
    transport methods, 325–329
MediaPlayerModel.as class, 89
    AS2, 151
    AS3, 153–154
MediaPlayerView class, 319–320
MediaPlayerView.as class, 89, 95–98
meetings, scheduling, **127**
Menu components, 132
merge method, 234
metadata, **155–156**
    cue points. *See* cue points
    overview, **156–159**
    reading, **159–164**, *161*
    scripted pseudo-streaming, **184–187**, *185–186*
    third-party tools, **187–188**, *188–189*
Metadata_duration.swf file
    AS2, 162–163
    AS3, 163–164
Metadata Injector, 187
Metaliq components, 42
methods in OOP, 58
Microphone class, 291
Model.as class, 89
Model-View-Controller (MVC) pattern, **60–62**,
    60, 62
models
    class methods, 325–330
    interface methods, 321–323
    in MVC, **60–62**, *60, 62*
Moock, Colin, 287
MoreMX host, 54
mouseClickHandler method, 249, 259–260
MP3s, streaming, 305–306
MPEG-2 files, *55*
MTASC compiler, **70–73**, *71, 73*
multiple browser and platform testing, **105–106**
Multiplication class, 103
mute method
    IMediaPlayerController, 321
    MediaPlayerModel, 329
mute/unmute buttons, 336–337
MVC (Model-View-Controller) pattern, **60–62**,
    60, 62
MVC Player, XML playlist integration into,
    148–154
MVCApplication.as class, 89
MVCMediaPlayer.as class, 89
MVCMediaPlayer framework, 344
mx.transitions class, 254–257, *257*

N

Name property, 165
National Television System Committee (NTSC)
    format, 20
navigation
    cue points for, **167–168**
    testing, **42**
Nellymoser codec, 304
NetConnection class, **87**, 291–292
NetConnection Debugger tool, 108
NetStream class
    cue points on, **168–170**
    FMS clients, 291
    NetConnection for, **87–88**
NetStreamExt.as class, 90
noise method, 234
nonpersistent properties, **158**
nonpersistent remote shared objects, 290
NTSC (National Television System Committee)
    format, 20
NTSC-J (National Television System Committee—
    Japan) format, 20

O

object-oriented programming (OOP), **57**
    AS2 vs. AS3 for, **64–66**
    benefits, **59**
    design patterns, **59–64**, *60, 62–63*
    elements, **57–58**
offline video, **54–55**
On2 Flix Pro encoder, 22
    metadata, **157**
    presets, 25, *25*
onAdPlay method, 317
onConnect method, 324, 344
onCuePoint method, 168
    CuePoint_trace_AS3.swf, 169–170
    CuePoint_trace_comp.swf, 172
    CuePoints_captions_AS3.swf, 176
    CuePoints_ns_captions_AS3.swf, 175
    VideoPlayer, 264
one-pass encoding, 28
onEnterFrame method
    AnimMask, 200
    Metadata_duration.swf, 164
    TransitionMask, 227–228
onFastForward method, 323, 344
onInitMedia method, 324, 344
onLoadComplete method, 107, 112, 116
onLoadDone method, 112

onLoadProgress method, 324, 343–344
onLoadStart method, 112, 116
onMediaEnd method, 324, 344
onMetaData method, **158–160**
    CuePoints_playlist_AS3.swf, 181
    FLVBitmapThumb, 242
    FLVPlayerBasic, 49, 52
    FLVPlayerBasicBwCheck, 115
    FotoBooth, 277
    ImediaPlayerView, 344
    MediaPlayerView.as, 97
    Metadata_duration.swf, 164
    videoconferencing, 301
    VideoMC, 202, 216, 226
    VideoPlayer, 264
onMute method, 323, 344
onNetStatus method, 301–302
onPause method
    ImediaPlayerView, 344
    MediaPlayerView.as, 97
onPlay method
    ImediaPlayerView, 344
    MediaPlayerView.as, 97
onPlayMedia method, 335
    ImediaPlayerView, 344
    MediaPlayerView.as, 97
onPositionChange method
    IMediaPlayerView, 324, 344
    MediaPlayerView, 336
onRewind method, 323, 344
onRollout method, 339
onRollover method, 339
onSetMediaPosition method
    ImediaPlayerView, 344
    MediaPlayerView.as, 97
onSetVolume method
    ImediaPlayerView, 344
    MediaPlayerView.as, 97
onStatus method, 107
    ImediaPlayerView, 344
    MediaPlayerView.as, 97
onStatusTriggered property, 88
onStop method
    ImediaPlayerView, 344
    MediaPlayerView.as, 97
onSync method, 290, 304
onUnload method, 240
onUnMute method, 323, 344
OOP (object-oriented programming), **57**
    AS2 vs. AS3 for, **64–66**
    benefits, **59**
    design patterns, **59–64**, *60*, *62–63*
    elements, **57–58**
open source products, **73–74**

optimal frame rate, **33**
optional Sorenson Squeeze properties, **158**
O'Reilly, James, 76
outgoing FMS streams, 289

P

packages, 89–90
PAL (Phase Alternating Line) format, 20
PAL-M format, 20
paletteMap method, 234
pans, 18
Parameters property, 165
pattern.mvc package, 89
pause method
    IMediaPlayerController, 321
    MediaPlayerModel, 327
    NetStream, 88
perlinNoise method, 234
persistent FMS connections, 282
persistent properties, **157**
persistent remote shared objects, 290
Phase Alternating Line (PAL) format, 20
photobooth application, **265–266**, *265*
    AS2, **266–270**, *267*
    AS3, **270–277**
PHP scripts, 142–144
piracy, *55*
pitfalls, anticipating, **6–8**
pixelDissolve method, 234, 246
pixels
    arrays of, 232
    aspect ratio, **32**
platform testing, **105–106**
play method
    IMediaPlayerController, 321
    MediaPlayerModel, 327
    VideoPlayer, 252, 262–263
play/pause button, 339–341
playback
    sequential, **144–146**
    shuffle, **146–147**
playerFadeCompleteHandler method, 250, 260
Playlist.as class, 90
PlayListAutoPlay.fla file, 145–146
PlaylistListBox.fla file, **137–138**, *138*
PlaylistListBox_XML.fla, **139–141**, *141*
playlists, dynamic. *See* dynamic playlists
PlaylistShuffle.fla file, 146–147
PlaylistUtils.as class, 90
playMedia method
    IMediaPlayerController, 321
    MediaPlayerModel, 326–327

playNext method
    IMediaPlayerController, 321
    MediaPlayerModel.as, 151
playPrevious method
    IMediaPlayerController, 321
    MediaPlayerModel.as, 151, 153
Playstation Portable (PSP), 55
playVideo method, FLVPlayerBasicBwCheck
    AS2, 113–114
    AS3, 117–118
port testers, 313
potential flaws, **6**
predesigned skins, **82**
preview property, 79
pricing in proposals, **11–12**
producing videos, **17–18**
"programming to the interface", 320
progress bars, **343**
progressive delivery and downloads
    AS2, **46–47**, *47–48*
    AS3, **48–49**, *50*
    scripted pseudo-streaming, **184–187**, *185–186*
    vs. streaming, **42–45**, *43*
progressive deployment, **119**, *119–121*
project fees in proposals, 12
project steps, **1**
    defining client needs, **2–5**
    pitfall anticipation, **6–8**
    proposals, **8–12**, *9–10*
    solutions, **5–6**
    wrap-up, **124–128**
properties
    OOP, 58
    Sorenson Squeeze, **22–24**, *23, 25*
proposals
    guidelines in, **8–10**, *9–10*
    pricing in, **11–12**
Proxus components, 42
Proxy.as class, 90
pseudo-streaming, **184–187**, *185–186*
PSP (Playstation Portable), 55
publishing choices, **52–55**

Q

quality assurance (QA), **105**

R

radio button groups, 132
random videos from playlists, **146–147**
rates in proposals, 11
read_dir_contents.php file, 142–144

readAccess method, 308–309
reading metadata, **159–164**, *161*
real-time data sharing, 290
Real-Time Message Protocol (RTMP), 55, 282–283
Real-Time Messaging Protocol over SSL (RTMPS), 309
recording, access control to, 308–309
red/green/refactor procedure, 102
Red5 project, 285–286
Red5-minimal project, 286
relative links, 106
release method, 201
releases from subjects, 17
remote shared objects (RSOs), 288, 290, 311
removeASCuePoint method, 166
removeEventListener method
    Component, 332
    VideoPlayer, 254
resetFilters method, FunWithFilters
    AS2, 211
    AS3, 218
resetMasks method
    FunWithMasks
        AS2, 194–195
        AS3, 204
    FunWithTransitions, 223
resetMetaData method, 322
rewind method
    IMediaPlayerController, 321
    MediaPlayerModel, 328
Richter, Stefan, 184
Riva Encoder, 24
RSOs (remote shared objects), 288, 290, 311
RTMP (Real-Time Message Protocol), 55, 282–283
RTMPS (Real-Time Messaging Protocol over SSL), 309

S

sample rate in audio, 27
Sanders, Bill, 64
Savage, Steve, 184
saving
    bitmap data, 232
    working file versions, **105**
scale method, 270
scaleMode property, 80
scaling UI components, 83
scheduling meetings, **127**
scratch method, 91
scripted pseudo-streaming (SPS), **184–187**, *185–186*

scroll method, 234
scrubbing
    limitations, 33
    streaming, 44
SD (Standard Definition Video) format, 20
SDP (state design pattern), **62–64**, *63*
search engines, metadata for, 156
SECAM (Sequential Color and Memory)
        format, 20
secure FMS applications, 309
Secure Sockets Layer (SSL), 55, 309
security through obscurity, *55*
seek bar, 343
seek method, 88
seekToNavCuePoint method, 166
seekToNextNavCuePoint method, 166
seekToPrevNavCuePoint method, 166
separation anxiety, 127
Sequential Color and Memory (SECAM)
        format, 20
sequential playback, **144–146**
Server-Side ActionScript (SSAS), 288, 311
Server.xml file, 312
servers. *See* Flash Media Server (FMS)
service providers, 284
setAdPlaying method, 324, 344
setBandwidthLimit method, 308
setBufferTime method, 88
setContinuousPlay method, 323
setFLVCuePointEnabled method, 166
setInterval method, 317
setMask method, *195*
setMax method, 342
setMediaPosition method
    IMediaPlayerController, 321
    MediaPlayerModel, 328
setMin method, 342
setPixel method, 234
setPixel32 method, 234
setPixels method, 234
setPlayState method, 341
setPosition method
    ISlider, 342
    seek bar, 343
setSound model, 321
setupLogin method, 302
setupVideo method
    AS2, 299–300
    AS3, 303–304
setValue method
    Component, 333
    ISlider, 343
setVideoInstance method
    ImediaPlayerView, 344
    MediaPlayerView.as, 96

setVolume method
    IMediaPlayerController, 321
    MediaPlayerModel, 328–329
shared objects, remote, 288, 290, 311
SharedObject class, 292
show method, 333
shuffle playback, **146–147**
simple arrays in ListBoxes, **137–138**, *138*
simple buttons, 132
simplicity, 6, **42**
Simulate Download feature, 107
sitUp method, 91
skin property, 80
skinAutoHide property, 80
skinBackgroundAlpha property, 80
skinBackgroundColor property, 80
skins
    FLVPlayback component, **82–86**, *84*
    video players, **98–99**, *98*
sliders, 337, 342–343
smart bandwidth streaming, 310–311
snapshots
    AS2, **235–239**, *235*
    AS3, **239–245**
    FotoBooth application, **265–266**, *265*
        AS2, **266–270**, *267*
        AS3, **270–277**
    from webcams, **278–279**, *279*
soft launches, **108**
solutions, determining, **5–6**
Sorenson Squeeze encoder
    metadata in, **157–158**
    settings, 22–24, *23*, *25*
sortData method, 182
sortValues method, 179
source property, 79
source videos from clients, **16–17**
spaghetti code, 59
Spark codec, 304
spatial (intraframe) compression, 28
spec sheets, **125**
speed
    FMS, 312
    testing, **106–107**
SPS (scripted pseudo-streaming), **184–187**,
        185–186
SSAS (Server-Side ActionScript), 288, 311
SSL (Secure Sockets Layer), 55, 309
Standard Definition Video (SD) format, 20
standards, video, **20**
startInterval method, FotoBooth
    AS2, 269
    AS3, 276
startPositionInterval method, 329
startProgressInterval method, 329

startup ventures, **12**
startVideo method, 226
startWipe method, 227–228
startXInterval method, 329
state design pattern (SDP), **62–64**, *63*
state functionality, 63, *63*
stop method
    IMediaPlayerController, 321
    MediaPlayerModel, 327
stopPositionInterval method, 329
stopProgressInterval method, 329
stopVideo method, 226
stopWipe method, 227–228
stopXInterval method, 329
storage and retrieval of FMS data, 290
storyboards, 17
Stream class, 292
streaming delivery
    AS2, **50–51**
    AS3, **51–52**
    MP3s, 305–306
    vs. progressive, **42–45**, *43*
    scripted pseudo-streaming, **184–187**, *185–186*
streaming deployment, **121–124**, *122–124*
streams
    access control to, 308–309
    FMS, 289
string tokens, 308–309
strokeHandler method, 194, 204
StrokeMask.as file, 199–200
suffixes, code with, 292
surveys, sample questions, 3–4
swapDepthsWith method, 252
SWF, embedding in, **43**, *43*
synching audio, 33

T

tags in interactive video, 134
takeSnapshots method, FotoBooth
    AS2, 270
    AS3, 276–277
target players, AS2 vs. AS3, **65**
temporal (interframe) compression, 28
test-driven development (TDD), **102–104**
test_playlist.xml file, 148–149
testConnection method, 111
testing, **40**, **102**
    bug identification in, **107–108**
    connection speeds, **106–107**
    limitations, **104**
    on multiple browsers and platforms, **105–106**
    navigation, 42
    for quality assurance, **105**

test-driven development vs. testing while
    coding, **102–104**
usability, **40**, **108**
versions, **106**
TestMultiplication class, 103
Third-Generation Platform (3GP) format, 55
third-party metadata tools, **187–188**, *188–189*
threshold method, 234
thumbnails
    clickable, 132
    dynamic
        AS2, **235–239**, *235*
        AS3, **239–245**
    options for, 245
time-based methods, 329
time property
    cue points, 165
    in NetStream, 88
timerCompleteHandler method, 263
timerHandler method, 253, 263–264
TiVo, 134
toggle method
    IMediaPlayerController, 321
    MediaPlayerModel, 326
togglePlayState method, 341
tools
    open source, **73–74**
    third-party metadata, **187–188**, *188–189*
toString method, 97
traceObject method
    CuePoints_playlist.swf, 179–180
    CuePoints_playlist_AS3.swf, 181
TransitionMask.as file, 227–228
transitions, **220–221**, *221*
    classes for, **221–230**
    dissolve, **246–247**
        AS2, 247–254
        AS3, 258–265
        transitions class, 254–257
    in state design pattern, 63
transparent videos, **19–20**
transport methods, 325–329
triggers in state design pattern, 63, *63*
tripods, 18
two-pass encoding, **28**
Type property, 165

U

ui.component.mediaPlayer package, 89
ui.component.mediaPlayer.playlist package, 90
ui.util class, 90
Unity 2 application, 287
unlock method, 234

unMute method
    IMediaPlayerController, 321
    MediaPlayerModel, 329
updateDuration function
    AS2, 162
    AS3, 163
updates, content, 130–131
usability tests, 40, 108
user interface (UI)
    components, 42
    customizing controls, 83–84, 84
util package, 90
utilities, open source, 73–74
Uvault host, 54

V

valueOf method, 112
variable bit rate (VBR) compression, 24, 28
vector video format, 24, 25
Veotag Player, 134, 134
versions
    detecting, 41
    testing, 106
    working files, saving, 105
vhost.xml file, 311
vidAnimMask method, 195
vidBlur method, FunWithFilters
    AS2, 212
    AS3, 218
vidColorMatrix method, FunWithFilters
    AS2, 213
    AS3, 218
vidColorTransform method, FunWithFilters
    AS2, 213
    AS3, 218
vidCompleted function, 145, 147
vidDragMeMask method, 195–196
vidDropShadow method, 219
video
    buffering, 109–110
    formats, 20
    interactive, 133–136, 135–136
    standards, 20
video players, 75–76
    code, 92–98
    components for. See FLVPlayback component
    creating, 86
    skins for, 98–99, 98
    structure, 89–92, 91–93
video snapshots
    AS2, 235–239, 235
    AS3, 239–245

FotoBooth application, 265–266, 265
    AS2, 266–270, 267
    AS3, 270–277
    from webcams, 278–279, 279
videocodecid metadata, 159
videoconferencing application, 293–294
    AS2, 298–300
    AS3, 300–305
    asset setup, 296–297
    server-side setup, 294–296
videodatarate metadata, 159
VideoMC.as file
    FunWithFilters, 215–217
    FunWithMasks, 201–203
    FunWithTransitions, 225–227
VideoPlayer.as file
    As2, 250–254
    AS3, 260–265
videos
    producing, 17–18
    transparent, 19–20
vidOneHandler method, FunWithTransitions
    AS2, 222
    AS3, 229
vidPlay method
    FLVDissolveTransition, 256
    FunWithTransitions
        AS2, 223–224
        AS3, 229
vidShow method
    FLVDissolveTransition, 255–256
    FunWithTransitions
        AS2, 223
        AS3, 229
vidTwoHandler method, FunWithTransitions
    AS2, 222
    AS3, 229
View.as class, 89
views
    class methods, 331
    interface methods, 323–324
    in MVC, 60–62, 60, 62
volume property, 80
volume slider, 342–343
VP6 codec, 22, 304

W

watermarks, 55
webcams
    FMS for. See Flash Media Server (FMS)
    snapshots from, 278–279, 279
WebService class, 292
widescreen video aspect ratio, 26, 26

width
    aspect ratio, 26, *26*
    metadata, 159
work environment, **66–67**
    Eclipse installation, **68–69**, *68*
    FDT installation, **69**, *70*
    MTASC configuration, **70–73**, *71, 73*
working file versions, saving, **105**
Wowza Media Server Pro, 286
wrap-up, **124–128**
writeAccess method, 308–309

X

XCode code editor, 67
XML
    for AS3, 65
    ListBox data, **139–141**, *141*
    playlist integration into MVC Player, **148–154**
XML class, 292, 306–307
xmlLoaded function, 140
XMLSocket class, 292, 307
XMLStreams class, 18, 292, 307